THE REAL
SAS

THE REAL
SAS

How it works and what it is like to be in it
Through the accounts of SAS members

Adrian Weale

SIDGWICK & JACKSON

First published 1998 by Sidgwick & Jackson

an imprint of Macmillan Publishers Ltd
25 Eccleston Place, London SW1W 9NF
and Basingstoke

Associated companies throughout the world

ISBN 0 283 06235 5

1 3 5 7 9 8 6 4 2

A CIP catalogue record for this book is available from
the British Library.

Typeset by SetSystems Ltd, Saffron Walden, Essex
Printed and bound in Great Britain by
Mackays of Chatham plc, Chatham, Kent

Conents

Acknowledgements

I would like to thank all interviewees who agreed to talk to me under conditions of anonymity for this book, as well as the staff of the Public Records Office at Kew, the Imperial War Museum Library in London, the Kensington Public Library and the Library of the Special Forces Club.

I would also like to thank my agent Andrew Lownie, William Armstrong for commissioning the book and, last but not least, my wife Mary for all her help.

Introduction and
Short History of the SAS

22 Special Air Service Regiment (the SAS), Britain's élite special forces unit, is probably one of the most famous contemporary military units in the world. Best-selling novels and autobiographies have been published, the Regiment features in Hollywood films, and snippets of gossip and rumours regularly appear in the British media: all this for a unit which, until 1980, when B Squadron stormed the Iranian Embassy in Princes Gate, London, was obscure and shrouded in mystery.

Now that the lid has been lifted on many aspects of the SAS role, and the men who take part in SAS operations have been subjected to the hyperbole of fiction writers and tabloid journalists – who, not surprisingly, have always focused on the more dramatic aspects of the Regiment's work – it has become easy to lose sight of what the SAS is about; what it does; and how it does it. In some respects this book is intended to redress this, but it is by no means a detailed history of the Regiment, several of which have already been published. Instead, it is an attempt to understand the way the SAS works and what it is like to be in it, through the accounts of men who have served in and with the unit: official, autobiographical and informal.

To achieve this aim I have used published accounts, official documents and records, and interviews with a number of veterans of the Special Air Service. When writing about this unique organization, authors are necessarily constrained by certain security requirements, one of the most important of which relates to the need to protect the identities of individuals who have been engaged in counter-terrorist operations. In order to fulfil this requirement, I have not identified any person who has served in the post-war SAS who has not been previously publicly identified, and I have protected the identities of all individuals who have helped by giving interviews or writing letters about their experiences. I would like to make an exception, however, in expressing my thanks and admiration for Sir Fitzroy MacLean, who sadly died as this book was approaching completion.

For those not familiar with the history of the SAS, the following brief outline will, I hope, serve as an introduction to this book.

L Detachment of the Special Air Service Brigade was the name given in 1941 to a small unit of volunteers (66 members) collected in Egypt by Lt David Stirling and Lt Jock Lewes to conduct raids against the lines of communication of Axis (German and Italian) forces facing the British Eighth Army in the Western Desert. Stirling and Lewes hoped to insert their raiding parties by parachute, but an early attempt to do so failed as a result of poor weather conditions. Although the unit was severely depleted by their first disastrous operation, the experiment was allowed to continue, with subsequent forays inserted behind enemy lines using vehicles driven across the desert, which formed a vast open flank to the south of the Axis armies. This proved spectacularly successful and during the remaining eighteen months of the campaign, the Special Air Service Regiment, as it became known, led by Stirling (Lewes was killed on an early operation), was responsible for the destruction of several hundred enemy aircraft on the ground, as well as large quantities of war *matériel*, and frequent disruption to infrastructure and communications targets. David Stirling was captured in January 1943 and eventually sent to the notorious POW camp at Colditz Castle. His command ultimately passed to Major (later Lieutenant-Colonel) Blair 'Paddy' Mayne, but for the Operation Torch landings in Algeria a second SAS regiment was raised, commanded by Stirling's brother, William.

Both SAS regiments were involved in operations in Sicily and southern Italy, but in early 1944 an SAS Brigade Headquarters was set up in Britain to command and co-ordinate the SAS after the D-Day invasion. For these operations two French regiments and a Belgian squadron were added to the brigade. Following the invasion on 6 June 1944, SAS parties were parachuted into France to work with Resistance groups, providing targeting information for Allied bombing and tactical expertise and weaponry for attacks on ground forces. When France was effectively liberated, the SAS were withdrawn to Britain, before returning in a light reconnaissance role for the final battles on German soil. At the end of the war, the British SAS were sent to Norway to assist in demobilizing and repatriating German forces.

In the autumn of 1945 the British SAS regiments were temporarily disbanded, pending a long-term decision on the future of SAS troops in the British Army. But in 1947 volunteers from the wartime SAS formed a territorial regiment, 21 SAS, to keep alive the SAS role and identity.

In 1948 a communist-inspired rebellion broke out amongst a minority of the ethnically Chinese portion of the population of the British colonies of Malaya and Singapore. Many of the guerrillas had been trained by British special forces during World War II, and were tactically relatively sophisticated and, in consequence, the British and indigenous security forces facing them were unable to achieve a speedy resolution of the situation. In 1950 a British Staff Officer, Major Mike Calvert (who had been the last commander of the SAS Brigade during World War II), was asked to study ways in which the communists might be defeated in Malaya. One of his main recommendations was the formation of a specialist unit for long-term patrolling deep in the jungle, which was being used as a safe haven by the communists. This recommendation was accepted and he was asked to lead the unit, which he named Malayan Scouts (SAS). After a patchy start, Calvert's unit proved successful and, in December 1951, it was formally accepted as a unit of the Special Air Service with the number 22.

When the Malayan Emergency was being brought to a successful conclusion in the late 1950s, there was speculation that 22 SAS might be disbanded as their jungle role would have disappeared. However, at the end of 1958, a sudden operational requirement arose to provide a low-profile unit to assist in an internal security problem in the Sultanate of Muscat and Oman. Initially one, and then a second, squadron of 22 SAS were sent there from Malaya. They achieved a notable success, demonstrating that the regiment was a flexible and discreet weapon with considerable use outside the jungle environment and, as a result, 22 SAS became a permanent part of the British order-of-battle, albeit with a reduced strength of two squadrons (at the height of the Malayan Emergency it consisted of five operational squadrons).

As the 1960s passed and Britain withdrew from the majority of its imperial commitments, 22 SAS was involved in campaigns in Borneo and Aden, whilst units of the Australian and New Zealand SAS took part in the Vietnam War. In all these campaigns SAS troops were relatively successful and, importantly, added to the pool of skills and abilities at the command of the SAS as a whole.

In 1970 22 SAS again deployed to Oman as a key element in yet another counter-insurgency campaign which, in this case, lasted approximately five years, at the end of which, in 1976, the Regiment was formally committed to operations in Northern Ireland, where elements of the SAS have remained ever since.

Throughout the 1970s, 22 SAS had been developing a specialist counter-terrorist capability in order to give the government a means of response to hijackings and kidnappings. This was graphically demonstrated in May 1980 by the successful assault on the Iranian Embassy, London, which had been seized by Iraqi-backed terrorists. However, in 1982 Britain was unexpectedly involved in a short war with Argentina following the Argentine invasion of the Falkland Islands. Elements of three squadrons of 22 SAS were deployed in their conventional war role against the Argentines, including an abortive mission to attack an airfield on Tierra del Fuego.

During the remainder of the 1980s the principal operational

commitment of 22 SAS was in Northern Ireland and this remained the case until 1990, when Iraq invaded Kuwait and precipitated the Gulf War. In the military build-up which followed, three SAS squadrons were deployed, together with reservist reinforcements from R Squadron. Following the end of the Gulf War, SAS troops have been taking part in operations in the former Yugoslavia, as well as in the continuing commitment to Northern Ireland.

In addition to military and counter-terrorist operations, the SAS has an important and wide-ranging role to play in training and helping friendly nations and organizations with their own security problems. Examples of this have included training Colombian anti-narcotics police and non-communist Cambodian guerrillas, hunting down ivory poachers in Kenya, and providing instructors at NATO special forces schools.

Currently, 22 SAS consists of four operational ('sabre') squadrons: A, B, D and G; a reserve squadron: R; 264 (SAS) Signals Squadron; a headquarters (including a large intelligence section); a training wing; and the headquarters squadron, which provides transport, catering and administrative functions. There are, additionally, two territorial regiments, 21 and 23, which have a similar overall structure but whose role is restricted to long-range patrolling in time of war.

1. **Beginnings:**
World War II 1941–45

A relatively small group of enterprising and aggressive misfits caused chaos and destruction

In March 1941 David Stirling, a twenty-five-year-old lieutenant commissioned in the supplementary reserve of the Scots Guards, arrived in Suez as a member of 8 Commando. Stirling's unit formed a part of 'Layforce', a raiding formation under the command of Brigadier Robert Laycock, which had been formed to participate in an offensive against the Axis-occupied Greek island of Rhodes. But the plan to set up a Balkan front, which had been developing as British forces dealt with the Italian armies in North Africa, under the sponsorship of Winston Churchill, was thrown into disarray in April by the German invasion of Yugoslavia and Greece and the seizure by airborne forces of Crete at the end of May.

The capture of Crete was to have a profound effect on British military thinking. The fall of France had shown that the British Army was hopelessly behind the times in comparison with the German *Wehrmacht*, with tactics still firmly rooted in the experience of the Western Front in World War I. The highly mobile armoured warfare demonstrated by the Germans as they drove for the Channel ports presaged a major tactical rethink by Britain's military leaders, whilst the German use of paratroops to seize key objectives ahead of their armoured thrusts was also noted. Britain had begun to experiment with paratroops in the summer of 1940, converting the newly formed 2 Commando into the airborne role with the cover designation '11th Special Air Service Battalion', but the original scheme was to produce a fairly small-scale parachute-delivered raiding force.

On Crete, the Germans demonstrated that the use of paratroops on a much larger scale was not only technically feasible but could also be strategically decisive. Attacking a garrison of nearly 30,000 New Zealand and British soldiers, the German 7th Parachute Division overwhelmed numerically superior defenders who should, theoretically, have defeated them. The allied forces were by no means at full strength, many of them having recently been evacuated from fighting on the Greek mainland. Nevertheless, the German attack was a clear lesson in the use of aerially delivered forces, combined with local air superiority. Much of their success was due to the demoralizing effect on the defenders of the sudden inundation of comparatively small areas by large formations of highly trained enemy.

The invasion of Crete was a source of fascination to many on the British side, not least because it seemed to be such a thoroughly modern way of going to war. Churchill demanded that: 'We ought to have 5,000 parachutists and an airborne division on the German model, with any improvements that might suggest themselves from experience.'

But, together with the appearance of the German Afrika Korps fighting alongside the Italians in North Africa, it meant the end for Layforce. Middle East Headquarters decided that there was little prospect of using commandos in the defensive campaign that they anticipated. It was felt that the best employment for the highly trained officers and soldiers who made up the 'Special Service Brigade' was as battle-casualty replacements. Whilst the commandos waited for the decision to disband, they spent their time in comparative idleness, conducting short day and night exercises to 'keep the troops busy'. During one of these, Lt Stirling, leading his platoon on a night march, received a thorn slash across his eye requiring hospital treatment. Already exasperated by Stirling's apparently lackadaisical attitude towards soldiering, a board of officers was convened to examine whether Stirling might be a malingerer lacking in moral fibre, who should be court-martialled for cowardice on active service.

On return to duty after receiving treatment for his eye injury – and unaware that his conduct was the subject of an official inquiry – Stirling met a friend, Lt (acting Capt) Jock Lewes, who told him he had received permission to carry out experiments with fifty parachutes which had been wrongly delivered to Egypt, and would Stirling like to take part? Stirling would.

At this stage of the war, no thought had been given to the use of paratroops in the Middle East theatre, at least by the British. The German airborne demonstration on Crete showed what they could achieve, and it was natural for exuberant, offensive-minded soldiers like Stirling and Lewes to want to experiment with this exciting technique. One of the original participants in this first exercise subsequently made a report on what took place:

Having been frustrated in his plans for a seaborne operation, Lt J S Lewes, Welsh Guards, decided to try it by parachute. He and his party first went to an RAF HQ located somewhere near FUKA and there he discussed the details with an RAF officer who, although none of the party had ever jumped before, was most helpful. He showed us the parachutes we were to use. From the log-books we saw that the last periodical examination had been omitted but Lt Lewes decided they were OK. Next day, along with Lt Stirling and Sgt Stone, who were hoping to do a job in Syria, we made a trial flight. The plane used was a Vickers Valencia. We threw out a dummy made from sandbags and tentpoles. The parachute opened OK but the tent poles were smashed on landing. Afterwards we tried a 10ft jump from the top of the plane and then a little parachute control.

We reached the landing field towards dusk, landed, fitted our parachutes and decided to jump in the failing light. We were to jump in pairs, Lt Lewes and his servant Gdsmn Davies first. The RAF officer was to despatch. The instructions were to dive out as though going into water. We hooked ourselves up, circled the field, and on a signal from the RAF officer, Lt Lewes and Davies dived out. Next time round, I dived out, and was surprised to see Lt Stirling pass me in the air. Lt Lewes made a perfect landing, next came Davies, a little shaken. Lt Stirling injured his spine and also lost his sight for about an hour, next, myself, a little shaken and a few scratches, and lastly Sgt Stone who seemed OK.

In fact, Stirling's comparatively rapid descent appears to have been the result of his canopy having briefly snagged on the tailplane of the aircraft as it deployed, tearing it severely. Being a large man, at 6ft 5in tall with a muscular frame, and having received no worthwhile training in parachute landing falls, Stirling hit the ground with considerable force and caused himself serious damage. He was hospitalized immediately whilst the remainder of the party continued with the experiment the next day. The second jump was just as amateurish as the first:

> The first three landed quite close to each other and doubled forward to the container, but Lt Lewes in trying to avoid some oil barrels, rather badly injured his spine, Gdsmn Evans also hurt his ankle. Sgt Stone, who jumped after us, landed OK. The intended operation was eventually cancelled.

When Stirling regained consciousness in hospital, there was some initial doubt as to whether he would be capable of walking again, but it soon became clear he would recover after he had had time to convalesce. It was a period that he was to put to good use. As he slowly regained the use of his legs, Stirling took to pondering on the concept of commando operations in the Middle East:

> I suppose the hospital confinement was a good thing; I had little else to do but think . . . I'd thought from the early days in Scotland that thundering around in droves, we lost something. Even if the raids along the coast had come off I doubt whether we would have achieved anything of real value.[1]

Stirling was referring to one of the essential truths of undertaking 'special operations' during major wars: that the more effort that goes into mounting them, the less value they actually are.

Despite their intensive training, the commando forces that were set up during 1940 were not a particularly subtle idea. Their concept of operations was, essentially, that they would seize a beachhead on an enemy-held coastline, defend it with naval

---

1 Quoted in *David Stirling* by Alan Hoe 1992, p. 58.

support whilst they proceeded with their mission, and then withdraw when the mission was complete. The relatively small size and light firepower of the commandos meant they would not be able to hold on to their beachheads for long. Therefore, their targets needed to be relatively close to comparatively undefended stretches of coastline: an unlikely state of affairs in the case of targets of strategic value. All such operations were likely to be extremely vulnerable to enemy observation before the landing, and to enemy air attack at any stage. This was not altered by the special conditions of the Middle East campaign. To Stirling, it appeared self-evident that the value gained from launching commando raids against the defended coastline of North Africa was not commensurate with the expenditure of men and *matériel* that it would require. It is worth noting that commando forces were raised as much for the propaganda and morale-boosting value of launching attacks against enemy targets as for the military effect they were expected to achieve.

Whilst in hospital, Stirling studied the geography of the North African campaign and made an appreciation that took a far more optimistic view of one of the key factors that was present: the desert. One of the most startling features of the North African campaign was that it was fought out along a comparatively narrow coastal strip, and both sides left what appears, on a large-scale map, to be a vast open flank to the south. In reality, most of this flank could be discounted because it was practically impassable to large bodies of troops. But Stirling recognized this meant it could also be a safe haven for very much smaller units to launch attacks deep into the enemy rear areas and lines of communication. Provided these attacks caused a certain amount of damage to the enemy, they would achieve an effect out of all proportion to the effort required to mount them. In hospital, he wrote an outline paper that summed up his argument and determined to present it to an officer as high up the chain of command as he could find. Stirling's paper does not appear to have survived the war, but it argued:

1 The enemy is vulnerable to attack along his lines of communications and at airfields, transport parks, supplies depots et cetera.

2 The scale of commando raids is such that surprise is unlikely to be achieved and the requirement for naval support and transport puts at risk assets that are of a value out of all proportion to the likely results of the raids.

3 There is an advantage to be gained from establishing a unit to attack l-of-c targets by stealth, taking full advantage of surprise and making minimal demands on manpower and equipment. Thus it might be possible to attack ten targets using the same level of resources used by a commando in attacking one.

4 Training for this unit would have to encompass all likely entry means, including parachuting, boats and foot infiltration, and should be designed to allow the unit to use available means of transport rather than having specially allocated and/or modified resources.

5 The unit must be responsible for its own training and operational planning, and the unit commander must operate direct to the Commander-in-Chief.

6 The unit should be ready to participate in the November 1941 offensive.

Stirling appended to this short paper an outline plan to attack enemy airfields at Gazala and Tmimi which involved parachuting sixty men into the desert south of the targets under cover of an air-raid, after which they would lie-up for the remainder of that night and the next day before infiltrating the targets on foot, blowing up any aircraft they could find, and exfiltrating to a rendezvous with the Long Range Desert Group (LRDG), who would then ferry them home.

Despite subsequent hyperbole, Stirling's concept was not startlingly original: the reason that it was subsequently accepted by General Claude Auchinleck, Commander-in-Chief Middle East, was that it was based on sound logic, practical military common-sense and, probably equally importantly, would require very few resources. At a meeting in mid-July 1941, Stirling was authorized to recruit a unit of six officers and sixty other ranks in order to put his scheme into practice.

The name given to the new unit was L Detachment, 1st

Special Air Service Brigade. The title was selected solely as part of a deception plan operated by MEHQ, designed to make Axis intelligence believe that the British had based an airborne brigade in Egypt (there was already a K Detachment, which was not related to Stirling's unit, and there was subsequently an M Detachment, which grew out of it):

> I liked what I saw from the word go, even though the whole thing was on a pretty amateurish basis, but the great thing was that David Stirling, really by sheer force of personality, had caught the imagination of General Auchinleck and, in spite of the fact that the first SAS operation was a disaster, managed to survive and managed to carry on with this idea. I think Stirling was already thinking about the development of the SAS concept, but the important idea at that stage, the idea that General Auchinleck realized was important, was the idea of the two armies involved in this back and forth in the narrow coastal strip, along the coast of North Africa, with this large hinterland to the south which meant that if you could get round, you could hit the other side where it hurt most. That was something that nobody else had grasped on either side.[2]
>
> Officer, L Detachment

The disastrous first operation was the attack on the airfields around Gazala and Tmimi first mooted by Stirling in his original proposal for the 'Special Service Unit'. Launched on 16 November 1941, it depended on the successful parachute insertion of five teams of saboteurs who would then march out of the desert, attack the airfields, and return to a rendezvous with the LRDG, who would ferry them back to safety.

The day of the operation brought bad news for Stirling and his team: weather forecasters predicted high winds and poor visibility at the planned drop zone. Even with military parachuting in its infancy – and Stirling's unit had only minimal expertise at this stage – it was known that winds above 20mph were likely to lead to a considerable scattering of each 'stick' and its equipment, and

---

2 Interview, Officer, L Detachment.

also enormously increase the risk of physical injury to the parachutists.

Stirling was faced with a considerable dilemma: should he cancel or postpone the operation and wait for more propitious conditions, but in so doing possibly undermine the morale of a group of men whose training and preparations had geared them for this one operation for months? Or should he go ahead, risking failure even before L Detachment had come to grips with the enemy. After canvassing the views of his officers, he decided to go ahead.

The poor weather conditions were to highlight a fundamental truth about special operations that remains current to this day: a successful entry phase is often considerably harder to achieve than the actual action on the objective. Apart from threatening the descent of the SAS group, the bad weather, with winds gusting to 35mph, was also causing confusion to the relatively inexperienced aircrew, who had never dropped paratroops operationally – cloud and sandstorms had reduced visibility and they were unable to use their usual navigational landmarks. One of the aircraft was shot down, a second was tricked into landing at a German airfield by an English-speaking air-traffic controller, leaving only three planes to drop their troops. For the soldiers leaving the aircraft, their problems were only just beginning:

The pilot straightened up and rose back up to five hundred feet. The green light had come on. As we stood up and got ready, Jock said the pilot was not exactly sure of our position because of the atrocious weather and the activities of the anti-aircraft gunners. He added that the wind-speed was force nine. The navigator came aft to wish us luck and gave us the wind direction. Then suddenly we were given the signal and the whole stick jumped together. I felt a terrific tug as my parachute opened and then I was swinging in comparative quietness except for the wind howling through my rigging lines.

I could see two other parachutes which both seemed to be drifting away at a vast speed. As it was impossible to see the ground I kept my legs braced, but when I hit the desert I suffered a tremendous jolt right through my body. Before I could gather myself properly I found myself being dragged across the desert floor at more than 30mph by the wind. Vainly I banged at the quick release box into which the straps of my harness were clamped, to jettison my parachute, only to realize that in a moment of panic I had failed to turn it first to unlock it. Finally I managed to get clear of the harness and, luckily for me, the parachute that was dragging me along got tangled in a camel thorn bush. I managed to roll clear just as it flew off into the air, never to be seen again.

Climbing stiffly to my feet, I felt for broken bones and realized that apart from bruises, scratches and slight dizziness I was still intact. Finding my compass I started to walk back along the bearing given by the navigator, and almost immediately bumped into another member of my stick. Miraculously, after about an hour, the entire stick was assembled and without injury. All but two containers, however, were missing, with our food, water, Lewes bombs and Thompson sub-machine guns.[3]

Much the same thing had happened to the other sticks that had jumped and, in any case, they were many miles from their planned drop zone. Under the circumstances, there was no question of launching the intended attacks, and the survivors of the infiltration instead converged on the LRDG rendezvous for evacuation.

It is to the great credit of everyone then concerned with the SAS, from the Commander-in-Chief at GHQ, down to the individual members of L Detachment, that Stirling's experiment was not abandoned after this fiasco. Of the sixty-two men involved, only twenty-two returned, and a good deal of equipment was lost.

The most important lesson learned by Stirling and his team – apart from the need to avoid glamorous but dangerous parachute insertions – was that the LRDG, who had picked them up and exfiltrated them to the safety of the Siwa oasis were also confident of their ability to insert SAS teams for attacks. For a few days after their return, Stirling set about organizing a second

---

3 Quoted in *One of the Originals* by Johnny Cooper 1991, p. 24.

operation involving all the survivors but with a drop-off provided by vehicles of the LRDG.

The second SAS operation was launched on 8 December 1941 when Stirling took Lt Blair 'Paddy' Mayne and ten men to attack airfields at Sirte and Tamet, whilst Lt Jock Lewes and his group headed out to attack Agheila on 9 December, and Lt Bill Fraser and his men made for Agedabia on 18 December. This time, L Detachment achieved a stunning success. All of the groups penetrated their target airfields, and Mayne, leading a team at Tamet, destroyed a significant number of aircraft:

It went without a hitch. We didn't meet anything on the way in and before we knew it we were groping around the airfields. Black as pitch it was, couldn't see a thing. Then Paddy spotted this Nissen hut affair and sneaked up to it. He obviously heard something inside because the next thing we knew he'd dragged the bloody door open and was letting rip with his tommy-gun. Screams from inside and the lights went out.

The buggers inside soon started firing. Paddy put a couple of guys on the ground to keep the Krauts' heads down and the rest of us went after the planes. We got through our bombs pretty quick – brilliant those Lewes bombs. Quick and easy. Afterwards Reg Seekings said there wasn't a bomb left for the last plane and Paddy got so pissed off that he climbed up to the cockpit and demolished it with his bare hands. What a feller!

We got moving fast, but even so the first bomb went off before we were clear of the airfield. We had to stop and look didn't we. What a sight, flames and muck all over the place. We headed straight out to the LRDG lads. There was a bit of a kerfuffle when the Krauts caught on to us using flashing lights to find the RV – they started flashing their own but we used our whistles as a back-up and we got back OK.[4]

The final score for the operation was sixty-one enemy aircraft claimed destroyed: an unprecedented result which secured the future of L Detachment. Instead of heading back to Cairo, Stirling decided to launch further immediate airfield attacks, and

---

4 RSM Bob Bennett, quoted in Bradford and Dillon, *Rogue Warrior of the SAS*, 1987, p. 64.

again they were spectacularly successful, courtesy of the LRDG's 'desert taxi' service. But this time, the Axis response was quicker and Jock Lewes's team were strafed from the air as they made their getaway. Severely wounded in the legs, Lewes, who had been Stirling's sounding board as he worked out the SAS concept, died shortly afterwards.

On their return, Stirling was given authority to replace his losses from the first operation and to begin the expansion of L Detachment. It was a crucial moment in the development of the SAS:

> After the first operation went wrong, I think there were a lot of people in GHQ Middle East – who didn't like David – who would have liked to have got rid of the whole thing, and thought it was useless. That is when the backing of Auchinleck came in.[5]

The expansion of L Detachment, apart from bringing in a number of new officers and soldiers, many of whom were to prove valuable acquisitions to the unit, also allowed the training programme to be put on a more formal footing. Even so, it retained a number of somewhat quirky aspects:

> Training had a dual purpose. Obviously it was intended to make us fit and equip us for the operations we were going to do, but there was an idea that it was testing our nerve as well. The parachute training, owing to the difficulty of getting an aircraft to jump out of, consisted of two things. One was jumping off a 14ft tower on to a bit of rather hard desert, and you were told to go into a roll, which was easier said than done. And the other was jumping out of the back of a truck going at 40 miles per hour across the same patch of desert. I think both of them were partly to check our determination and were also a way of eliminating people who were unfit or unlucky: it was training by ordeal![6]

With a sound means of insertion available, the bread and butter of SAS operations became attacks on enemy airfields and main

---

5 Interview, Officer, L Detachment.
6 Ibid.

supply routes. The benefit of using SAS troops in this way was that it caused disruption and chaos in the enemy rear area at very low cost in terms of manpower and equipment, and without in any way imperilling operations by the Eighth Army. The SAS were not then, and have never been, 'suicide' troops: nevertheless, part of the value of the operations they carry out lies in the reality that there is relatively little to lose in attempting them, whereas the gains are potentially enormous. The flavour of the operations carried out in World War II is well captured by the following report of a typical mission:

MOST SECRET

REPORT ON WESTERN DESERT OPERATION CARRIED OUT BY CAPT BP SCHOTT K.A.R. AND PARTY IN JULY 1942

OBJECTIVES   Landing grounds 121 and 05 at Sidi Barrani to destroy aircraft and stores

PERSONNEL   Capt BP Schott – Capt PE Warr – Sgt Almonds J – Sgt Brough W – Cpl White H – Cpl Baird C – Pct Thompson J – Pct Meyer J – Pct Ridler F – Dvr Hope J

TRANSPORT   One Jeep – One 3 tonner

The party left Kabrit on 3 July 1942 together with all other parties and contacted LRDG under Capt Robin Girdon and Major Stirling at Eighth Army HQ Ameria, Alexandria, on 4 July '42.

All parties left together with LRDG the same day, our route being to endeavour to slip through the Southern end of the line unobserved, skirting the NORTH side of the Quattara Depression. This was successfully achieved and the convoy made their rendezvous with three further LRDG patrols on the p.m. of 6 July '42 at approx. point 712231, off the Mersa Siwa track.

One day and half were spent at the RV sorting stores and making final arrangements for various parties' objectives, some enemy recce planes came over but failed to observe anything.

Major Stirling gave all parties their final briefing, our party operating the furthest WEST having two objectives LG 121 and LG 05. Our party was to come under Capt Alister Timpson, LRDG G2. Patrol until we were dropped for offensive operations, we were to be in wireless communication with HQ LRDG. Major Stirling ordered that LG 121 and LG 05 were not to be attacked unless 12 or more aircraft could be destroyed.

After all parties and stores had been divided up, we departed from our RV in different directions. There was nevertheless a great shortage of petrol with our party when we left and at one time it was thought to be necessary to wireless for aircraft to drop supplies. From the time we parted with the main body up to the day of our planned attack things were comparatively uneventful. We had one or two very narrow escapes from enemy aircraft which failed fortunately to observe us: also we found a petrol dump en route to Sidi Barrani which was used to fill up all available empty cans and our empty reserve. From then on the petrol situation and food situation was solved, also quantities of water were found in dumps. Unfortunately all these dumps were our own left behind by our own troops in their retreat to El Alamein.

Our lying up base was at first in the wadis South of Sidi Barrani at point 583340. Considerable amount of our abandoned equipment was observed. Since parting with the main party I became slightly ill and Capt Timpson was suffering from extensive desert sores – the LRDG Sgt was also suffering from bad jaundice and running a very high temperature. The remainder of the party were in excellent spirits.

The attack on the airfields was carried out as ordered on the night 12–13 July. Capt P E Warr i/c one party consisting of Sgt Almonds – Pct Meyer – Pct Ridler, objective LG 05 and myself with party consisting of Sgt Brough – Cpl White – Cpl Baird – Pct Thompson, objective LG 121. We were to be dropped by LRDG approx. 4 miles from our objective at 2350 hours on night of 11 July '42. Unfortunately owing to errors on maps Capt Warr's party found themselves some 10 miles from the target and myself only two or three miles away.

We had some two hours' sleep that night then proceeded to a lying up posi before first light. Capt Warr found an excellent OP but our party was not so successful. We came across an enemy (German) patrol of 6 with a JMG and a dog before we could reach a point to observe the LC. Owing to this unfortunate meeting and our certainty of being observed we decided to take up an all round defensive position in a BIR and fight it out when a recce party arrived. We lay up the entire next day expecting enemy to attack but fortunately the patrol could not have seen us as no one came during the day. We were able to observe the German transport AC arriving at 05 LG and made accurate plots of their courses on the maps. We were also able to ascertain that LG 121 was *not* being used by AC but only used as a decoy at night when our bombers flew over. A further recce by Cpl Baird confirmed this.

The same took place on Capt Warr's target at night all AC were flown off in a WEST direction leaving the LGs empty except for one crashed JU87.

On the night 13 July we were picked up by Capt Timpson at 1130 hours, but Capt Warr's party failed to make the RV with LRDG. We had to proceed back without them, the base had been changed during the day as the LRDG had been chased out of the wadi by armoured cars and aircraft. Another lying up position was taken 35 miles South of point 543340. On route we left water for Capt. Warr's party at the old RV.

The following night a recce party went out to see if Capt Warr had arrived, he had not, in the meantime Capt Timpson and myself had planned to strafe the road at Bug Bug on the night 15–16 July. We set out to carry this out and passed through our old RV en route. There we found Capt Warr and party, all very tired and fatigued owing to lack of water and food for 4 days.

We set out same night for Bug Bug but failed to make our objective owing to the bad nature of the ground for the vehicles. We all returned to RV and spent part day servicing vehicles etc. Capt Warr's party recovered from their lack of food and water and were fit once again. All information re enemy transport AC was wirelessed back to LRDG HQ.

Capt Timpson then decided to strafe the road at Kilo 86 between Sidi Barrani and Mersa. We later proceeded to point 212–632315. I remained with Sgt Almonds – Pct Thompson and Dvr Hope, 1x 3-tonner and Jeep at RV point 212.

Next day at 0930 hours a column of vehicles was observed approaching our RV from the wrong direction to Capt Timpson pre-arranged position. We decided to abandon the broken down Jeep and make a break in the 3-tonner, to the pre-arranged RV with Major Stirling's party. This we did and arrived at point 695305 at 1530 hours in time for tea! During the dash across the desert we were chased by an ME110 who failed to cause any damage owing to the speed and dust caused by the Ford 3-tonner.

It was later found out that the column we observed approaching our RV was none other than Capt Warr but the haze and mirages caused by this one vehicle gave the impression of at least 25 Italian Lancia trucks loaded with troops.

I returned to Egypt with my party together with LRDG heavy section under Capt Lazarus LRDG via the Quattara Depression and arrived at Hena on 7 August '42. Enemy aircraft attempted to locate us but failed owing to quick dispersion and camouflage.

It was later found from Capt Timpson and Capt Warr that all enemy transport on road West of Mersa stopped from dusk until dawn owing to our previous raids, therefore no vehicles were destroyed or observed but that they had blown the water pipeline between Barrani and Mersa.

The results of this operation were as follows:-
   — Water supply between Mersa and Sidi Barrani destroyed at lowest point therefore draining all water in pipeline.
   — Ten confirmed fully laden transport aircraft destroyed over Sidi Barrani by RAF on information wireless to HQ and 4 destroyed on the ground at LC 05.
   — Quantities of equipment left behind by our own troops destroyed, including broken down vehicles, tanks and dumps.

There were no casualties and I should like to mention the efficiency of Capt Timpson's LRDG patrol throughout the operation. Capt Timpson and the patrol Sgt were both extremely sick, with desert sores and jaundice. Capt Warr - Sgt Almonds - Pct Thompson and Sgt Brough also showed courage and determination throughout the operation. Capt Warr recovered the broken down Jeep from point 212 and assisted by LRDG towed same back to the Delta area, through the Depression.

However, in addition to the extremely valuable raids on airfields and lines of communication, David Stirling soon came under pressure to launch more obviously spectacular attacks; this pressure came from both within the SAS and from Middle East Headquarters.

One of the fundamental tenets of special forces operations is that they are implemented at the strategic level with the intention of creating strategic impact: they are meant to significantly affect the outcome of campaigning in a particular theatre. But the principle beauty of 'special operations' is that they are themselves conducted on a small scale, are simple in character and tie up very few resources in their execution. The strategic impact of the SAS during their first year of operations came from the sheer numbers of relatively small-scale attacks against enemy airfields that they were able to carry out, and the consequent drain on Axis resources that this caused, and certainly not because any one of their targets was particularly valuable. Nevertheless, there is a strong temptation for military planners, and for special forces themselves, to reach the conclusion that an attack on a particular target can have a disproportionate impact in itself: this is undoubtedly an illusion, albeit a very common one. The first occasion in which the SAS was misused in this way was in the simultaneous raids on Benghazi and Tobruk, launched in September 1942.

The Benghazi/Tobruk operation was a brainchild of the planners at MEHQ rather than being developed, as had previous operations, from within the SAS. It envisaged SAS groups attacking the two locations from the landward side whilst commandos attacked from the sea, supported by naval gunfire. Part of the infiltration plan involved the use of a specially formed unit of Palestinian Jews of German descent, the Special Interrogation Group (SIG), who had been trained as a bogus Afrika Korps detachment for use in tricking POWs into revealing information. The aim of the raid was for the attacking forces to destroy as much *matériel* as possible in the towns, hold them for a short period, and then withdraw via the Jalo oasis, which was to be captured by the Sudan Defence Force. In the event, both parts of the plan went disastrously wrong:

To: The Commanding Officer
          SAS Regiment

By: Lt T B LANGTON

Sir,
In August of this year, I was instructed to report to Lt-Col HASELDEN to accompany him on a raid against TOBRUK

23

which I subsequently learned was to be in conjunction with a naval landing.

On August 22 the following party left CAIRO in seven 3-ton lorries:

   Lt-Col HASELDEN in Command
   1 Squadron 1st SS Regt – Major CAMPBELL in Command
   1 Detachment RE – Lt HARRISON
   1 Detachment RA Anti-Aircraft – Lt BARLOW
   1 Detachment RA Coastal Defence – Lt POINTON
   1 Detachment RC Signals – Capt TROLLOP
   1 Medical Officer – Capt GIBSON
   and myself

We were later joined by Y1 Patrol LRDG, Capt LLOYD OWEN and a detachment of the SIG (Capt BUCK) and F/O SCOTT, RAF
The party proceeded to TOBRUK via KUFRA.

Intention
The intention was to drive into TOBRUK in three of the 3-ton lorries disguised as British Prisoners-of-War, with a guard made up of the SIG party in German uniform (increased in number by Lt MACDONALD, Lt HARRISON and myself).

The lorries were to turn along the South side of the harbour and drive to the Wadi near MARSA UMM ES SCLAUSC 418431. Here troops were to debus, and divide into two parties. Lt-Col HASELDEN with the SIG, RA detachments, Lt TAYLOR's section, Lt SILLITO's section and Lt MACDONALD's section were to take the small house and gun positions on the West side of the bay 417431. The remainder of the Squadron, under Major CAMPBELL was to take the positions on the East side. Success signals were to be fired by each party on completion of task, and then Major CAMPBELL's party was to proceed two miles East to find out if there were any guns there ('BRIGHTON' Rest Camp) 41974300 and to deal with them. Unless it proved to be extremely simple for Lt-Col HASELDEN's party to push on Eastwards and take the AA positions there, they were to hold until the Coy of A and S Highlanders and 1 Platoon RNF were landed from MTBs in the bay.

I was responsible for 'signalling in' the MTBs and meeting the party when they came ashore. The signalling was to take the form of 3 'Ts' flashed every 2 minutes in Red from a point on the West shore of the bay (41784315) and also from a point just outside the bay to the East (41834313).

On the journey up, Major CAMPBELL developed dysentery badly, and, although he insisted on seeing the job through, Lt-Col HASELDEN told me to accompany him as 2nd-in-Command as far as the first objective. My own plan was to station two of the RE party at the Eastern signalling point, with a torch and instructions as to how to signal in case I couldn't get back to them. I was then going back to the small house on the West side (which was to be Col HASELDEN's HQ) to report and to collect F/O SCOTT and his two Aldis lamps. I would substitute F/O SCOTT for the two REs and return myself to signal from the Western point. Signalling was not due to start until 0130 hours so there should have been plenty of time.

The rest of the Plan does not affect the remainder of the report.

Entrance
Owing to a slight miscalculation the party was late getting on to the EL ADEM road and it was dark soon after we had turned on to the main road towards TOBRUK. However, the entrance went smoothly and no check posts were encountered. Further delay was caused by the fact that, apparently considerable alterations (wire fences etc.) had been made where the track along the Southern bank of the harbour joined the main road. We were still some way off our debussing point when the bombing started.

After debussing, sorting stores, hiding German uniforms etc. the two parties set out.

Action

Immediately on leaving the trucks Major CAMPBELL's party had to negotiate a small minefield (41754308). This was done by an RE party with a detector, and caused considerable delay and necessitated the party walking in a long single file. In the middle of this operation a rifle was fired from the other side of the Wadi (4178305). This caused further delay. Eventually one section was sent forward (under Lt ROBERTS) to investigate and I asked permission to reconnoitre the sandy beach. I walked right across the beach without encountering any-thing, and directed Lt ROBERTS to take his party up on the high ground to get round the back of whoever had fired the rifle. I then went back to Major CAMPBELL and guided one section across the beach, the rest following at intervals. Lt ROBERTS in the meanwhile engaged and put out of action a section of enemy who were manning a spandau.

We had taken almost an hour to get across the Wadi. The same procedure of advance was adopted up the Wadi-side and on. I waited on top to guide Lt ROBERTS and the REs who were labouring under heavy burdens of explosives etc. and it took some time to catch up with the rest, who I eventually found, had struck Eastwards away from the bay. Soon after that I met Lt DUFFY who said that all the positions near the bay were empty and unused.

By this time the success signal from Lt-Col HASELDEN's party had been fired.

We proceeded to catch up Major CAMPBELL and soon afterwards came on a small wireless station (approx. 41874306) which was put out of action with its personnel – mainly by Lt ROBERTS.

In climbing out of that Wadi I discovered it was already

0130 hrs. I urged Major CAMPBELL to fire the success signal, which was done. I then returned alone and as fast as I could towards the bay. This journey was made more difficult by the fact that I had to skirt a small enemy camp in a Wadi (approx. 41854310) which we had missed on the way out. I found the Eastern Signalling point and was relieved to see that F/O SCOTT was signalling from the West side although he was far too high up. The REs had disappeared by this time, and, I presume that they returned to HQ on finding no guns to destroy. I had no watch and only an inadequate torch. I tried to time my signalling with F/O SCOTT's.

After a short while I saw two MTBs come in (41854310). After that however no more appeared. My problem now was whether to stay signalling or to go to meet the landing troops and conduct them to HQ as I was supposed to be doing. I decided to try a compromise by wedging my torch in a rock and leaving it alight. I did this and started back but, before I had gone 200 yds I saw a light flashing out to sea and it appeared to be on an MTB proceeding *away* again (approx. 41954317). I rushed back to the torch and started to signal again. But nothing materialized. After another half hour I left signalling and started back towards the landing point. On the way back I found that my haversack and T/G had been taken from the Sangar where I had left them before climbing down to the rocks. I later ran into two enemy one of whom I hit with my revolver.

On reaching the landing point I found the two MTBs unloading. Lt MACDONALD appeared to be organizing the landing, so I took one man with me with a T/G and returned at once to continue signalling. During all this time F/O SCOTT was still signalling from the West side.

By the time we got back to the Eastern signalling point the searchlights were sweeping the entrance to the harbour and our own shore. However I resumed signalling.

Heavy fire was coming from the opposite shore of the harbour out to sea. Once the MTBs got caught in the searchlights and I could see their wake, and tracer bouncing off one of them. They were well to the East of us however, and it was obvious that there wasn't much chance of them getting in. One of the two MTBs slipped out past me during a slight lull, and appeared to get away safely. At 'first light' I decided to abandon signalling and I returned to the landing point. By the time I got there dawn was breaking and I saw one MTB apparently aground. Sounds of rifle and LMG fire were coming from just over the West ridge of the Wadi, near where we had left the trucks. I hailed the MTB, but getting no answer, I walked around the bay and up the small Wadi to the house which was Lt-Col HASELDEN's HQ (41744311). Rifle fire was coming down the Wadi. I got to the house to find it deserted and I saw the heads of about a platoon of enemy lying covering the house from about 300 yds away. I walked back down the small wadi, and thinking I heard a shout aboard the MTB, I boarded her, but found no-one. I filled my water bottle and took what food I could find. Lt RUSSELL, Lt SILLITO, Pte HILLMAN and Pte WATLER then came aboard. Lt RUSSELL opened up with the twin Lewis guns forward on troops on top of the hill. I went to the engines to see if there was any hope of getting them started, but not even Pte WATLER - a mechanic - could help there. We then took all we could in the way of food and water and boarded one of the assault craft lying alongside. We paddled out into the bay but were forced to go ashore by being fired on from the rocks on the West side. We saw some of our own men dodging along the West side of the bay and there were large explosions coming from behind them. It was impossible to tell who they were, but I think they may have been the REs dealing with the guns on the point (417431). We climbed through a minefield and into a wadi. Here we were joined by Sgt EVANS (Welsh Guards) 1st SS Regt. We made for the hills, having to hide frequently from low-flying aircraft. I looked back from the higher ground and saw what I now know to have been HMS ZULU with HMS SIKH in tow. The latter appeared to be burning and shells were bursting round. We were fired on heavily, going over a ridge, from the direction of BRIGHTON, but got safely into a large wadi where we found about 15-20 others waiting. These included 2/Lt MACDONALD SS Regt and Lt BARLOW RA (AA) also those of the RNF who had been landed from the MTBs. We decided it was now useless to resist. No one knew what had become of Major CAMPBELL's party. It seemed clear that Col HASELDEN had been killed. We decided to take to the hills and make for Wadi SHAGRA North of BARDIA, where we had been told we would be picked up 5 days (?) later.

Hearsay evidence

I have pieced together the following stories from information gathered in short talks with Lts BARLOW, MACDONALD and RUSSELL, and Sgt EVANS and Pte HILLMAN. The last named will be able to furnish his own report.

A The action of Lt-Col HASELDEN's party on the West side of the bay went quite well. The SIG party went first to the house and found only one man there. All the rest were at their posts. These posts were taken fairly easily, but four Italians escaped and went off towards the town shouting the alarm. During the course of this brief action Lt GRAHAM TAYLOR was severely wounded.

At dawn a strong party of enemy attacked from the West (a battalion perhaps?). It would seem that most of the party took to the trucks but these were ambushed. However Lt BARLOW who was driving one truck, drove straight through the ambush, and came out the other side. They then got on foot again and brought the two Lewis guns which had been brought ashore, into play from a flank. The RSM had apparently taken a party to protect the wounded and HQ personnel. Lt-Col HASELDEN then shouted to those that were left to charge the enemy and led the charge himself, but was hit when within a few yards of some screaming Italians. Lt MACDONALD told me that he got to Colonel HASELDEN just after he fell, but as he bent down to him, a grenade burst practically on the Colonel. Lt MACDONALD was temporarily stunned and his face was blackened. Lt BARLOW appears to have rallied the small force again but the fire from the twin Lewis on the MTB at that moment came a bit too close so they decided to withdraw, covered by the RNF section, who later disabled their two guns and followed.

B After I left Major CAMPBELL, the party apparently proceeded Eastwards, putting out one or two small positions on the way. Lt ROBERTS section appears to have been left behind for one of these jobs, for when they caught up again they could hear heavy firing ahead but could not find the others. Just before dawn Major CAMPBELL returned to join them. He had been wounded in the foot. Apparently the positions at BRIGHTON were heavily manned and there were CD guns there (I had seen these firing out to sea). The old concrete emplacements had been repaired and enlarged. When attacked the enemy had shut himself in and our troops – and the whole area – were shelled from the North side of the harbour.

Lt ROBERTS started to help Major CAMPBELL back and sent Sgt EVANS on ahead with some men. They got split by enemy fire and Sgt EVANS was just coming through when he saw us coming across the bay in the assault craft.

Escape

We did not stop long in the big wadi. Lts SILLITO and MACDONALD took their respective sections. I believe their intention was to make towards the coast further East and try to get taken off by the MTBs the same day. I have not heard of any of them since.

Lt BARLOW, Lt RUSSELL and myself went off up the wadi with eight men. We found a small wadi and lay up all that day among the bushes. At dusk we disposed of everything we did not require, divided what food we had into three and ourselves into three parties. We split up and made for the perimeter that night. Later in the night – after avoiding two enemy posts – I joined up again with Lt BARLOW's party. Soon after we met, we bumped another enemy post and had to take hurriedly to the nearest wadi. When we regathered Lt BARLOW was nowhere to be found, and I have not seen or heard of him since. After 'bumping' several more posts we eventually got through the perimeter wire and lay up next day in a cave in a wadi. My party now consisted of:

    Sgt EVANS (WELSH GDS)
    Cpl WILSON (RNF)
    Fus LESLIE A (RNF)
    Fus LESLIE G (RNF)
    Fus MACDONALD (RNF)
    Pte HILLMAN (SIG)

The last named had no boot to one foot and a very lacerated heel as well. He also had the added burden of knowing he would be shot if caught. We changed his name there and then to KENNEDY and he was known thus until we were safe.

We had two nights of dodging camps etc. during part of which we walked on the road. We hid up every day in caves in the wadis. On the fifth night, just as we were desperate for food and water we found the first Arab village where we were taken in, fed and given water. Pte HILLMAN acted as interpreter. The Arabs knew all about the TOBRUK raid. They also said they could not understand how the English managed to come all the way from KUFRA.

Going from village to village, we eventually reached the Wadi AM REISA. There was a large Carabinieri post at the shore end of this wadi, the strength of which had recently been doubled, according to the Arabs. They also told us of boats cruising up and down at night – they said they thought they were British. One had landed a party one night and someone had shouted 'Any British here?'

The Arabs then showed us to the Wadi KATTARA about 5 miles North of BARDIA. Here we found an Indian soldier of the 3/18th Garwhal Rifles who had escaped 3 times from TOBRUK and had been living there for 2 months.

We also found Pte WATLER of the 1st SS Regt. His story is as follows:

On leaving us on the night of the 14th, Lt RUSSELL, Pte WATLER and one member of the SIG got through the perimeter and walked 'all out' towards BARDIA along the road. They arrived at MERSA SHAGRA one day late. That night they ran into the enemy post in Wadi AM REISA and were fired on. In making their getaway Pte WATLER got left behind because of bad boots. Nothing further is known of the other two. The man with Lt RUSSELL spoke only German.

We lived in the Wadi KATTARA for four weeks being fed by the Arabs as best they could. We tried making fires by night to attract the attention of aircraft, but only got a stick of bombs extremely close. The only news or information we got was obtained from Italian, or German soldiers via the Arabs who sold eggs etc. on the road and engaged the soldiers in conversation. It was apparent that the enemy was very low in morale and very short of food. We had to take great care not to get caught because the Italians would undoubtedly have 'wiped out' the village. As it was we saw no one during our four weeks there.

After three weeks Sgt EVANS unfortunately got dysentery and later we had to help him to the road by night and leave him to be picked up the next morning. The same happened a few days later to one of the Leslie twins and his brother went with him. The rains had come heavily and it was very cold and damp. I decided to move. The Indian stayed behind, and so the party consisted of Cpl WILSON, Pte WATLER, Pte HILLMAN and myself. I was lucky to have a German compass and a small German map, though the latter was not much use being 1:5,000,000. We had some tins of bully-beef, some goat meat and bread and ten water-bottles. We started on Oct 26th.

Apart from getting fired on on the second night our journey was uneventful. We did not see anyone from the day after we climbed through the frontier wire until we were picked up at HIMEIMAT on Friday Nov 18th with the exception of one convoy which looked very like an SAS patrol – near the SIWA MERSA MATRUM track on Nov 5th. We walked south of the QATTARA depression for the last four days and thereby missed the 'retreat'.

Known casualties

Prisoners   Sgt VANS (WELSH GUARDS)

Fus LESLIE G (RNF)

Fus LESLIE T (RNF)

Fus MACDONALD (RNF)

Casualties not absolutely certain

Killed   Lt-Col HASELDEN

Wounded Major CAMPBELL

and POW Lt GRAHAM TAYLOR

Lt DUFFY

Gdsmn HOGAN (IRISH GUARDS)

(sd) TB LANGTON LT

IRISH GUARDS

SAS REGIMENT

The failure of the Tobruk/Benghazi operation removed, for the remainder of the war, any enthusiasm within the SAS for using the regiment to mount spectacular raids and attacks against prestige targets. Instead, in the aftermath of the battle of El Alamein, as the Eighth Army began to pursue the Afrika Korps and their Italian allies across North Africa, the SAS resumed raids, at an increased tempo, against the Axis lines of communication.

During this period, two significant events occurred for the SAS. The first of these was the formation, under David Stirling's brother William, of the second SAS regiment (2 SAS), from volunteers drawn from 62 Commando, which was intended to pursue a parallel role in First Army to 1 SAS in the Eighth Army. The second was the capture of David Stirling by Italian troops in January 1943.

The plan for 2 SAS was that they would undergo basic training in Britain before moving to the Middle East for advanced training and 'desert hardening' at the SAS headquarters at Kabrit, and then deploy with the First Army in Tunisia.[7] Stirling had by this stage conceived the notion of an SAS 'brigade' consisting of his and his brother's regiments which would operate throughout the Middle Eastern, North African, Mediterranean and Adriatic theatres of operations. He already had under his command the Special Boat Squadron, together with Free French and Greek SAS squadrons, alongside his original L Detachment members. For the post-Alamein operations 1 SAS was organized into A Squadron, under the command of Major 'Paddy' Mayne, which consisted of more experienced unit members, and B Squadron, under Stirling, whose soldiers were mostly new to operations but which included a cadre of relatively long-serving SAS veterans.

With each squadron allocated a sector of the German lines of communication, they raided roads, railways, airfields and supply depots almost at will; however, it was a showy and unnecessary attempt to become the first ground troops to link up with the First Army that was to lead to Stirling's capture. Taking a small party through the 'Gabes Gap', Stirling had the misfortune, in the last week of January 1943, to make a rest stop in an area being used for working-up exercises by a German security battalion being specially trained for anti-SAS operations. Stirling suffered the indignity of being captured by the unit's dentist and, although he briefly escaped, he was soon in permanent captivity.

Anxious that he might attempt to escape, Stirling was quickly

---

7 Some 2 SAS patrols did operate in Tunisia in March/April 1943, but conditions prevented full-scale deployment of the regiment.

removed to Italy, where he was subjected to interrogation by a British traitor, Theodor Schürch, a private in the Royal Army Service Corps who had been taken prisoner by the Italians near Tobruk.

Schürch was a Londoner with a British mother, a Swiss father and a strong sense of class resentment. He had joined the British Union of Fascists as a schoolboy and, on the instructions of a 'Mr Bianchi', an Italian intelligence officer, had enlisted in the army, as a driver in the Royal Army Service Corps (forerunner of the modern Royal Logistics Corps) in 1936. From July 1936 to November 1937, Schürch supplied low-level intelligence to the Italians through his contact, Edward King, an employee of Spinks & Co, the London jewellers. At the behest of King, Schürch obtained a posting to Jerusalem as a staff car driver and from November 1937 he was in a position to supply his Italian contacts with good quality intelligence on the movements of senior British officers and political figures in Palestine.

Schürch remained in the Middle East after the war began and, by the time of his capture by an Italian unit, he was a committed and relatively successful agent. Once in Italian hands he wasted little time before seeking out an intelligence officer and was swiftly 'sprung' from captivity. He was soon back in action on behalf of the Italians. In September 1942 he was inserted into a POW cage to interrogate survivors of the Benghazi raid and in October he crossed the line, the first of several such missions, and gave himself up to a British officer, telling him that he was an escaped prisoner.

After several successful spying operations, Schürch was re-tasked by his Italian controller:

During this time two or three patrols of the Special Air Service were captured and by this time Colonel Revetria had made it my responsibility to get information from all prisoners of the Special Air Service. I mixed with the officers and also the other ranks of these captured patrols, again as Captain John Richards, and from information received in this manner, and also from captured documents we found where other patrols were located, and also their strength. From this information received we were able to capture two other patrols, and acquired information as to the operation of other patrols in that area in the near future.

From this start as a specialist interrogator of SAS troops, Schürch was given the opportunity to interrogate Stirling after his capture:

I was then sent to a special prisoner of war camp in Rome to get information from a British colonel. I was put in with Colonel Stirling, CO of the SAS, whom I found to be the Colonel referred to and whom I recognized from a description and his badges. I was posing as Capt John Richards of the RASC, and as all the necessary information respecting the SAS had already been obtained, I was told only to obtain the name of Colonel Stirling's successor. This I found out to be a Captain 'Paddy' Mayne.

Schürch's claim is interesting, bearing in mind the resistance to interrogation training that is currently given to SAS and other 'prone to capture' personnel. The shock and isolation of captivity is particularly difficult for soldiers captured as individuals rather than with groups of comrades. Stirling subsequently denied that he had given Schürch any worthwhile information and it is certainly difficult to see what benefit the Italians gained from knowing who his successor was. When the German Army seized control of Allied POWs in Italy in 1943, Stirling was removed to Germany, eventually ending up in Colditz Castle, the camp for 'difficult' officer prisoners. As for Schürch, he was passed by his controllers to the Abwehr (the German military intelligence service) after the Armistice and was ultimately captured in the south of France. After being court-martialled by the British Army for treachery, he was executed in December 1945.

Although it was not difficult to replace Stirling, initially with Lord Jellicoe, who had been commanding the SBS, and subsequently with 'Paddy' Mayne, as tactical commander of 1 SAS, his capture created enormous problems for the unit because of his tendency to run it as a one-man band. Although he had

8 WO79/1109.
9 Ibid.

discussed many aspects of his future plans with members of the regiment and with Colonel 'Shan' Hackett, the staff officer at MEHQ with special responsibility for supporting the SAS, it seems that no single individual other than Stirling had the full picture. In fact, as the North African campaign reached its climax, with the Axis forces squeezed into an ever smaller section of Tunisia, the opportunity to use the SAS in their classic role was disappearing.

It wasn't until the Normandy invasion on 6 June 1944 that the SAS returned to a role that resembled Stirling's vision of a strategic special force. Following the invasion of Sicily and during subsequent operations on the Italian mainland, SAS (now divided into the Special Raiding Squadron under Mayne and the Special Boat Squadron under Jellicoe) and 2 SAS under Bill Stirling conducted a series of raids against targets that were, in some cases, of purely tactical significance and in others required the SAS to operate, in effect, as commandos rather than special forces. What became evident was that without the benefit of a huge open flank, and faced with a complex security and logistic infrastructure, small-scale raids were much more difficult and achieved considerably less impact. Some operations were set up on a purely speculative basis, including sending parties into enemy-held territory to find and cut telegraph wires, but others, particularly the SRS operations at Bagnara and Termoli, were launched with the aim of achieving specific results.

The Bagnara operation, in early September 1943, was a coastal assault in which the SRS, commanded by Mayne and accompanied by other commando units, were directed to seize the Italian port of Bagnara and hold it, thus disrupting German lines of communication and forcing them to retreat in the face of the Eighth Army who were, by now, advancing from the Salerno beachhead against dogged opposition. Although a success – SRS achieved their objectives with relatively light casualties (five dead and six wounded) – it was a pointless misuse of a highly specialized capability. The value of lightly armed, mobile and stealthy special forces does not lie in their ability to seize and hold ground, even though they possess the bravery and tactical skills to do so; in Bagnara they were lucky to get away relatively lightly.

The Termoli raid in October 1943 was to be 1 SAS's last operation before returning to the UK for re-training. In some respects it was a re-run of the Bagnara attack, in so far as the SRS were to land with a force of commandos (from 3 and 40 Commandos) and then go on to seize and hold two key bridges. The aim was similar: the attack was launched in order to disrupt German counter-moves against British and US forces in the south of Italy. Nevertheless, it was a misuse of the skills of the SAS and on this occasion they were not so lucky.

With surprise on their side SRS quickly achieved its objective in the coastal town of Vasto to the north of the main commando bridgehead and secured a defensive position around the area. As expected, the Germans launched a swift counter-attack, bringing members of their elite 1st Parachute Division into action to expel the British raiders from their objectives. Knowing that they couldn't hope to hold their position for any length of time, Mayne and his men began to conduct an orderly withdrawal. As the Germans brought armour, artillery and mortars to bear on the lightly armed British:

> . . . this bloody great shell landed right in the middle of the truck. It blew us to hell. We were carrying detonators for the '78' 2-lb grenade in our packs – you never loaded the grenades till you needed. Mine was the only pack not to explode.
>
> A family who lived opposite the truck – three or four girls who did the washing for us – the women were just blown open. The eldest son was running around screaming, with his guts hanging out like a huge balloon. I caught him and shot him – it was the only thing to do. Wounded all over the place. I was covered in blood and bits of flesh – I stank for days after it. Lance-Corporal Grant picked up his own arm, his own arm, and set it to one side. 'I've had it this time,' he said. He died of wounds that day.[10]

In all 29 members of SRS were killed – more than ten per cent of their strength – in an operation that could quite easily have been handled by a less specialized, less highly skilled unit.

---

10 Lt Reg Seekings, quoted in Bradford and Dillon, *Rogue Warrior of the SAS*, 1987, p. 134.

The question of appropriate employment for the SAS remained a problem throughout the rest of the war. By the end of 1943 there were two British SAS regiments, two French *Regiments de Chasseurs Parachutistes* (one composed of Free French volunteers, one of 'Vichy' soldiers recruited after the liberation of Algeria: relations between these two units were somewhat fraught) and a Belgian independent squadron. These were grouped together into an SAS Brigade under the command of Brigadier R W McLeod, a Royal Artillery officer, and based in Scotland to train for operations in Europe. After a certain amount of indecision it was decided that the SAS would operate in France after the invasion, providing a stiffening of disciplined but flexible troops to operate in support of, and in some respects to guide, the French Resistance forces who would be harassing the German lines of communication. This was a task that had been carried out by 2 SAS during their operations in Italy, when they had linked up with partisan groups operating in rural areas of the country against the German occupiers.

This was considered an important role for the SAS, and it was hard won. One of the early plans for the Brigade had been to provide diversionary raids to cover the real invasion – a role of almost suicidal danger – and which was resisted by Bill Stirling to the point of resignation. At the same time, it put the SAS into competition with SOE – the Special Operations Executive – an organization set up in the dark days of 1940 to actively support resistance to Nazi rule throughout occupied Europe. Apart from SOE agents and networks active in France since 1941, the organization planned to send uniformed 'Jedburgh' teams, consisting of a British, an American and a French member, as liaison to Resistance groups in order to co-ordinate resupply from England and to pass on orders and instructions.

There was a difference between the envisaged roles of the SAS and of the 'Jeds', but it was a subtle one. SAS troops would be present in sufficient numbers to conduct their own operations, attacking bridges, railways, supply depots and other traditional LOC targets; they would also have their own vehicles, armoured jeeps, dropped with them which would add to their mobility and operational flexibility.

One crucial stipulation which affected both the SAS and the Jedburgh teams was they could not be dropped into France prior to the start of the main invasion (Operation Neptune), for fear that their capture might compromise details of the overall plan. As a result, the forty-three members of the SAS Brigade who dropped into France as reconnaissance and advance parties on the night of 5/6 June 1944 – amongst the first members off the Allied forces to arrive on French soil – were the first members of the SAS to serve in north-west Europe. The SAS Brigade Headquarters summary, prepared at the end of June 1944, describes their tasks:

TOP SECRET

Place	FRANCE
Date	6 June 44 to 30 June 44
Operation	OVERLORD
Event	Operation NEPTUNE – Summary of SAS participation for JUNE

Pre-arranged SAS participation in NEPTUNE, the assault phase of OVERLORD, comprised the establishment by 4 FRENCH PARA BN of two base areas in BRITTANY (SAMWEST, SW of GUINGAMP and DINGSON in the LANDES DE LANVAUX NE of VANNES), and by 1 SAS Regt of two bases in central France (BULBASKET in the BRENNE marsh west of CHATEAUROUX and HOUNDSWORTH in the MORVAN Mountains N25).

In addition 1 SAS Regt found a small party for a deception operation (TITANIC 4) in connection with the main air-borne assault in NORMANDY. From the bases it was intended that small parties should work outwards against enemy road and rail communications, particu-larly the latter, and such chance targets as dumps, and telephone cables. In BRITTANY, a direct drop (operation COONEY) onto various railway targets was planned for D +

1/D + 2 for a troop of 4 French Para Bn, who were to work back into base afterwards. It was accepted that the first need was to establish a firm base in each area, before feeding in the further offensive parties.

In the event, reconnaissance parties were safely despatched and reported favourably on all areas. The two BRITTANY bases expanded rapidly – too rapidly for they both drew enemy attention after growing to 115 and 328 men plus over 2000 Maquis respectively, and were dispersed by direct attack, but casualties were not excessive, and the whole remainder of 4 French Para Bn (including those dropped as planned for COONEY) was dispersed in small parties in central BRITTANY and spent the rest of the month organizing the local Maquis and arming it with weapons flown from the UK.

1 SAS's bases both developed securely; HOUNDSWORTH was reinforced up to 80 men and able to begin offensive operations. The BULBASKET party moved further SW than had been foreseen, to conform with active Maquis groups in support of which it was operating and was reinforced up to 44 men. Part of this reinforcement was carried out by dropping parties direct onto rail targets in the area (operation LOT) and a similar operation (GAIN) was mounted later in the month in the PARIS-ORLEANS area, where about 25 men were dropped to form a small base. LOT and GAIN were both mounted at very short notice.

By the end of the month a total of 585 SAS Tps had been dropped almost all by 38 Group RAF (a few by 3 Gp) for the loss of only one aircraft and 15 men.

Resupply sorties, principally to BRITTANY, had dropped nine jeeps and 1892 containers of stores. JUNE, therefore, saw nearly a third of the Brigade's operational strength deployed, and laid the foundations for future offensive operations on a wider scale than had been possible while bases were being established.

The bases established by the SAS parties were, by and large, in remote forested areas away from towns and major centres of population, and normally co-located or, at least, close by camps used by the Maquis: French partisans operating as guerrillas on a more or less permanent and semi-overt basis. For short periods, the lifestyle of the SAS with the Maquis produced an almost idyllic illusion:

> When we finally reached the campsite, out came the wine and a sumptuous meal was prepared. Tucking into vast portions of meat and potatoes we were surrounded by grinning Maquis trying to communicate in French and broken English. We were located in the Morvan just to the north of Chateau Chinon, an area of steep hills which was an ideal hiding place for the Maquis. Having eaten our fill, we settled into our sleeping bags and drifted off to sleep. The following morning the Maquis showed us the location of our own bivouac area and told us where we could get wood for cooking and drinking water.[11]

As the SAS bases increased in size, they were joined by signals specialists from the GHQ Liaison Regiment 'Phantom', whose F Squadron was assigned to work with the SAS supplying long-range communications to the tactical HQ of the SAS Brigade at Moor Park in north-west London. Theoretically trained to the same standards as their SAS colleagues, they shared the SAS's precarious existence inside France. An interesting insight into the degree of security that the SAS parties felt whilst working with the Maquis is provided by the following extensive list of military equipment carried by members of a 'Phantom' patrol working with the SAS:

---

11 Johnny Cooper, p. 89.

Personal Kit Taken by No. 3 Patrol, SAS PHANTOM

Per man

1	.45 Automatic and holster
1	.45 Automatic spare mags and pouches
1	Tin dubbin
1	Life belt Mk 2
1	Knife, fighting
1	Knife, single blade folding
1	Trousers, paratroops
2	Vests, string (too heavy for hot weather)
1	Flashlight US 122A with 1 spare Bty (excellent)
1	Ruc-sac, Bergan, rubber lined
1	Bedding roll, Icelandic with cover (cover too heavy)
1	Entrenching tool with cover
1	Map case, 'Z' type
1	Oil bottle, gauze, and rod
20	Rds amn .45 spare
1	Mess tin
1	Waterbottle
1	Ground sheet
4	Prs socks, spare
1	Shirt, spare
1	Pullover, worn
1	Gym shoes prs
1	Washing kit
3	Pencils
3	Message pads, small
1	First field dressing
1	First aid pack (add foot powder)
1	Steel helmet with net (never used after jumping)
1	Smock, airborne, camouflaged

1	Jumping jacket (never used after jumping)
1	Pr short puttees (gaiters would be better)
4	Boxes matches
1	Escape pack
2	Secret compasses
1	Escape money purse (£12)
1	Language booklet
3	24 hr ration packs
2	Face veil camouflaged
4	Handkerchiefs
1	Compass, oil
1	Pr binoculars
1	Watch GS
1	Housewife[12]
1	Luminous ball (not really of use)
1	Anti-dog smell (never used)
1	Maps sets of the area
1	Gas cape (optional) (most useful for bivouacs)
1	Knife, fork, spoon, mug set
1	Carbine American with 5 mags .30
1	Haversacks American type

Carried in the Patrol

2	Jedburgh sets complete with 6 crystals
2	MCR1 with 2 bts each
2	Protractors
2	Code books and 3 silks
2	India rubbers
4	Sets rubber heels and soles
5	Escape maps (2 were paper, 1 silk) sets
5	Grenades No. 36
2	Sets of colour filters for torches

12 A sewing kit

The SAS Brigade's operations in France undoubtedly achieved many successes at the tactical level. The German garrison troops (often Russians, Cossacks and even Indians, bribed and black-mailed out of POW camps) against whom they were normally pitted were ill-equipped and ill-motivated to deal with the highly trained, enthusiastic SAS. Nevertheless, the question of whether they achieved their aim, the disruption of the German lines of communication to the extent that it hampered the main German military effort is more debatable.

One of the principal objectives of the SAS and Resistance in the immediate aftermath of the invasion was to delay the arrival of the 2nd SS Panzer Division 'Das Reich' in the operational area. Despite its number, the 2nd SS Division was in fact the oldest combat division of the Waffen-SS, probably the best equipped and certainly the best led (1st SS Panzer Division 'Leibstandarte Adolf Hitler' was also well equipped and well led but contained a higher number of officers who owed their position to political and family influence). As the SS-Verfügungs Division it had spearheaded the German invasion of France in 1940 and of the Soviet Union in 1941, and it had taken part in many of the crucial battles in Russia since then. In early 1944, the division was moved to the Toulouse area of southern France to rest and refit and to upgrade its armoured complement. It was recognized by Allied planners that, should the division arrive at the Normandy beachhead during the first few days of the invasion, it would pose an enormous threat to the success of the entire operation.

Deception operations designed to persuade the German high command that the main Allied landings would take place in the Pas de Calais area successfully delayed 'Das Reich's' move for several days, whilst Allied air superiority limited the Germans' ability to move by day at all. Resistance units in the path of the SS division had been tasked to launch delaying attacks and did so, but the limited firepower available to the Resistance meant that these attacks were little more than pinpricks against the powerful German formation. Even so, the casualties caused by these efforts outraged the SS, who regarded the Resistance as terrorists outside the scope of the Geneva Conventions, sufficiently for them to mount two horrific and brutal reprisal operations against local French civilians. The first of these was the hanging from lampposts in the town of Tulle of ninety-nine civilians, the second, on 10 June 1944, was the massacre of 648 men, women and children of the village of Oradour-sur-Glane.

The lightly armed parties of 1 SAS's Operation Bulbasket, who were in the path of 'Das Reich', not surprisingly avoided direct contact with it, but they did report on the position of elements of the Division and on the presence of a number of fuel trains in rail sidings at Chatellerault. This fuel was intended for 'Das Reich' but bombing raids by the Allied tactical air force destroyed much of it, imposing more delays on the Division.

In the event, it took 'Das Reich' some seventeen days to reach the combat zone; a journey that shouldn't have lasted more than a week (some writers have suggested that the Division could have made the journey in three days but this is highly unlikely). The principal reason for this was the air threat to the Division's convoys which inhibited daylight movement, but as the SAS were directly involved in reporting information to the Allied tactical air force, it is fair to accord them a measure of credit for their role. Nevertheless, the delaying strategy was put in place on the assumption that the Division would be a threat if it was thrown into battle straight from the line of march against newly arrived troops, and this does not appear to have been part of the German plan. Instead, even after 'Das Reich' had reached the combat zone, they were held in reserve for operations that didn't commence in earnest until early July.

In the meantime, Operation Bulbasket had been compromised and attacked by German security units. One SAS officer, Lt Tomos Stevens, had been killed (beaten to death with a rifle butt as he lay wounded on the ground); three troopers were seriously wounded and captured together with twenty-seven lightly wounded or uninjured members of the Bulbasket party: all thirty – more than half the party – were executed by the German Army in accordance with Hitler's savage *Kommandobefehl*, which claimed that commandos and special forces fell outside the Geneva Conventions.

The reality of capture for most members of the SAS since the end of the Western Desert campaign has been grim. The nature of special forces is that they are rarely captured by front-line soldiers, more often than not they fall into the clutches of militias or security units composed of frightened individuals of limited competence, who have had little or no contact with their enemies and have not developed the empathy that opposing combatants traditionally feel. Oddly enough, the same can be true for the SAS themselves: they are normally held back a considerable distance from the front line until they are committed operationally. This tends to give them a dangerously abstract view of their enemies, an attitude reflected in the decision of Capt Robin Edwards and his patrol to shoot a non-combatant goatherd during their tragically ill-fated patrol in the Radfan in 1964 (*see pages 127–31*).

The *Kommandobefehl* is worth looking at because it encapsulates an attitude that persists even now:

1 For some time our enemies have been using, in their warfare, methods which are outside the international Geneva Conventions. Especially brutal and treacherous is the behaviour of the so-called Commandos, who, as established, are partially recruited from freed criminals in enemy countries. From captured orders it is established that they are directed not only to shackle prisoners, but also to kill defenceless prisoners on the spot at the moment in which they believe that the latter, as prisoners, represent a burden in the further pursuit of their purposes, or could otherwise be a hindrance. Finally, orders have been found in which the killing of prisoners has been demanded in principle.

2 For this reason it was already announced, in an addendum to the Wehrmacht report of 7 October 1942, that, in future in the face of these sabotage troops of the British and their accomplices, Germany will resort to the same procedure: that is they will be ruthlessly killed by German troops in combat wherever they appear.

3 I therefore order:
Henceforth, all enemies on so-called Commando missions in Europe or Africa, challenged by German troops, even if they are to all appearances soldiers in uniform or demolition troops,

whether armed or unarmed, in battle or flight, are to be slaughtered to the last man. It does not make any difference whether they are dropped by parachute. Even if these individuals, when found, should be prepared to give themselves up, no pardon is to be given to them as a matter of principle. In each individual case information is to be sent to the OKW for publication in Wehrmacht despatches.

4 If individual members of such Commandos, such as agents, saboteurs, etc., fall into the hands of the Wehrmacht by other means, through the police in occupied territories, for example, they are to be handed immediately to the SD. Any imprisonment under military guard, in POW camps and so forth, is strictly prohibited, even if this is only temporary.

5 This order does not apply to the treatment of any soldiers who, in the course of normal hostilities, large-scale offensive actions, landing operations and airborne operations, are captured in open battle or give themselves up. Nor does this apply to enemy soldiers falling into our hands at sea, nor to enemy soldiers trying to save their lives by parachute after air battles.

6 I will hold responsible, under Military Law, all commanders and officers who fail to carry out this order, who neglect to instruct their subordinates about it or who question its implementation in specific cases.

Adolf Hitler
18 October 1942

The activities of the SAS, and their SOE and Resistance counterparts, behind the lines in occupied France certainly did cause considerable disruption, but whether it was sufficient to seriously affect the Germans' war fighting ability – as the SAS had demonstrably done in North Africa – remains clouded by the fog of war. The toll of spending long periods behind enemy lines was large. Apart from losing men through death, injury and capture (which they were unlikely to survive, bearing in mind the criminal ruthlessness of the *Kommandobefehl*), psychological stress was severe. On 10 August 1944, Brigadier McLeod, overall commander of the SAS, visited the *2ème Regiment de Chasseurs Parachutistes* (usually known as 4th French Para or 4 SAS) and recorded his impressions in the SAS Brigade war diary:

> Discipline is first class and morale is extremely high. The unit regards itself as having been largely responsible for liberating Brittany and are more than anxious to get back to grips with the Germans. The majority will jump again if called upon to do so, but in spite of their apparent high morale I consider that they have undergone a very severe nervous strain and should not again be asked to operate with the Maquis behind enemy lines if it can be avoided. There is no doubt that a proportion of the men could not stand the nervous strain of this sort of life again, but are more than anxious to meet the enemy in overt as opposed to clandestine warfare.

By the end of September 1944 the French campaign was over as far as the SAS were concerned. Now that the Germans were being forced back behind the pre-war borders of the Reich there seemed to be little prospect of using the brigade for much other than armed reconnaissance and this did, in fact prove to be the case; from January 1945 onwards SAS parties acted in a reconnaissance and liaison role. Strategic operations by special forces in the dying months of the war would have been a waste of resources and a dilution of the main effort. Nevertheless, the SAS did play an important role as a reconnaissance force and their flexibility was such as to give a notable 'edge' to formation commanders in areas where they were operating. In the last few weeks of the war, SAS troops were amongst the first to reach the Belsen concentration camp, where they found scenes of indescribable horror; and the British component of the SAS Brigade played a vital role in supervising the German surrender in Norway at the war's end.

There is no doubt whatsoever that in the Western Desert in 1942, David Stirling's idea of using small raiding parties to hit Axis airfields and lines of communication, had a strategic impact on the outcome of the campaign. A relatively small group of enterprising and aggressive misfits – for want of a better word – caused chaos and destruction out of all proportion to their own strength and, importantly, at very little cost to the main effort. They did not need to be closely co-ordinated with operations at Army level and could, to some extent, be left to get on with matters themselves. It was a buccaneering, freebooting style of warfare whose character owed a lot to the personalities of the principal leaders involved. It is equally clear that as the war progressed out of the desert wilderness, it became much more difficult to achieve the same 'value for money'. The costs in terms of troops involved, support effort and casualties became progressively higher. SAS operations in North Africa were unequivocally successful with 250 men involved: in France, ten times that number produced a rather less clear-cut result. Nevertheless, the SAS under David Stirling, 'Paddy' Mayne, Roddy McLeod and, in the last few months of the war, Mike Calvert, had turned heads at the very highest level, and the end of hostilities in Europe did not spell the end for the Special Air Service.

2. **Renaissance:**
Malaya 1948–60

Soldiers joining 22 SAS are still essentially trained as jungle soldiers

During his captivity as a prisoner of war, David Stirling spent a good proportion of his time musing on how his creation, the Special Air Service, could be used after the European phase of World War II had ended. Japan, of course, fought on after the German capitulation in May 1945 and, although the Japanese were clearly heading for defeat, it was by no means clear how soon it might be achieved.

Although Japanese air and sea power had all but evaporated by 1945, their ground forces remained relatively strong and capable of fierce, even fanatical, resistance. Japanese troops were still fighting in Burma, the Philippines, Borneo and, particularly, China, where their infrastructure was still sufficiently intact to be able to provide supplies to the besieged Japanese home islands. It was here that Stirling proposed to employ the SAS, raiding the Manchurian railway, and perhaps also hitting the main supply routes maintaining Japanese forces in Malaya.

But Stirling, and the great majority of those working on plans for larger scale operations, were unaware of the new factor in warfare that was to become available in August 1945: the atomic bomb. The attacks on Hiroshima on 6 August and Nagasaki on 9 August, together with the threat of further strikes as the new weapons were constructed, precipitated Japan's unconditional surrender, and with that disappeared any obvious requirement for a military special operations force in the Far East. In possession of an SAS Brigade Headquarters together with two operational regiments, 1 and 2 SAS (the French and Belgian SAS units had been handed over to their respective national commands in September 1945), the War Office took the view that the SAS should be temporarily shelved pending investigation as to what future role, if any, it might have. On 8 October 1945, the British SAS contingent was formally disbanded.

This was not the end for the SAS, however, and contrary to modern myth, it was not intended to be. Even as the majority of members of the regiments returned to civilian life, Mike Calvert, the last brigade commander, was soliciting views from senior SAS officers enquiring about their thoughts for the future of the regiment:

FUTURE OF SAS TROOPS

To:

Lt-Col W Stirling	Lt-Col The Earl Jellicoe
Lt-Col D Stirling, DSO	Lt-Col D Sutherland
Lt-Col RB Mayne, DSO	Lt-Col D Lloyd Owen, MC
Lt-Col BMF Franks, DSO, MC	Major J Verney, MC
Lt-Col IG Collins	Major R Farran, DSO, MC
Lt-Col EC Baring	

The Director of Tactical Investigations, Maj-Gen ROWELL, has been ordered by the Chief of Imperial General Staff that his directorate should investigate all the operations of the Special Air Service with a view to giving recommendations for the future of SAS in the next war and its composition in the peace-time army. The actual terms of reference were:

An investigation of SAS technique, tactics and organization without prejudice to a later examination of all organizations of a similar nature which were formed and operated in various theatres of this last war.

Brigadier Churchill is Deputy Director of Tactical

Investigation and lives at Flat 110, 4 Whitehall Court, London, SW1 (Whitehall 9400 Ext 1632), just behind the War Office. The Officer immediately concerned is Lt-Col CA Wigham. Lt-Col Wigham has in his possession all the reports on SAS operations in W. EUROPE. The reports on SAS operations in ITALY and in the MEDITERRANEAN Theatre are also being obtained and forwarded. I have given Lt-Col Wigham your names so that he may either have a talk with you to obtain your views and to find out about incidents which are not clear in the reports, or to ask you to write your views to him.

We all have the future of the SAS at heart, not merely because we wish to see its particular survival as a unit, but because we have believed in the principles of its method of operations. Many of the above-named officers have had command of forces which have had a similar role to that of the SAS, as well as being in the SAS at one time.

The object of this investigation is to decide whether the principles of operating in the SAS manner are correct. If they are correct, what types of units should undertake operations of this nature, and who best to train and maintain such units in peace, ready for war. I will not start now by writing about the principles of SAS, which have been an intrinsic part of your life for the past few years, but I will mention what I think are some of the most important points which need bringing out. The best way to do this is to consider the usual criticisms of the SAS type of force.

1 *'The Private Army'*

From what I have seen in different parts of the world, forces of this nature tend to be so-called 'Private Armies' because there have been no normal formations in existence to fulfil this function – a role which has been found by all commanders to be a most vital adjunct to their plans. It has only been

due to the drive and initiative of certain individuals backed up by senior commanders that these
forces have been formed and have carried out their
role.

2 '*The taking up of Commanders' valuable time*'
This has often been necessary because it has very
often only been the Comds of armies who have realized
the importance of operations of this nature, and to
what an extent they can help their plans. The difficulty has been that more junior staff officers have
not understood the object or principles of such forces. They have either given us every help as they
have thought us something wonderful, or they have
thought we were 'a bloody nuisance'. I felt that the
best way to overcome this is, that once the principle
of the importance of Special Raiding Forces operating behind the vital points of the enemy's lines
is agreed to it should become an integral part of the
training of the army at the Staff College, military
colleges, and during manoeuvres, etc. Students
should be asked not only what orders or directives
or requests they have to give to the artillery, engineers, air, etc., but also what directives they
would give to their raiding forces. There should be
a recognized staff officer on the staffs of senior
formations whose job it is to deal with these forces,
i.e. the equivalent of a CRE or CRA. This should be
included in the textbooks FSR, etc.

3 '*These forces, like airborne forces, are only required when we pass to the offensive, which – judging
by all previous wars – is when the regular army has
been nearly wiped out in rearguard actions whilst the
citizen army forms, i.e. about 3 years after the
beginning of the war*'
The answer here, I feel, is that it is just when we
are weak everywhere that forces of this nature are
the most useful, and can play a most vital part in

keeping the enemy all over the world occupied. Also there is little difference between the roles of SAS and 'Auxiliary Forces' who duck when the enemy's offensive rolls over them and then operate against the enemy's L of C from previously constructed bases. An SAS formation, by its organization and training, is ideally suited to operate in this defensive role.

4 '*Overlapping with SOE and other clandestine organizations*'

My experience is that SOE and SAS are complementary to each other. SAS cannot successfully operate without good intelligence, guides, etc. SOE can only do a certain amount before requiring, when their operations became overt, highly trained, armed bodies in uniform to operate and set an example to the local resistance. SOE are the 'white hunters' and produce the ground organization of which SAS operates. All senior officers of SOE with whom I have discussed this point agree to this principle.

5 '*SAS is not adaptable to all countries*'

This has already been proved wrong. SAS is probably more adaptable to changes of theatres than any regular formation. Also, as I have said in 4 above, SAS work on the ground organization of SOE. It is for SOE to be a worldwide organization with an organization in every likely country. Then when necessary, SAS can operate on this organization using their guides and intelligence, knowledge, etc.

6 '*Volunteer units skim the regular units of their best officers and men*'

Volunteer units such as SAS attract officers and men who have initiative, resourcefulness, independence of spirit, and confidence in themselves. In a regular unit there are far less opportunities for

making use of these assets and, in fact, in many
formations they are a liability, as this indi-
vidualistic attitude upsets the smooth working
of a team. This is especially true in European
warfare where the individual must subordinate his
natural initiative so that he fits in to a part of the
machine. Volunteer units such as the Commandos and
Chindits (only a small proportion of the Chindits
were volunteers although the spirit was there) have
shown the rest of the army how to fight at a time when
it was in low morale due to constant defeat. A few
'gladiators' raises the standard of all. Analogies
are racing (car, aeroplane, horse, etc.), and Test
teams.

7 *'Expense per man is greater than any other formation
and is not worthwhile'*

Men in units of this nature probably fight 3 or 4
times more often than regular units. They are always
eager for a fight and therefore usually get it. If
expense per man days *actually in contact with the
enemy* was taken into account, there would be no
doubt which was the more expensive type of formation. I have found, as you will have done, the 'old
familiar faces' on every front where we have seen
trouble. I consider the expense is definitely worth
it without even taking into account the extra
results. One SAS raid in North Africa destroyed
more aeroplanes in one day that the balloon barrage
did during 6 years of war.

8 *'Any normal battalion could do the same job'*

My experience shows that they definitely cannot. In
NORWAY in 1940, a platoon of marines under a Sgt ran
away when left on its own, although they had orders
to stay, when a few German lorries appeared. Mainly
owing to the bad leadership of this parade-ground
Sgt, they were all jittery and useless because they
were 'out of touch', and could not receive orders.

By avoiding action, the unit went into a waterless area and more perished this way and later by drowning than if they had attacked.

My experience with regular battalions under my command in Burma was that there were only 3 or 4 officers in any battalion who could be relied on to take positive action if they were on their own, and had no detailed orders. This 'I'll 'ave to ask me Dad' attitude of the British Army is its worst feature in my opinion. I have found the RAF and Dominion officers far better in this respect. I have not had experience with the cavalry. They should also be better. Perhaps cavalry could take on the SAS role successfully? I admit that with training both in Burma and North Africa there were definite improvements amongst the infantry, but in my opinion, no normal battalion I have seen could carry out an SAS role without 80% reorganization. I have written frankly and have laid myself open to obvious criticism, but I consider this such a vital point that I do not mind how strongly I express myself. I have repeated this for 5 years and I have nowhere seen anything to change my views, least of all in Europe.

I have mentioned some points above. You may not agree with my ideas but I write them down as these criticisms are the most normal ones I know. Other points on which the DTI wants to obtain information are:

- *Obtaining of recruits.* Has anybody got the original brochure setting out the terms and standards required?
- *Obtaining of stores and equipment.* Here again, I imagine SOE has been the main source of special stores. My own HQ is producing a paper on this when in England.
- *Signal communication.* This is of course one of the most important parts of such an organization and it has, as in other formations, limited the scope of our operations.

- *Foreign recruits and attached civilians.*
- *Liaison with RAF and Navy.*
- *Command.* How is an organization of this sort best commanded and under whom should they be?
- Suggestions re survival in peacetime including auxiliary formation, command, technical development etc.

You may expect a communication from Lt-Col Wigham. Please give your views quite candidly. They certainly need not agree with those I have written down. I am sending Lt-Col Wigham a copy of this letter so that it may give you something to refer to if necessary. I hope, from the army point of view, and for all that you have worked for and believed in during the last few years, that you will do everything you can to help Lt-Col Wigham to obtain all the information that he requires. We can no longer say that people do not understand if we do not take this chance to get our views put before an impartial tribunal whose task it is to review them in the light of general policy and then make recommendations to the CIGS. Send along any reports or documents you have got. Lt-Col Wigham is thirsting for more information.

Sloe House	JM CALVERT
Halstead, Essex	Brigadier,
12 Oct 45.	Commander,
JMC/LGM.	SAS Troops

The outcome of this consultation exercise was the conclusion that:

1 There was unlikely ever again to be a war with static front lines, except perhaps for short periods.

2 Small parties of well-trained and thoroughly disciplined troops operating behind the enemy lines achieve results out of all proportion to the numbers involved.

3 Their operations are, and should be quite distinct from

non-regular groups such as Special Operations Executive, or Secret Service.

4 The full potential of such units is not yet fully known but there is clearly scope for tremendous development.

5 The role of SAS troops should never be confused with the normal role of the infantry. The SAS task is more specialized. The SAS does not necessarily drain the infantry of its best men but will often take a person who is no better than average in his ordinary tasks and transform him into a specialist. A man of great individuality may not fit into an orthodox unit as well as he does to a specialist force. In wartime the best leaders were independent, well-travelled men who were often good linguists; university men, who had made full use of their brains at and after university and were mature, often successful.

As a result of which it was decided to create an SAS Regiment when the Territorial Army was brought back into being in 1947, and recruiting for 21 SAS Regiment (Artists) began in September 1947.

21 SAS was placed under the command of Lt-Col Brian Franks, the former CO of 2 SAS, and, originally at least, a majority of members of the new unit were former members of the wartime SAS units:

I met Billy on the Charing Cross Road and we went for a drink in a pub on the Cambridge Circus. We were talking about old times, as you do, and he mentioned that he had joined the Territorials, and that they had re-formed the SAS as a territorial regiment and he was back in it, and it was a lot of the old boys from the war. My first reaction was 'good luck to him', but over the next few weeks I started thinking about it more and more, and I suppose it began to sink in just how much I missed all the old chaps.

After a while I wrote off and was invited to go down to the barracks in Euston and sign up, which I did, and virtually the first chap I met there was Billy and his first words were 'I knew you'd show up eventually', but really, it was tremendous to be back in that atmosphere.'

21 SAS was essentially being formed for operations in Europe in the event of general war and would become operational in the event of a large-scale mobilization, but in the wake of the end of World War II and the decision to withdraw from India, the cornerstone of the Empire, Britain was to find itself embroiled in a plethora of relatively small-scale conflicts, ranging in intensity from the Korean War, which took up the attentions of an entire Commonwealth division, through to minor skirmishes and policing operations in Africa, the Pacific and the Caribbean which might be handled by a force no larger than an infantry or Marine company. But in the summer of 1948, an uprising started in a colony that was to be a thorn in the side of the British military for the next twelve years: Malaya.

The Malayan Emergency, as it became known, was a bizarre offspring of the Chinese civil war, which was, at the end of World War II, about to move into its final phase. The Malayan Communist Party had begun to organize as early as 1930, but it received its real impetus as a result of the Japanese occupation of Malaya, Singapore and the other European colonies of south-east Asia in 1942. Apart from the military defeat they had suffered, the blow to European prestige and 'face' was enormous and one from which it was unlikely that the colonial powers would ever recover, whatever the final outcome of the war. In Malaya and Singapore, a large but poorly equipped and inadequately led Commonwealth force was defeated by less than half their number of Japanese invaders. Singapore was, at that time, Britain's principal strategic naval base in the Far East and the island had been fortified against possible attack at enormous financial cost during the 1930s, but a lack of foresight and military imagination left the Malayan peninsula itself relatively undefended, and the Commonwealth forces had effectively crumbled when the Japanese attacked.

In the face of military defeat, an attempt was made in the

---

1 Letter. NCO. 21 SAS.

dying days of the campaign to deploy 'stay-behind' teams of guerrilla saboteurs into the jungle. Few survived very long, but from this experience an SOE-type unit, Force 136, was created to develop and nurture resistance to the Japanese.

Although they preached a form of anti-colonialist Asian nationalism, the new Japanese rulers of south-east Asia were not much less racially supremacist than their German counterparts in Europe and it was not long before the brutality of their occupation policies began to stir up genuine indigenous resistance. The object of Force 136 was to harness this feeling and allow it expression by supplying training, leadership and, most importantly, *matériel*. In Malaya it soon became apparent that the best organized resisters were to be found in the Malayan Communist Party and their Malayan People's Anti-Japanese Army (MPAJA) and, similarly to Fitzroy Maclean in Yugoslavia, Force 136 actually provided most assistance to an avowedly communist grouping.

One particularly interesting feature of the Malayan Communist Party and the MPAJA was in its ethnic make-up: it was largely drawn from the minority Chinese population, which, by and large, lived in 'Chinatown' ghettos in the towns. Despite their urban background, however, the MPAJA showed no reluctance to operate in jungle areas and their relative ethnic exclusivity also proved an advantage in providing a ready-made support infrastructure within the Chinese population. This support structure, known as the 'Min Yuen', probably involved a majority of the Chinese population at one stage or another, and was as much a result of family ties as of political affiliation. As will be readily appreciated, the conjunction of politically committed communist guerrillas, an extended ethnically homogenous logistics and intelligence system and military support and, to some extent, leadership from the British Empire and its allies created an effective resistance force.

Even so, the end of the war in south-east Asia caught the MPAJA by surprise. Although the Japanese home islands had been utterly devastated by American bombing, including the two atomic strikes, some of the outlying garrisons were relatively unscathed, and there was no reason to suppose that the Japanese forces would collapse as quickly as they did. When Japanese authority in the Malayan peninsula ended, the MPAJA and the Malayan Communist Party (MCP) were in no position to attempt to seize power or fill the temporary vacuum that was created and instead they made every effort to stockpile as many weapons as they could lay their hands on.

It appears there was some confusion amongst the MCP regarding their next move and also a somewhat naive belief that 'a People's Republic in Malaya could be achieved by co-operation with and the eventual support of the British authorities'.[2] Consequently, it took some time for their strategy and tactics to evolve. For the first two and a half years after the end of the war, the MCP consolidated their military infrastructure (their military wing was called the Malayan Race's Liberation Army but they were almost always referred to as Communist Terrorists or CTs as the result of a British psyops campaign) and built up a campaign of subversion, infiltration of trades unions and other associations, disruption of industry, agriculture and commerce, and the assassination of (mainly Malayan and Indian) managerial personnel until in the summer of 1948 the government declared a state of emergency.

The British response to the outbreak of violence was characteristically patchy: the Labour government of Clement Attlee had no wish to hang on to Malaya as a colony but it clearly could not grant independence whilst an armed insurrection was taking place. Only when the Communist Terrorists were being contained could meaningful progress be made towards self-rule. The problem was: how to contain the terrorists, now operating in the alien and seemingly impenetrable jungle?

The British Army of the late 1940s was something of a hotchpotch. The majority of men who had fought in World War II had left after demobilization in 1945, leaving a hard-core of regular soldiers supplemented by National Servicemen of variable motivation at best. The relatively short duration of each conscript's service meant that many units comprised a large proportion of soldiers with no real experience and little enthusiasm,

---

2 Alan Hoe, Eric Morris. *Re-enter the SAS* 1994. p. 14

and yet this was the army which, for the next ten years or so, was expected to fight the battles associated with Britain's withdrawal from the empire.

Although the regular British Army prior to World War II had a good deal of experience dealing with counter-insurgency and low-intensity warfare, it had not, in recent years fought against such a well-organized enemy in such unforgiving surroundings. As a result, the first few years of the campaign, which was to be Britain's principal overseas operational military commitment, were marked by a distinct lack of success at both the tactical and strategic levels. The guerrilla strength amounted to about 3–3,500 operating permanently in the jungle in small groups, with at least 5,000 committing terrorist acts on a 'part-time' basis whilst living in towns; the Min Yuen support organization consisted of at least 400,000 members and probably as many as 600,000. The small relatively flexible guerrilla gangs would attack plantations, small villages and other centres, and unwieldy British infantry units would respond by launching slow search-and-destroy operations which rarely achieved their aim. The CTs hoped that by their strategy of concentrating on rural areas they would cripple the economy and then isolate the British and their allies in the towns; an urban uprising orchestrated by the Min Yuen would then force the British out completely. Faced with the failure of their initial response to the CTs, the apparently bewildered British leadership cast around for a new method to get them out of their predicament. The man selected to study the problem in the spring of 1950, at the suggestion of General Sir William Slim (Chief of the Imperial General Staff), was then working as a staff officer in Hong Kong: Major Mike Calvert, DSO, former commander of the SAS Brigade.

Calvert had an outstanding reputation as an unconventional fighting soldier. As a senior member of Major-General Orde Wingate's Chindits he had spent long periods commanding troops behind the Japanese lines in Burma and, although he was in fact a relatively junior major in the Royal Engineers, he had ended the war as a temporary brigadier commanding the SAS Brigade, taking over from Brigadier Roddy McLeod in early 1945. He had presided over the disbandment of the British SAS regiments but had initiated the studies which had eventually ensured that the SAS would remain part of the order of battle after the reorganization of the TA. Reverting to his substantive rank of major, he had then been sucked back into the career stream of the regular officer, attending staff college, working on the Boundary Commission for Yugoslavia and Italy and winding up in Hong Kong as the G1 (Air). His brief in Malaya was to come up with some recommendations to bring the emergency to an end.

Calvert's fact-finding mission has since become almost legendary in Special Forces circles. He covered a distance of around 30,000 miles over some seven months of exhaustive study, during which he interviewed soldiers and officers, accompanied patrols and operations, and made a recruiting trip to Rhodesia. His two most important observations were that military success against the CTs was being hampered by the confused chain of command that prevailed in Malaya, and that insufficient effort was being made to win control of the jungle and its inhabitants.

The first point was fast becoming glaringly obvious to the government in London: it was evident that ill-feeling and rivalry between the Colonial Administration, the Police and Special Branch, and the Army in Malaya were blocking any kind of resolution to the problem, but Calvert's second idea was more interesting. Freddie Spencer-Chapman, one of the original 'stay-behind' officers in 1942, had coined the phrase 'the jungle is neutral', by which he meant that with the correct approach, fighting in the jungle environment offered as many advantages as disadvantages, and that it was up to the jungle soldier to make use of them. The reluctance of the British forces to operate deep in the jungle – they would not usually stay in for more than a week or so – meant that it had become a haven for the CTs (who as urban Chinese had no greater 'instinctive feel' for the jungle environment than their opponents).

A second factor that Calvert identified in relation to this issue concerned the position of the aboriginal jungle tribesmen. About 100,000 of them lived deep in the jungle in longhouses, subsisting on what they were able to catch and gather in their tribal area and showing little interest in the outside world. Although they had no particularly good reason for supporting the CTs, many of them were doing so, providing food shelter and intelligence, partly because of intimidation but also because the CTs represented their major contact with outsiders. In the early stages of the conflict British troops treated the locals with an entirely unwarranted degree of brutality, an attitude exemplified by the massacre of (at least) twenty-five innocent Chinese by a small patrol of Scots Guards in 1948, an incident that was covered up for many years. The occasional appearances of British patrols in the aboriginals' tribal areas were an irritation to the aborigines, who would avoid them when possible and make little or no effort to help, even when they would have suffered no loss to have done so.

Calvert understood that by inserting patrols for much longer periods, and by making an effort, using medical and other forms of aid, to win the 'hearts and minds' of the local population it might be possible to make the jungle an extremely hostile, and possibly even untenable, environment for the CTs. Even so, he was less than sanguine about being able to achieve this aim with conventional infantry, and he recommended that a special long-range patrol unit be formed. The majority of his report was accepted for incorporation in the 'Briggs Plan', the document that served as a strategic blueprint for the Malayan campaign, but Calvert himself, with his background in the jungle as a Chindit, and as a wartime SAS officer, was given the task of raising the special unit. The name selected for Calvert's unit, 'The Malayan Scouts', reflected the Army's intention that it remain a purely local force raised to meet the conditions of the Malayan theatre only, but Calvert was keen to associate it with the SAS – as a military special force – and successfully lobbied to have SAS incorporated into the name, making it 'Malayan Scouts (SAS Regiment)'.

The genesis of the Malayan Scouts was by no means smooth. Although armed with the authority to raise the new unit, Calvert was given very little logistic or administrative support and found himself acting as recruiter, trainer, planner and quartermaster for the unit when he should have been commanding it. Personnel issues were also problematic: Calvert was to be allowed to select his officers by interview but his men were, by and large, selected for him by unit commanders who, not unnaturally, took the opportunity to unload their troublemakers and wasters. At one stage Calvert was even given ten deserters from the French Foreign Legion who had jumped ship in Singapore en route for the war in Indo-China. Not surprisingly, such recruits were worse than useless in a unit with the Malayan Scouts' projected role, but their presence, and that of similar low-grade soldiers, was to give the Malayan Scouts, and subsequently 22 SAS, an unde-served reputation that took many years to shake off:

They had a dreadful reputation, the SAS in Malaya. Whenever one came across them they were dirty, scruffy and drunk. The problem lay in their leadership because Calvert, for all his undoubted qualities, was also dirty, scruffy and drunk a lot of the time as well! When they first started working, they were not very much use to us: it was only when they'd been in the jungle for a few years that they started to achieve results.[3]

Calvert's training methods for the unit were also somewhat unconventional:

At one time he had us practising jungle movement by stalking each other with air-guns. We went into this patch of jungle and had to creep around until we found our opposite number and then shoot him! We wore fencing masks to cover our faces but the pellets from those guns bloody hurt!

On one occasion I was up against Mac and I was closing in on him when I heard the whistle blowing so I stood up straight and called to him to come out. And do you know what the bugger did? As I stood up he shot me right in the balls.

Well I was lucky because the pellet didn't go through my trousers but it was like someone had slapped my balls and you know how much that hurts. I'm a fighting Irishman, I didn't join the Army to let my mates shoot me with air-rifles, so I chased after him and gave him what for: a

3 Interview. Officer. Scots Guards.

damned good thumping. Anyhow, I thought I might have a spot of bother about it but Calvert thought it was all very funny and just let it drop.

But the pressure to achieve success with very limited means undoubtedly had an effect on the preparation of the unit. When A Squadron of the Malayan Scouts was deemed ready for its first training operation in August 1950, the standard of training left a good deal to be desired:

I had assumed that the officers and senior NCOs would be in the picture about everything because the other ranks weren't. I could probably just about get around with a map on Salisbury Plain but the deep jungle was a different kettle of fish and map-reading is no easy task. In the first six months of patrolling, I should say we were lost for five of them! It was a surprise to find that the officers couldn't really navigate either and we did spend a good deal of time fooling around trying to find where we were, rather than looking for the enemy.

It is certainly true that the Malayan Scouts developed a reputation for carousing when out of the jungle. Calvert, a hard-drinking man, felt that after long operations, parties and drinking sessions gave his men the opportunity to unwind, but it is probably true that he was both too busy and pre-occupied to take as close an interest in his men as he should have done at this stage, and matters began to get out of hand. A similar mistake was made with regard to the men's appearance:

In the jungle we all used to grow beards 'cause we'd get awful infections and rashes and so on from the nicks and cuts. But Calvert didn't mind if we kept them on afterwards and that caused a wee bit of friction with the Monkeys [Military Police] and some outside officers. I didn't keep mine on after we came out because it itched like billy-oh, but some of the fellows did.

---

4 Interview, NCO, Malayan Scouts (SAS).

For many fighting soldiers, the question of their men's appearance has often seemed profoundly trivial, but it can have an important effect on the way in which a military unit is perceived by outsiders. Traditionalists certainly made up the great majority of the officer corps in the 1950s, and probably still do today, and they have always been likely to form a poor opinion of soldiers who are scruffy in barracks, however effective they may be in the field. This prejudice can certainly lead to suspicion and misuse of units with a potentially important role to play, and Calvert's failure to enforce basic standards was a serious error.

The vicissitudes of founding a special force 'on the run' meant that A Squadron's early operations were not a success. On their first deployment, in August 1950, they failed to make contact with the enemy at all, but importantly, the more able officers and soldiers in the unit did begin to develop an understanding of what long-term jungle patrols entailed, and it was this 'jungle awareness' that was to have a major role in the relative successes of later years.

With A Squadron formed and ready for operations, the Malayan Scouts had a continuing need for volunteers to bring the unit up to a projected strength of four squadrons. The first source to be tapped back in Britain was, perhaps, the most obvious one, although it does not seem to have been at the forefront of the recruiters' minds: 21 SAS Regiment in London.

Following the North Korean invasion of the South on 25 June 1950, General MacArthur, the American commander of the United Nations forces, had requested two regiments of SAS troops from Britain to operate in the classic World War II role. This was evidently not possible, but nevertheless volunteers were called for from 21 SAS and the Z Reserve of SAS (wartime SAS soldiers with a peacetime training commitment) to form a squadron, known as M Independent Squadron, for service in Korea. Amongst those who put themselves forward were a number of World War II veterans, including at least one member of L Detachment:

After leaving the Guards at the end of the war I soon decided to re-enlist but I couldn't face the Guards' bullshit so I joined the Royal

Artillery where they made me a Bombardier. I came home from Greece in 1949 and found myself based in Wales. I heard about M Squadron and volunteered. I was given instructions to get myself down to Aldershot and on the railway platform I ran into Alistair McGregor, Tony Greville-Bell and Jock Easton, so, of course, we went straight to the pub. It was a lovely reunion. Tony virtually made me SSM on the spot![5]

In fact as the situation in Korea improved in early 1951 it was decided that there was no continuing need for M Squadron's services and, instead, the volunteers were offered the opportunity to go to Malaya instead. Sufficient came forward, 'between thirty or forty',[6] for the squadron to go out to Malaya as a formed unit where they were to become B Squadron of the Malayan Scouts.

Arrival in Malaya was something of a shock to the well-trained, highly motivated soldiers of B Squadron:

It was a hell of a problem. We had pretty good·discipline in our Squadron and it made things difficult all round when I was making my guys shave and do all the normal things soldiers do in camp while A Squadron seemed to just do as they pleased. Roadknight, the RSM, wasn't a lot of help in things like that. We soon heard the stories of Calvert's boozing and the wild parties that went on when the lads were out of the jungle.

B Squadron were joined shortly after their arrival by C (Rhodesia) Squadron, commanded by Captain (later Major) Peter Walls[7] and soon after that by D Squadron, which had also been raised from UK-based volunteers and had gone through a short period of training at the Airborne Forces Depot in Aldershot. All the new squadrons were put through a jungle training course organized by Major John Woodhouse, who had assumed temporary command of B Squadron when their original OC resigned his command in disgust at the apparent slackness and disorganization of the Malayan Scouts under Calvert, and shortly afterwards

---

5 Alan Hoe, Eric Morris, *Re-enter the SAS* 1994, p. 63.
6 Ibid. quoting RSM Bob Bennett, p. 64.
7 As a 3-star (Lieutenant) General he commanded the Rhodesian Armed Forces at the height of their struggle against ZIPRA and ZANLA in the 1970s.

assumed full command of D Squadron. At the time that these changes were taking place, in mid-1951, Calvert's health was beginning to collapse under the strain of a series of major tropical diseases, combined with the sheer hard work of commanding the new special force, heavy drinking and other stresses resulting from his private life. The combination of these was to lead to him being invalided back to Europe for a period of convalescence, leaving the field open for a new commanding officer to take control of the fledgling unit.

The officer selected to take command of the Malayan Scouts was Lt-Col John Sloane, an officer of the Argyll and Sutherland Highlanders, who had just finished a tour of Korea with his battalion:

Sloane was a damned good man to take over from Calvert. Mike Calvert was a visionary, if you like, but he had no great tolerance for the nitty-gritty of running a unit like the Malayan Scouts.

I think Sloane saw that Calvert's strategic concept was right but was also a good enough regimental officer to see that you needed to get the discipline and the admin on a firm footing as well. Together with John Woodhouse, he laid the foundations for the survival of the SAS after a fairly rocky start.

The second half of 1951 saw a steady increase in the efficiency and effectiveness of the Malayan Scouts as the squadrons gained experience on longer jungle patrols and began to move into areas hitherto only visited by the CTs and aborigines, and the usefulness of the unit was fully appreciated by Headquarters Far East Land Forces:

GHQ, FARELF

22 December 1951

To: The Under Secretary of State

The War Office

Whitehall, London, SW1

Subject: MALAYAN SCOUTS – SPECIAL AIR SERVICE REGT.

The employment of the Malayan Scouts (Special Air Service Regiment) has been under consideration at this HQ and the following conclusions have been reached.

ROLE

The role of the Malayan Scouts (Special Air Service Regiment) is to operate in the deep jungle areas not already covered by other Security Forces, with the object of destroying bandit forces, their camps and their sources of supply.

No other units in Malaya are so suitably organized or equipped for this task which is vital in bringing the bandits to battle.

The result is that the unit is becoming a 'Corps d'Elite' in deep jungle operations and is a most valuable component of our armed forces in Malaya.

ORGANIZATION

In order to increase the efficiency of the Special Air Service Regiment, certain changes are now considered necessary in the establishment, but these changes are largely on the administrative side, which has been the weak link in the past. The Regiment is now to be organized on a four-squadron basis as shown on the outline War Establishment, at Appendix 'A' attached. This reorganization shows a decrease of two British officers, but an increase of 52 British other ranks. However, certain of the administrative appointments can be suitably filled by National Servicemen, thereby economizing in the use of more experienced volunteers.

TACTICAL OPERATIONS

The regiment is having increasing successes in their operations all the time.

Their initial operations involved many weeks of

patrolling deep in the jungle, which had the effect of disturbing bandits in their camps and providing a great feeling of insecurity among them.

The next main operations the Regiment took part in were deep jungle penetrations in connection with other operations by Infantry battalions. These were very effective and provided many bandit kills.

The Regiment is at present taking part in a most difficult operation in North Malaya, from which valuable results are expected.

TERMS OF SERVICE

This paragraph is covered by Reference 'B', *[Author's note: this reference is omitted]* which in short recommends a two year tour, with the option of extending for a period of one year.

TRAINING

The unit is authorized to recruit a percentage of parachutists, as there is a role for them during the emergency in Malaya and in wartime in the Far East. With the longer tour it may be possible to retrain a number of volunteers as parachutists by arranging local refresher courses for them. This is now under investigation, but there is no intention of carrying out basic parachute training in this theatre.

TITLE

It is felt that the present title of the Regiment indicates that the unit will only operate in Malaya and that the volunteers would be more attracted if the words 'Malayan Scouts' were deleted from the title and that the Regiment should be known as Special Air Service Regiment, with a suitable number to be selected by the War Office. It is believed that '22nd Special Air Service Regiment' would fit in with the present order of battle.

It is presumed that the Rhodesian Government should be consulted before the change of title is approved.

RECOMMENDATIONS

(a) That the Regiment, reorganized as on the attached outline War Establishment remains in this theatre during the emergency (Note: the revised complete War Establishment will be forwarded to the War Office in the normal way with the Minutes of the War Establishment Committee).

(b) That the Regiment includes a proportion of National Servicemen in certain selected administrative appointments.

(c) That the initial tour be increased from 18 months to 2 years.

(d) That the title of the Regiment should be a 'Special Air Service Regiment', with a number selected by the War Office, and if this is approved, that action should be taken to inform the Rhodesian Government of its wider implications.

$$\text{(Sgd) . . .}$$
$$\text{for General . . .}$$
$$\text{Commander-in-Chief . . .}$$

This coincided, however, with the low-point in the fortunes of the British forces. Despite the presence of 40,000 British and Commonwealth troops and some 75,000 policemen, incidents generally were running at around 500 per month, whilst in October 1951, the Governor, Sir Henry Gurney, was assassinated during a CT ambush. The Government's response was to appoint General Sir Gerald Templer as the 'one man with one plan' recognized as essential in resolving the emergency, but at the same time the Malayan Scouts were beginning to expand their operational repertoire. One technique that they decided to try was parachute insertion:

The first jump was in early 1952 into the Belum Valley and resulted in several men becoming hung up in jungle trees by their parachute harnesses. As a result it was decided to carry out experimental jumps to perfect a method of getting down from trees once ensnared . . .

The problem was that high winds made jumping into the clearings around aborigine settlements extremely hazardous. If you found yourself deposited on top of a two hundred foot high tree, how the hell could you get down? We decided that the answer was to drop our bergens and then attach a hundred and fifty foot coil of rope, knotted at eighteen inch intervals, to a strong branch. The idea was then to simply climb down to the ground. [8]

In practise however, 'tree-jumping' was fraught with danger. The first problem was that in hitting the tree, the parachutist could not know how the branches would be arranged below him, and had no way of preventing himself from hitting thick boughs, or of catching branches at odd angles, and thus causing himself serious injury. The second problem was that there was no guarantee that the canopy of the parachute would actually be caught in the tree; if it didn't catch, but simply collapsed, the parachutist might then fall up to two hundred feet down to the jungle floor:

Parachuting into trees was somewhat interesting! From above the jungle looked quite inviting and the trees look soft and comfortable but when you actually hit them you were bounced from branch to branch like a rubber ball! Even though it was rare for anyone to be seriously injured, there were a few broken backs and necks over the years, and a lot of other broken bones and sprains and so on. I should think that almost everyone who jumped got at least a few cuts and bruises every time, and I have to say that helicopters were undoubtedly a big improvement! [9]

Together with the deep penetration patrols, the SAS also became involved in the construction and protection of 'jungle forts' as

---

8 Johnny Cooper. *One of the Originals*, p. 122
9 Interview. Officer. 22 SAS.

they came to be known. The idea underlying this tactic was to place aboriginal families in protected environments where they could not be 'got at' by CT groups, without removing them from their traditional areas. Once the forts had been established, by the SAS and other units, they would be guarded by the Malayan police and by an aborigine 'Home Guard' of men armed with shotguns and given basic training by the SAS. The attraction of living in the forts was the availability of food and medical aid, often supplied by SAS patrol medics, who began to develop their skills beyond the rudimentary first aid training given by the Royal Army Medical Corps.

In the period 1952–55 as the deep jungle became a more hostile environment for the CTs, there was a shift in emphasis by the SAS towards operations on the jungle fringe, using the skills acquired during the early stages of the campaign to mount searches and ambushes against terrorist groups around their area of operations. At the same time, back in the UK, a selection process was being organized to ensure that a consistent standard of volunteer was coming out to the Far East for operational service. This came about by coincidence. In 1952 John Woodhouse had returned to Britain to take up an appointment as the adjutant of a Territorial battalion, but, having some weeks to spare before reporting to his new unit, he was asked to take control of a draft of new volunteers for 22 SAS who were assembling at the Airborne Forces depot at Aldershot. Starved of resources, he took them to Snowdonia for a period of strenuous hill-walking combined with map-reading instruction and basic tactics, with the intention of giving them the best possible preparation before they left and also to weed out any unsuitable soldiers: it was from this small beginning that the now famous SAS selection course developed and it normally meant that officers and soldiers arriving in Malaya were of a high baseline standard, even if their jungle skills were not up to those of the veterans:

We landed in Singapore and were unceremoniously put on the overnight train to Kuala Lumpur. I can remember listening all night for the first shots fired from a terrorist ambush position. The trip, however, was uneventful. Arriving in Kuala Lumpur we were soon breakfasting at Wardieburn Camp. But, before we could consider settling down we were taken to the operations room and given a general briefing and then a specific operational brief for D Squadron. We were to join them in the Ipoh area the next morning.

We spent the remainder of that day being kitted out. Our feet didn't touch the ground. We were allowed to choose what weapon we wanted. I selected a US M1 carbine – it looked the smallest, lightest one available, and I had seen John Wayne use one to great effect on the cinema screen. After an overnight stop at Brigade Headquarters we were flown in by helicopter to the D Squadron Headquarters at the 'Dorset LZ' in primary jungle east of Sungei Siput. We were welcomed by John Woodhouse the squadron commander, to be told that he had no room for us until the next day. We would have to look after ourselves that night and find a basha site nearby. He gave us an escort to help us settle in. Peter de la Billière (who had arrived a few days earlier) was already with D Squadron. He, too, was expelled from the main base to join us!

That first night in the jungle was terrifying. I didn't know what to expect. The night noises were very loud. I later learned to wake up when it went quiet at night. And I had never built a basha before. Somehow we survived and the next day returned to the 'Dorset Base'. It was a well-built jungle camp with good bashas and log sangars. We were taken there for a few days receiving excellent practical tuition from John Woodhouse.

Just after dark one evening a single shot rang out, amazingly loud amongst all the other jungle noises; we dived for our stand-to positions and stared into the darkness. We then heard John Woodhouse speaking to the dog handler. A second shot rang out. We were then told that we could stand down. What had happened was that Trooper McComb had been cleaning his handgun and let off an accidental discharge. When he was showing John Woodhouse what had happened he let off a second round. Apparently Woodhouse then snatched the gun from McComb, took out a 36 grenade, removed the pin and thrust it into McComb's hand saying: 'Now let's see you let that off accidentally.'

McComb worked for quite a few days thereafter armed only with his grenade minus its safety pin!

After about a week at 'Dorset', we were sent off on an individual navigation exercise. We had to rendezvous with the Training Troop at Long Jim's ladang. It was a two-day march and we were given an escort of two troopers who were forbidden to help us in any way.

On the first day I was travelling as number two in the patrol when the leading scout stopped, put his hand to his ear to indicate that we should all listen. He pointed and then gave a thumbs down sign signifying enemy presence. I suddenly heard a noise as if the whole Chinese army was charging us. Bravely I stood my ground and released the safety catch on my carbine. The magazine dropped from the weapon – I'd pressed the magazine release lever instead. At that instant I realized it was only a troop of monkeys in the tree tops (a fact that the lead scout had known only too well). My escorts laughed their heads off and I learned that never again would I select a weapon with which I was not familiar.[10]

The success of SAS patrols in dominating the deep jungle led to a steady pressure to increase their numbers and, as already mentioned, within two years of its foundation as the Malayan Scouts, 22 SAS had reached a strength of three regular British squadrons together with the Rhodesian volunteer squadron. However, in December 1952 the Rhodesians' tour of duty ended and the regiment began to search for a replacement. The solution eventually reached was to request assistance from the government of New Zealand, and to seek volunteers from the Parachute Regiment, thus increasing the strength of 22 SAS in 1955, when both contributions became ready for duty, from three to five operational squadrons. At the same time, this created a lasting affiliation between both the New Zealand Armed Forces, who have maintained an effective and efficient SAS capability ever since (with further operational experience in Borneo and Vietnam), and the Parachute Regiment, which prides itself on providing a majority of operational SAS soldiers to this day. All

10 Alan Hoe, Eric Morris, quoted in. *Re-enter the SAS*, p. 67.

faced the same ordeal, learning to live in the jungle for extended periods, surviving on what they could carry and on what could be dropped to them:

When they teach you jungle training at the school, they teach you to have a dry set of clothes which you keep in a plastic bag. So every night you put your basha up and you take all your clothes off and you powder your feet and you put on your dry set of clothes and you get into your hammock. But in reality that didn't work for us. We binned all the spare army kit, never used the issued hammocks at all. For the first week we'd rough it. Then when they dropped our supplies we'd cut four panels off a parachute, fold them over and stitch them up with para cord, cut two six foot poles and slide them through the side which made a stretcher and that's what we'd sleep on. One each, off the ground. The we'd put up our poncho, cut a piece of wood, bend it to hold the hood in place, tie the corners with para cord and you had a waterproof basha. Then we'd strip off, and because your kit was either wet with sweat or rain you'd put a couple of sticks in the ground and hang up your boots and socks, but they'd still be wet in the morning. We used to sleep in green, very lightweight cotton underpants which we called 'drawers, Dracula'. We'd wear the same pair of pants for maybe weeks. At night we'd sleep in a sleeping bag made out of two parachutes stitched together.[11]

The discomfort of daily existence in the jungle was added to by the poor quality personal equipment that was issued at that time:

We wore green cotton shirts and trousers which were generally OK, though they would start to chafe you when they were wet and you'd been wearing them for a week or so, but we also had these terrible boots which, believe it or not, had been specially designed by some boffin for use in the jungle. They were made of green canvas with a rubber sole and they laced up to just below your knees, and they had little eyelets which were meant to help ventilate your feet and let the water out. In fact what happened was that these holes let sand and grit in, which caused blisters and sores on the soles of your feet and round

---

11 Peter Geraghty, quoted in *Men of the Red Beret* by Max Arthur, 1990. p. 452.

your ankles. and the canvas and rubber started to fall apart after a week or so anyway. particularly if you went anywhere near any paved roads or stony or rocky ground, so they weren't much good!

The webbing we had wasn't much help either, and again it was meant to be special jungle issue: the only bits that were any good were the water-bottle pouches and the water-bottles themselves were shit! The belt was made up of three separate bits of canvas which were joined together with metal fasteners, so it would just fall apart as soon as it was under any pressure, and the ammunition pouches fitted high up on your chest so that when you hit the deck for cover, you'd get a great thump in the ribs *and* you'd be sticking up like a sore thumb. Most of us binned the belts and used sections of cargo strap from heavy drop pallets and eventually we got a load of pouches made up locally which were a lot better: at least they would survive a couple of patrols![12]

Together with mediocre equipment, other hazards soon made themselves known:

You would see snakes and monkeys and various sorts of birds, particularly when you'd been in ambush a few days, because they would just ignore you, and there were all the usual creepy-crawlies and nasties as well. Ants, scorpions, hornets and my pet hate: leeches. Those fuckers would fasten on to you any chance they got and start to fill themselves up, drinking your blood 'til they were full and then dropping off. Every time you stopped you'd check yourself over, round the tops of your boots, round your waist and so on, and you'd usually find some; and when you stopped for longer, you'd check your genitals and you'd get your mate to check your arsehole 'cause they loved it in there as well. When you found them you had to be a bit careful about getting them off 'cause they'd leave their little jaws inside if you just pulled them off and you'd get an infection, so you had to get a smoker to burn them off with his fag. Some of the lads saw tigers out in the jungle, though I never did. I drank a few in Singapore though.

---

12 Interview. NCO. 22 SAS.

The tide began to turn in favour of the government forces in Malaya when political and military command was unified under Sir Gerald Templer in 1952, but the process of finding and destroying the fighting elements of the MRLA was slow and laborious and Malaysia did not become independent (within the Commonwealth) until August 1957. 22 SAS remained on operations in Malaya until the middle of 1959, although by that stage the NZSAS Squadron had returned home, the Parachute Squadron had been disbanded and A and D Squadrons were operating in the Oman, leaving only B Squadron 'in at the death' under Lt-Col Tony Deane-Drummond. CT activity had declined drastically from the early days and many operations consisted largely of searches for specific small guerrilla bands. A good example of this was Operation Thrust, B Squadron's successful search for the CT gang led by Ah Hoi ('the Babykiller') in the Telok Anson area in January and February 1958.

At its height the Malayan Emergency employed the services of 22 battalions of British and Commonwealth infantry, 180,000 police (including special constables and auxiliaries) and 250,000 Home Guards. During the period of the Emergency – 1948 to 1960 – some 6,400 CTs were claimed killed with a further 3,000 captured or surrendered, 34,000 individuals were interned without trial, 10,000 deported and 226 hanged. Set against this, the contribution of 22 SAS, which was operational for nine years of the Emergency and had a peak strength of 560 men, was a total of 108 confirmed terrorist kills. Clearly there was no sense in which the role of 22 SAS was decisive: the Regiment was a relatively small cog in a large, and after an extremely shaky start, effective security apparatus.

But the SAS's part was by no means insignificant. Calvert correctly saw the importance of denying the deep jungle as a safe haven for the CTs and recognized two ways in which this could be achieved: by sending effective troops to live in it, and thus dominate it, for extended periods, and by winning the allegiance of the jungle people who could sustain the CTs. In pioneering these activities, the SAS developed a strand of the security policy that would lead to ultimate victory.

The campaign was also important from the SAS point of view

in helping to refine the Regiment's method of selecting and recruiting its soldiers, and in defining its role. From the end of 1952 a formal procedure existed whereby individuals could volunteer from their parent regiment or corps for service in 22 SAS, and a formal selection and training course existed to check their suitability. This was a crucial development which laid the foundations for future successes: a special forces unit can only hope to achieve its normally ambitious objectives if its members are up to the tasks set for them. Calvert's original Malayan Scouts struggled despite the sound underlying concept because many of its soldiers did not have the aptitude or the self-discipline to handle the particular demands of special forces soldiering. Jungle warfare makes great demands on its practitioners – a situation recognized implicitly by the fact that soldiers joining 22 SAS are still essentially trained as jungle soldiers – and by only selecting those who are likely to succeed, rather than relying on the 'lottery' of blind posting or over-ambitious volunteering, the SAS ensured that it became a regiment that could achieve its aims.

3. Parachuting

In 1941 parachuting was envisaged as the best insertion option for SAS troops in the desert, but it was soon discovered that the prevailing weather conditions militated against this and instead it became very much a secondary method. But as the war moved into mainland Europe, parachute insertions behind enemy lines were often the only realistic approach and the technique resumed its importance within the SAS. In Malaya there was some experimentation with parachuting SAS patrols into the jungle canopy, but it was soon recognized that this caused an unacceptably high level of casualties and it was abandoned in favour of other methods.

Since then, parachuting has remained an entry option for all SAS soldiers, but it is recognized that for SAS-type operations, standard military static-line parachuting has few advantages over helicopter or vehicular insertions and it is unlikely to feature as a first choice entry option in future operations. But the same is not true of free-fall. In 1961 22 SAS was re-organized so that each squadron maintained four troops each specializing in a different 'entry skill': mobility (using vehicles), mountain, boat and 'air', whose job was, in fact, to explore the possibilities for insertion by free-fall parachute.

Nevertheless, despite the fact that all operational members of the Regiment, and many of the support personnel, are parachute trained, parachuting per se is not now and never has been universally popular outside the Air Troops:

> After I did my para course I was in danger of getting over-enthusiastic about it all and even though I was in 'Boats' I took off on a few spare weekends to do some civvy sport free-fall. But on about my fifth or sixth weekend I had a bad 'line over' and then had a bit of a nause with getting my reserve up. I landed OK in the end but I'd had a bad panic and I was a bit wound up by it all.
>
> I went off to get a cup of tea to calm down and I met this bloke who was a Sergeant Major in the gunners and was in their free-fall display team, and he was telling me how at one stage in his career he'd been testing free-fall rigs and was getting a total failure on his main chute on fifty per cent of his jumps, 'cause the Velcro was too stiff or something. I was thinking: 'You must be fucking barking, mate! One's enough for anybody'.

A similar sceptical attitude dates back to 1943:

> Before we made our first jump, I looked across at Colonel Brian, who was taking over from Bill Stirling, and I saw that his face was literally as white as a sheet, and his lips were the same colour as the purple of the ribbon of his MC . . .[2]

But for those who enjoy it, there is little to match the exhilaration of parachuting:

> Your basic static line jumping is just a conveyer belt: you line up, you jump, the canopy opens automatically, you release your equipment, you hit the deck. The sensation of freedom you get when you leave the aircraft is momentary, to say the least. But a free-fall descent from high altitude gives you time to enjoy it.
>
> I don't know if you've ever been in a car crash? That feeling you get of time stopping, when you feel totally in control of things, is extraordinary.

---

1 Interview, NCO, 22 SAS.
2 Interview, Officer, SAS Brigade.

It's all about the surge of adrenaline that hits your system, speeding up your reactions as fast as they'll go, but you get the same thing every time in free-fall and I can't understand why people need to take drugs. I really can't.

---

3 Interview, NCO, 22 SAS.

4. A Growing Role:
the Jebel Akhdar, Oman, 1958–59

22 SAS were flexible enough to be discreetly moved from one theatre of operations to another

As the Malayan campaign was drawing to a close in the late 1950s, it was evident that 22 SAS Regiment had established a niche for itself as a specialist long-range jungle patrol unit. What was not so clear was whether there would be a job for the regiment when the campaign finished. The 'parent' SAS Regiment, 21 SAS, was a territorial unit with an established role to play in a general war against the Soviet Union, building on the experience of the SAS Brigade of World War II. 22 SAS had conducted no operations outside Malaya and there was no particularly strong reason to think that it would be able to, other than that it was composed of a number of experienced, and presumably reasonably flexible, officers and soldiers. Although there were no immediate plans to disband 22 SAS at the end of the Malayan campaign, it was agreed in principle that it would be reduced in strength to two regular squadrons – A and D – and held in readiness in England for any tasks that might come up.

Reducing the size of 22 SAS wasn't, in reality, as drastic a step as might be imagined. On paper the Regiment consisted of five squadrons but one was from New Zealand, one from the Parachute Regiment and the other three were chronically understrength. The plan to disband B Squadron meant a consolidation rather than a reduction of the Regiment's main asset: the soldiers. The question of wider employment for the Regiment was also resolved at around the same time, by events several thousand miles away in the Arabian Gulf Sultanate of Muscat and Oman.

Oman is a thinly populated country which inhabits some 1,300 miles of the coastline of the Arabian peninsula, encompassing a coastal strip, mountainous inland regions and part of the uninhabitable Arabian desert known as the 'Empty Quarter'. The population is divided between those living in the towns and ports of the coastal strip, a group who generated much of the country's wealth and influence through trade (particularly in slaves) prior to the discovery of oil, and traditionalist tribes which live in the mountainous inland areas, notably the plateau of Jebel Akhdar in the north and in the mountains of Dhofar to the south. Historically Oman, which also at times controlled Zanzibar and parts of the coast of East Africa, was ruled by a religious Imam who combined spiritual with secular authority, but in the eighteenth century the two roles were split and the country came under the authority of an hereditary Sultan based in the port of Muscat. In the early nineteenth century the Sultan of Oman began to develop a relationship with Britain, particularly because of British anxiety to curtail the slave trade in the Arabian peninsula, but this was reinforced in the middle part of the century after the loss of Zanzibar. Discontent resulting from this had been so great that in 1866 a group of Omani tribal leaders, with the backing of Saudi chiefs, assassinated the Sultan and replaced him with his son.

For the traditionalist leaders of the Jebel Akhdar tribes, the association of the Sultan with the Saudis, who were members of a different Islamic sect, was an outrage, and in response they elected a new Imam to lead them in rebellion. Under extreme pressure, the Sultan was obliged to call on Britain for help, which was duly provided, and although the Sultan himself was killed, he was succeeded by his uncle, who managed to stamp out the rebellion. This created a pattern for effectively the next seventy-five years: the coastal-based Sultan ruling with the backing of British military force and control of the ports, a relationship formalized in 1920 with a treaty between the inland tribes and the Sultan which kept the peace until 1954.

The cause of the rebellion that ultimately led to the deployment of 22 SAS in the Oman was the death of the Imam who had negotiated the 1920 treaty. After his death in 1954, leaders of the influential Bani Riyam and Bani Hinya tribes conspired to have a young Bani Hinya man, Ghalib ibn Ali, elected to the Imamate. Having achieved this, the new Imam's brother, Talib, used his new found authority to attack a group of oil prospectors working in a neighbouring tribe's area. This in turn provoked a reaction from the Sultan's Army, which forced the new Imam and his Bani Riyam allies to take refuge in their tribal villages, and which led Talib to leave for Saudi Arabia, where he hoped to raise and arm a force of expatriate Omanis.

The rebellion began at an interesting time in Arab history. In Egypt, Gamel Abdul Nasser had seized power and was attempting to reassert Egyptian control over the country, which had been virtually occupied by Britain for many years; whilst the huge wealth created by oil deposits in the Gulf states was giving some Arab leaders a level of influence they had not enjoyed since the time of the Crusades. It was therefore a propitious time for Talib to seek help to oust a Sultan characterized by his enemies as a puppet of the British. When he returned to the Jebel Akhdar in June 1957 with weapons, his Saudi-trained Omanis and the support of the two tribes, he was quickly able to seize control of the central part of Oman and declare its independence from the Sultan.

Although Talib's rebellion was not widely supported outside the Bani Riyam and Bani Hinya, he was in a strong military position because of his control of the Jebel Akhdar. The massive plateau effectively controlled the land routes inland from Muscat and was supposedly impregnable to attack by land forces. Once again, the Sultan called on the British for assistance.

In reality, the military problem presented by the rebellion was not that great. Talib's force of Saudi-trained soldiers numbered no more than five hundred and would be no match for a British infantry battalion, for example, provided one could be got on to the plateau. The real problem was political: by the time that Britain came to consider committing regular forces to resolve the situation the ill-judged invasion of the Suez Canal zone had taken place and British prestige was at an all-time low amongst the Arab states. Committing regular British Army units or formations for long-term operations in any part of Arabia would be met with enormous hostility and suspicion, and could not be countenanced. Instead, in 1957 an infantry brigade was deployed from Kenya to seize low-lying areas held by the rebels, and a number of British officers and NCOs were attached to the Sultan's forces to 'stiffen' them with experienced leadership and more up-to-date tactics as they attempted to enforce a blockade of the Jebel Akhdar, to which Talib's forces withdrew after the arrival of the British brigade. At the same time RAF squadrons based in the region began a campaign of bombing against suspected rebel strongholds.

In the meantime, Major Frank Kitson, a staff officer working in the Military Operations branch of the Ministry of Defence, was set to study the problem with a view to finding a long-term solution:

. . . I put forward a suggestion that a small and comparatively simple special operation should be mounted. In outline my suggestion was that four or five specially selected officers should be established in suitable posts around the foot of the Jebel Akhdar. Each one would be provided with a substantial sum of money and a few strong and resourceful soldiers to act as guards, drivers and escorts. Each officer would also need a reliable English-speaking Arab to act as an interpreter and some trackers. The first stage of the operation would be for the officers to install informers in nearby villages by judicious use of the money allotted to them. The job of the informers would be to discover when and where groups of the Bani Riyam, coming down from the plateau, might be contacted. Stage two would be to ambush and capture some of these people. If carefully handled, a proportion of the captives would doubtless change their allegiance and work for us. I visualized forming one or two teams of prisoners augmented by some of our soldiers in disguise. During stage two we would also build up a detailed and accurate picture of the way in which Talib organized his force. The third stage would be for one or more of the teams to get onto the plateau. With reasonable luck they should be able to get through the piquet at the pass by virtue of their disguise. If the worst came to the worst they would certainly get up to the guards before they were spotted and they would then have to overcome them. Once on the plateau. they would discard their disguise and start operating against Talib's irregulars . . . I judged that the total number of British troops required would not exceed forty and that a cash sum of £15,000 would be required.'

After approval had been gained from the Foreign Office for Kitson's plan in the early autumn of 1958 he prepared to visit Muscat for a reconnaissance:

Just before I left, the Director of Military Operations had an idea. Some years earlier a unit had been formed to carry out patrols in deep jungle. It was in effect a descendant of the old wartime Special Air Service and in due course it became known as 22 SAS. By the summer of 1958 the Malayan Emergency was nearly over and it was decided that 22 SAS should move to England and hold itself in readiness to carry out patrol tasks in other parts of the world if necessary. General Hamilton reckoned that 22 SAS might provide most of the soldiers needed in our teams, which would be a quicker and more efficient way of getting individuals than collecting them from the army as a whole.[2]

A signal was duly despatched to HQ Far East Land Forces asking the CO of 22 SAS to meet Major Kitson in Aden in order to discuss the possible deployment of elements of the regiment. Its arrival seemed a godsend to Captain de la Billière, then serving as 22 SAS's operations officer:

I took the message to Deane-Drummond, who seized on the opportunity as eagerly as I had, though for different reasons [de la Billière did not want to return to regimental soldiering with the Durham Light Infantry]. He saw this not merely as another operation, but as a chance for the SAS to prove to the world that it could fight effectively in environments other than the jungle.

Because the Regiment had been in Malaya ever since its re-formation,

---

1 Major Frank Kitson. *Bunch of Five* 1977. p. 168.
2 Ibid.. p. 170.

its soldiers had become known to outsiders as 'Jungle Bunnies', and the general assumption was that all we could do was to creep about in thick cover. Moreover, many people believed that when the Malayan campaign came to an end, the SAS would be disbanded. As Deane-Drummond at once realized, Oman would give us another chance.[3]

The reconnaissance by Kitson and Deane-Drummond showed that Kitson's scheme was workable, but posting problems suggested that it would be unlikely that sufficient suitable officers would reach Oman in time to put it into effect in the short term. Consequently it was decided that an SAS squadron would come out from Malaya and begin patrolling around Jebel Akhdar, probing the rebels' defensive positions. The squadron selected was 'D', under Major Johnny Watts:

We were pulled out of the jungle and started re-training but they wouldn't tell us where we were going. We were doing anti-ambush drills and all the rest of it but much more like infantry, and we were issued with FN rifles and Bren guns rather than the carbines and SMGs and shotguns that we were used to. Most of us guessed that it would be somewhere in Africa.

Anyway, just before we left we had a briefing and they told us: 'You're all off to Oman,' which didn't excite me that much as I'd never heard of the place . . .

We flew from Singapore to Colombo, and from there we went on to an RAF aerodrome on Masiryah Island which is off southern Oman and spent the night there, which was really miserable. The humidity was as bad as anything I'd come across and it was the sandfly capital of the world: I got bitten all over by the little buggers! And then the next day we flew on up to Muscat and a half-built tented camp that the Sappers were setting up for us.

After Malaya, and particularly Singapore, it was like going back in time a thousand years. There were no big buildings or proper roads, even, and hardly any vehicles apart from the ones that belonged to the

---

3 Sir Peter de la Billière, *Looking for Trouble* 1994, p. 129.

Sultan's Armed Forces: everything went by donkey or camel. We set up ranges and had about a week to acclimatize, then we had to get down to work.[4]

D Squadron arrived in Oman at the end of November 1958 and began operations the following week, but it is worth remembering that they were not the first to conduct operations against the *Jebali* rebels:

. . . during the week ending 12 September, Shackletons dropped 148 x 1000lb bombs; 40 rockets were fired by Venoms and a large quantity of 20mm ammunition was expended. During the latter part of this month HMS *Bulwark* [a Royal Navy aircraft carrier] arrived in the Gulf of Oman and her full complement of Sea Venoms and Seahawks joined in the air attack. In one week, forty-three offensive sorties against the plateau targets were flown from the ships as well as ten reconnaissance sorties. Within the confines of a relatively small target area, air attacks on this scale continuing for week after week against simple agricultural tribes was a terrifying experience . . . There were increasing reports that villagers were pleading with their Imam Ghalib to go down the mountain and surrender . . .[5]

The first moves by D Squadron were careful probes of unguarded routes onto the plateau. The aim laid down by Deane-Drummond was that:

D Squadron 22 SAS [would] carry out offensive recce on all slopes leading up the mountain and on the plateau with a view to:
a. Gaining knowledge of all possible routes up the mountain.
b. Ambushing and killing pickets on the wadis or anywhere else.
c. Killing Talib.

It was a considerable contrast to operations in Malaya:

---

4 Interview. NCO. 22 SAS.
5 Sir David Lees. *Flight from the Middle East* 1980, p. 133.

It was just about completely different from Malaya! For a start, you could see. In the jungle you've got an absolute maximum thirty or forty yards' visibility but on the *Jebel* – particularly in the early morning before the haze got up – the air was so clear you could see for miles. These *adoo* were all over the place, basically everybody up there was enemy, and so you had a big temptation to take a pop at them, but this could be at ranges of six- or seven-hundred yards: they could have cooked their Sunday dinner by the time the bullets got to them. But you couldn't afford to get slack because although they only had ancient weapons, they were sharp and they knew the ground. Duke Swindells was shot on about the second or third day by a sniper 'cause he stood in the same place too long. He stood up for a look around and – bang! – down he went, dead as a doornail.

The climate was also a big change. One thing you don't have to worry about in the jungle is water but up there you really had to ration your supply because it was so hot you just wanted to drink all the time. At night, on the other hand, it would get really chilly so we'd all have our Denisons [camouflaged combat smocks], and pullovers and balaclavas on – those of us that had 'em anyway, and you needed a proper sleeping bag as well.

There were blazing hot jagged rocks that wore your boots out in no time, and all sorts of snags and thorns to catch on your uniform. In Malaya, your kit fell apart because of the damp and the rot, but up on the *Jebel* it was battered and torn apart by everything it touched.[6]

Early patrolling by D Squadron established that it was possible for the SAS to get on to and stay on the Jebel and that, despite the death of Swindells and their enormous numerical inferiority, they were perfectly capable of holding their own against the rebels in any confrontation. The next step was to exploit their foothold.

With D Squadron having pioneered the routes on to the Jebel it was now decided that the best way to bring the campaign to a swift conclusion was to bring A Squadron out from Malaya to take part in an assault on the main rebel strongholds. This operation

---

6 Interview, NCO, 22 SAS.

was launched at last light 26 January 1959 and involved a long climb up the southern slopes of the Jebel for both squadrons. There was some opposition from snipers during the next morning, during which a chance hit exploded a grenade which severely wounded three SAS troopers, two of whom subsequently died of their wounds, but by now the rebels were exhausted and demoralized, and they melted away from the Jebel as quickly as they could. By 31 January all resistance had ceased and within two weeks both squadrons were on their way back to Malaya to prepare for the Regiment's move to temporary accommodation in Malvern, in the west of England.

The task that was set for the SAS – or rather, the task that it set itself, because Kitson's special operation was never mounted – was not especially daunting from a military point of view. By the time D Squadron arrived in Oman the rebels' morale was close to collapse as a result of bombing and the blockade. What created an enormous impression was how quickly and efficiently it was achieved, despite a climate and environment that were hostile to say the least. The Jebel Akhdar campaign demonstrated that 22 SAS were flexible enough to be discreetly moved from one theatre of operations, using one set of tactics, to another in which the tactical requirements were completely and profoundly different; and still accomplish their task at a low cost in terms of men (three dead) and resources. The two SAS squadrons deployed less than one hundred fighting soldiers combined and this was a lesson that was not lost on the ever cost-conscious War Office. As Frank Kitson subsequently wrote:

> From the point of view of the army as a whole, the most important effect of the campaign was that it ensured the continued existence of the Special Air Service. The regiment had been formed in Malaya for operations deep in the jungle and might well have been disbanded at the end of that campaign had it not been able to demonstrate that it had a use outside the jungle as well.[7]

---

7 Major Frank Kitson, *Bunch of Five* 1977, p. 201.

5. **Intelligence Gathering:**
Borneo 1963–66

Their involvement in border surveillance and patrolling was an important element in gathering intelligence

The origin of the Borneo confrontation lay in a revolt that broke out in Brunei in December 1962 against the rule of the hereditary Sultan. Brunei, along with Sabah and Sarawak, was one of three former British colonies which occupied the northern third of the island of Borneo (the southern two-thirds of which comprised the Indonesian province of Kalimantan) and which were, at that time, ear-marked to federate with Malaya and Singapore to form Malaysia. The Brunei revolt was locally inspired and led – and was quickly put down by British troops brought in from Singapore – but it came at a time of tension between Malaysia and Indonesia to its south and was interpreted as an Indonesian move to destabilize Brunei, and the British soldiers remained in place.

In fact the revolt was not Indonesian inspired but it did suggest to President Soekarno, the expansionist and bombastic Indonesian leader, that it might be possible to foment trouble throughout 'British' Borneo and he began to cast around for a means by which to start the ball rolling. He found it in the 'Clandestine Communist Organization', an ethnically Chinese terrorist group based mainly in the towns of Sarawak, and also by sending his own Indonesian soldiers across the border in small groups to raid villages and intimidate the locals. Soekarno was by no means a communist, but was prepared to use the ready made terrorist infrastructure for his own ends. The British Director of

Operations, Major General Walter Walker, found himself with a 900-mile-long jungle border to guard as well as the prospect of an internal uprising, and with very few troops with which to do it. Not surprisingly, he accepted the offer of an SAS squadron, and A Squadron, under Major John Edwardes, was swiftly despatched, arriving in January 1963.

Walker's original intention was to use the SAS as an airborne quick reaction force. Never having worked closely with the unit he believed that the SAS ability to parachute into jungle canopy might allow them to intercept Indonesians involved in cross-border raiding before they had managed their getaway. Lt-Col John Woodhouse, who had now taken command of 22 SAS, persuaded Walker that this would not be the best use of their talents. Instead they were set to much the same task they had performed in Malaya: long-range patrols aimed at winning the friendship and support of the jungle inhabitants and, at the same time, maintaining surveillance on the border. These two tasks were, of course, complementary. When the tribesmen realized that the SAS patrols were friendly benevolent men prepared to dispense medical aid to them and their families, they were happy to pass on information they had gleaned from their own travels in the jungle, and even from relatives and friends on the other side of the largely arbitrary border. Thus a single strategically placed patrol was actually able to keep an eye on a very much larger area than might have been anticipated.

It is worth recalling that in early 1963 22 SAS only consisted of two operational squadrons, A and D, which meant that only one could be operational in Borneo at any one time. The strain, physical and mental, of extended patrolling in the Borneo jungle was such that squadrons were restricted to four-month tours. A Squadron covered January to April and then August to December, whilst D Squadron covered April to August. D Squadron's second tour, December 1963 to June 1964, covered the period when A Squadron were operating in the Radfan (*see pages 127–31*). With this level of demand, it is not surprising that 22 SAS were given permission, in January 1964, to reactivate B Squadron ready to be committed to the Borneo campaign in November.

It was during 1964 that 22 SAS's role began to evolve from

what was essentially defensive information reporting within British Borneo to offensive intelligence gathering across the border in Kalimantan. Patrols would cross the border covertly, investigating reports of Indonesian terrorist and special forces camps, in order to target them for larger, more conventional attacks. In conjunction with this, the number of SAS troops available for operations was increased, as it had been in Malaya, by introducing Commonwealth SAS, from Australia, who provided a squadron, and New Zealand, who provided a half squadron; and by re-training British infantry, in this case C Company of 2 Para and the Guards Independent Parachute Company.

Cross-border patrolling was perhaps the most significant activity conducted by 22 SAS during the Borneo confrontation and was perhaps also the most revolutionary – after all, despite everything that had happened, Britain and Indonesia were not at war. Sgt Don Large, of D Squadron, led several such patrols and his account of one is reproduced here in full:

D Squadron's tour of duty in Borneo was nearing its end. We were due to be relieved by A Squadron, and would return to the UK for a short break before going to our next job. There was, however, time for the squadron to have one last try at a job which had already been tried six or seven times by patrols from B and D Squadrons. It was a mental thorn in the mind of our squadron commander. Brigade HQ were warm under the collar about it.

We all knew that no job could be termed 'impossible'. In fact it looked dead easy. The main problem was the opposition also knew it looked dead easy, and, as previous patrols had found out, were dead set on making it dead hard!

Everyone on our side of the border wanted to know if the Indonesians were using the River Koemba to build up their troops and supply them. If they were, to what extent? And what could we do about it? Everyone on the other side of the border had seemed, so far, to be very much against the idea.

We didn't even know if the river could be reached along most of its length near the border because of vast swamps in the jungle. The swamps made most of the area operationally impassable. The other bits were well patrolled and more easily watched by the opposition. Reading the reports of previous patrols I got the impression if the swamps didn't get you the Indos would.

For some inexplicable reason the squadron commander got it into his head that my little band of comedians would crack it. (Or was this his final attempt to rid the scene of too much operational hilarity?) I seem to remember asking him if he really believed that about the white armbands.

Before briefing me for the job the squadron commander asked me if I felt completely fit and 'up to scratch'. I assured him I had no problems. Then he asked me about Pete, and told me to give Pete the option of dropping out of the patrol for this last job. When I asked the reason, he told me Pete and myself had been continually on operations, mostly difficult ones, for too long – according to 'medical advice' – so it was only fair to give Pete the chance of a rest.

I didn't fancy changing the team, but gave Pete the option anyway. Just as I expected, Pete blew his top. His reply was unprintable, very much to the point – and just what I wanted.

I was given all the 'gen' to study. Then the big question. Did I think we could crack it? I thought we could give it a damn good try, and said as much.

The other patrols who had made the attempt had all been sent to specific areas of the river with boundaries which they could not cross for operational reasons, such as patrols in adjoining areas, artillery target areas, etc. My first request was for freedom of choice for the route in, and freedom of movement anywhere within reason. This was granted.

I went down to Brigade HQ and my good friend Staff-Sergeant Watson. We went over those maps and air photos with about everything. All the information we could glean from other patrol reports we related to the maps and photos until I formed an idea of the only possible route which would be worth trying.

There was a spur of higher ground running south from the border towards the river. The spur vanished from both maps and air photos a long way from the river, but, following the line of that pointing finger, there was a corresponding bend in the river. It was little enough to go on, but it was all we had. A detailed study of that particular bit of jungle revealed almost nothing. The only 'holes' in the trees on the air photos revealed water. Even Watson couldn't estimate the depth of water through little holes in the trees. I remember there were only two holes anyway, in an area of several square miles. There was an Indonesian military set-up, a small garrison base, less than 1,000 metres from where I thought I might reach the river. It was on the north bank of the river, the near side, and was probably the base from which their patrols covered the area to the border.

It was obviously on high ground, clear of flooding from the river, so, at a push, I could get close to the base and use 'their' high ground. The main task was to get all the information we could. The secondary task was to disrupt any military traffic we found. To help with our secondary task I requested a Bren light machine-gun to be carried by myself, for added firepower. Being the biggest patrol member, well able to use a Bren like a rifle, I thought it was a good idea.

The squadron commander, however, thought the extra weight and more cumbersome weapon just might tip the balance the wrong way and interfere with our primary task. The Bren was not granted. He did suggest I take an AR 15 (Armalite) but at that time we only had two in the unit. One was being carried on operations already, and the other – you would never guess – had been taken to Labuan, a safe base area hundreds of miles from Kuching, by a gentleman who, in that situation, didn't need a weapon at all! Having a fancy gun to parade around would do his ego a power of good, but very little to help the unit effort in the field.

I counted it a small price to pay for peace and quiet, so, although a few alternatives were available, I opted to take my tried and trusted SLR. At least it had the punch we wanted, if not the rate of fire.

The patrol worked out on the jungle training areas, firing and checking our weapons as well as all our contact drills and operational detail. Confident in ourselves, in each other, and in our ability to do the job. We knew we were going to reach that river – come hell or high water!

Our departure was marred by something we could do nothing about. Our weapons had been checked, cleaned and oiled to perfection, our lives were likely to depend on them. They were then handed into the squadron armoury for the night and brought with the vehicle which picked us up to take us to the airfield in the morning. It was several miles from Squadron HQ to where we were then billeted, then a few more miles away from SHQ to the airfield. When the vehicle arrived we piled in and immediately grabbed our beloved rifles. There was a yell at once from Pete: 'Where's my rifle? – I don't want this bloody thing!'

Somehow the wrong rifle had arrived and Pete didn't want to know it. There was no time to go back for the right weapon so we had to take it. I told Pete it must be OK. We would try to test fire it at Lundu, to where we were flying by fixed-wing aircraft, a Twin Pioneer. In the event there was not time, as we went straight from the 'Twin Pin' to a chopper which couldn't wait because of a tight schedule. Arriving at a very dicey LZ right on the border in a 'hot' area, there was no chance of test firing the weapon. Pete went into the jungle a very unhappy man that day.

None of us was too happy with the situation. We worked together like a well-oiled machine, there was no room for a suspect part. Pete had stripped the weapon on the aircraft, checked every bit. Tested everything that could be tested short of firing it. But he distrusted the damn thing, losing no chance of letting the rest of us know his feelings.

The first night in the jungle we all checked the suspect weapon. I for one pronounced it perfect, advising Pete to ignore the possibilities, we had enough problems already. Pete said he felt better about it, but I knew him too well.

Information from another patrol's report (Old Joe's) told where the best route lay for most of the distance, so I kept well away from it. We might need it on the way back. There are many problems with jungle movement under operational conditions. One is tracks. No matter how good you are, you are bound to leave tracks in most places. So on the first day or two we moved on a steady bearing towards a point west of where we were really heading. After that we made for a point east of our real heading. After that we hit swamps and our choices finished. We were limited to where was possible.

On the second day. I heard a slight sound up ahead. Leaving the patrol I went forward and found an Indonesian unit of probably platoon strength right in our path. We pulled back a little, made a detour to the east of them and pushed on. The enemy platoon were stationary. Some were cutting small branches, making the noise which gave them away. So we had no idea which way they were heading or what they were doing. It was too early in the day for them to be making a night stop camp. There was no track anywhere we could see which they might be ambushing. But as we didn't find their tracks we knew they must have come from west of our route, so it was possible, or probable, they would cross our tracks when they resumed moving. Not good news. We did what we could with our track problem. Kevin kept an extra sharp look and listen to the rear.

The edge of the swamp was just a matter of splashing in and out of areas of shallow water onto areas of low firm ground. Further in, the water became gradually deeper, the ground above water level became less firm, then just mud. A jungle swamp is not a nice place. Under the black water tree roots tangle and jam unwary feet. Deep holes are not usually common, but they exist. The jungle is still there, above and below the water, in all its tangled glory, but now decorated with hanging moss and drapes of jungle rubbish up to the high water mark. In this case several feet (up to nine or ten feet) above the present water level. Fallen trees and branches are still obstacles to progress, but often no longer visible.

Sometimes a thick green scum covers the surface of the swamp over large areas. This particular swamp had an extra hazard. Huge leaves, mostly four or five feet long and two or three feet wide, which had fallen from a type of tree which was apparently very common in that area. The leaves crackled like a tin roof when walked upon, and still kicked up a row when moved to one side on the water.

By the time I had been waist deep for about half an hour at a stretch, trying in vain to move silently southward, I had this recurring vision of a grinning enemy watching me approach noisily to the muzzle of his heavy-machine gun. The water crept above my waist and I stopped. The decision, silently made a long way back, was that no way was I going to fight a war more than waist deep in that lot.

Turning onto a westerly bearing we moved until we found dry ground. There we took a break. having spent about ninety minutes in the water. Leaving Paddy and Kevin to look after the packs, Pete and I went south again. looking for a way through.

We were probing the east side of where the spur should be – if it still existed – and would continue pushing south towards the river as far as we could on each probe, moving west after each failure. At one point I came to a fallen tree. about a foot thick, lying in the water. It was just under the surface, the water was nearly waist deep. As I reached the tree and prepared to climb over it the water swirled on the other side and I glimpsed a large patch of light brown 'scales' going down under the tree towards my legs. I was nearly airborne by the time I realized it was only a turtle or a tortoise.

After about an hour, we were stopped in waist-deep water while I checked the map, compass and memory for anything which tallied with the terrain we had crossed.

Pete was probably as smashed as I was. It was bloody hard work. I glanced back at him, he was about twenty metres back, right where he should be. Seeing my glance he whispered something. I couldn't hear the words so signalled him closer. Closing up to about ten metres, he whispered, 'I hope we're the Goodies!'

In a daze of problems I stared at him. 'What?' He repeated the same sentence. Losing patience fast I said, 'What do you mean?'

Pete closed up a couple more metres, his face and eyes serious, 'Well,' he said, 'if we're the Baddies, we'll just as likely finish up with our hats floating on top of this lot!' Then he let the grin slip, and I had difficulty in keeping the laughter silent. After that I felt more relaxed, and inwardly blessed that comedian for his sense of humour.

For two or three days we pushed and probed, then we cracked it. We had been so close on occasions, we had heard the heavy diesel engines on the river, within one hundred metres of us. When we got through we were all moving together as a patrol. I could hardly believe my eyes. There were the muddy swirling waters of the elusive Koemba. Part of the shock was seeing it about seventy metres away, down a steep slope through a rubber plantation. I checked the area, then brought the patrol forward so they could see what had stopped us, and deploy to cover me while I checked all around. The rubber plantation was not in use, although cups still hung on the trees. Tappers' tracks were old and overgrown. There was a track along the top of the bank from where I first saw the river but that too was disused.

As I moved forward to check down to the river, the whole plan became clear. I signalled the patrol to follow as soon as I knew it was safe. They came down through the rubber taking care not to leave tracks. The place was made to measure. There was an old ditch, about three feet deep and ten feet wide, just short of the river bank. A few bushes hid the ditch from all sides. We moved in.

In front of us now was a good view of the river, right on a sharp bend. The bend would slow and turn river traffic so we could get a good view. The ambush possibilities were beautiful. Our only problem was tracks. We thought back over our last bit of dry land after the swamp, and decided it was worth taking the chance. To go back and look would only create more problems so we decided to stay put.

At first, it puzzled me why the rubber plantations didn't show on the air photos. Then, when I looked around, I could understand it. The rubber trees were planted haphazardly, not in rows. There were odd jungle trees growing among them down at the river edge and along the lower slopes. The higher ground put the rubber trees up to the height of the jungle near the edge of the plantation, giving an overall flattish canopy right across.

Assessing our position, we decided our weak spot was the high ground from which we had first seen the river. But the only time we would be exposed to view from that side was when in our actual ambush firing positions. On normal watch there was no problem.

The whole situation tickled our sense of humour. Morale was sky high. What kind of fool would hide under a few bushes in a rubber plantation, within a few hundred metres of an enemy base – when there was a whole damn jungle everywhere else? It looked ridiculous as a hiding place. Enemy patrols would concentrate on the jungle, they wouldn't give our bushes a second glance, even if they came anywhere near.

Night came. we cooked a good curry and slept on it. 'Top exponents' of jungle warfare. and young lads wanting to learn the art – each group trying to impress the other – should read no further. Very likely on real pain of death. From apoplexy in the one case and from trying to do the wrong thing in the wrong place in the other.

To the good. tough. resolute fighting men of the British Army who had suffered ambush positions of complete silence, no smoking, no hot drinks, no cooked food (no farting?) for days on end, sometimes a week or two. maybe more, the hard truth (never told before) which follows, may be too much to bear. Or believe. I could cloud the whole scene in bullshit. without mentioning realities, but so far I have stuck faithfully to the truth of my memory and see no reason to change.

We all knew the rules laid down by the regiment, concerning ambushes, observation posts. movements in enemy-held areas and a whole bible of operational situations. I make no excuses, I had my reasons. I know I have been unorthodox. but on purpose, with a logical reason.

Our position would be good until the shit hit the fan. We had passed the 'cut off' tracks, freshly cut in nice straight lines, we had seen sign of enemy patrols and almost bumped one. We were not far from an enemy base and knew we had to go nearer to it when we bugged out – if we were to make a fast escape from the potential trap we were in.

I wanted fitness and morale at its peak for the 'bug-out', which we all knew would come. I wanted a cock-a-hoop patrol which would take on the world with a grin. So I got one.

We smoked. Even Pete, the non-smoker, had the occasional cigarette. We had a brew of coffee or tea about every two hours. We had a good meal of curry and rice every evening. Relaxation, as far as is possible under those conditions, was the order of the day. We got most of the information required in the first twenty-four hours. Although we had to stay put as long as possible to gain as much information as possible we were not too bothered about picking a fight to finish the job any time anyone wanted to try us. We felt very secure in our own confidence.

The first thing we saw on the river nearly finished us. Kevin was 'fishing' for water. He had his water bottle on a cord, dangling it in the river, which was about seven or eight feet below the sheer bank in front of us, when a canoe carrying two men came silently upstream from the west. They came just past the position then turned to face us. I watched them closely. They could have been locals, but I didn't think so.

One was working his paddle hard and staring at the bank just to the left of me. The water bottle cord was away to the right, thank God. The other man was staring into the muddy water and working with a 'stick', which turned out to have a hook on the end when he pulled up a fish trap. Situation explained. I continued to watch them closely as they moved upstream and lifted other traps. There was no sign they had seen anything of us, so we let them go. Being a suspicious lot, the patrol had all been looking the other way, in case the fishermen were being used as a distraction.

Several diesel launches had passed us during the second day. Heavily laden going upstream, empty on their way back. Then an open boat with an outboard motor appeared. There were three men in it, all wearing blue shorts. They looked too big, too military in appearance to be locals, but I wasn't sure. They beached the boat about twenty-five metres upstream from us, then went to work on baling out the boat and refuelling the engine. The patrol was in an all round defence posture. I watched the men closely. I can't remember seeing any weapons, but there could have been some among the kit in the boat.

I thought of taking them prisoner. They could probably give our people all the information they wanted if we could get them back over the border. Three or four things were against taking them prisoner. First, I wasn't sure they were military. Second, it would be difficult enough to reach the border even without a prisoner. Third, they might have had no knowledge of use to us, whether or not they were military. Fourth, I had explicit instructions not to initiate any type of offensive action until my primary role was completed, and I received authority from base. So they finished their work and went on their way, never knowing how lucky they were.

The days passed. We informed base of everything which moved on the river. On one occasion a raft came down the river with three or four men on it, all singing. One was doing the lead singer's job quite well, he had a good voice. I glanced back at the patrol. They all had their arms waving in the air like they were conducting an orchestra. Morale was high.

The time came when I calculated we had done enough. Time was running out. so I sent a signal requesting permission to carry out our secondary task. Being of an extremely distrusting nature, I didn't trust the opposition not to have the necessary radio equipment to get a fix on our position when we used our radio to send messages. As a result, all our messages were as short as possible, with Paddy and I spending a lot of time finding the shortest possible way to code each message.

It was 1965. The James Bond films were at their height. Checking for a short way through the codes, we found the shortest. The message read: 'Request "00" Licence'. Everyone at base would be expecting the request. I thought it was unmistakable. Everyone at base understood exactly what was required – except the clown who was in charge of the Operations Centre at the time. With everyone else in the place telling him it was obvious, he sent back a signal saying, 'Message not understood'. The difference in time sending the next shortest alternative coded message was about twenty seconds instead of the original four or five seconds.

There is no way around stupidity in high places, when you're out on a limb. I only wished the squadron commander had been in the Ops Centre at the time, but he wasn't. We sent the request the hard way, and hoped (as we always did when working to base from close to enemy positions) that no enemy signals type was getting his pop music interfered with by our Morse code. Having penetrated the thick skull with a long hammering message, we received permission to proceed with stage two of the operation.

Now it was a matter of finding the right target at the right time. I wanted the biggest possible military boat moving upstream in the late afternoon. The rest of the patrol wanted any floating object as soon as possible and to get the hell out of there.

We agreed on a deadline of one hour before dusk. If we had not found a target by then we would wait until the next day.

Our big problem was not the ambush, but the getting clear away after it. The enemy base just down the river would be sure to hear the attack and could well be in a position to send troops along the deployment tracks to the north of us, thereby cutting off our escape. If they reacted quickly they could reach the crucial point before us, as they had less distance to go and good tracks to move on. There was not a lot of room between the swamp and the open rubber plantation, both of which we must avoid. If the enemy could get troops to the north end of that strip of jungle we would have big problems.

I estimated we could get past the deployment tracks in about half an hour if we moved fast. Once out of the bottleneck our chances would be good – if we could keep moving fast.

I also estimated the enemy would deploy without their packs, being so close to their base, so would have two chances late in the day: either to return to base before dark, or to spend the night cold and miserable in the jungle. Either way we would have the advantage next morning – if we had cleared that bottleneck. The enemy patrols further north might, or might not, still be there. Luck would likely be the major factor in their case, so there was little we could do about them. There was also the chance we may get into problems and be glad of darkness to cover our escape. The jungle is not impassable at night in that situation.

A straight beeline for our extraction LZ (the same one we entered by) would not be wise, with those patrols to the north, so I planned to put an easterly 'crank' in our route, partly to avoid interception further north (which could be organized by enemy troops following our tracks, and sending the position and bearing to those ahead of us), partly to take advantage of the 'good going' mentioned in Joe's patrol report. The patrol had haggled through all the pros and cons. We were all satisfied we had taken care of all foreseeable possibilities (plus a few others). We all knew what to do once the ambush was over.

So we waited. Noon passed and the optimum time was approaching. Two or three launches passed. They were too small or going the wrong way. Those going downstream were obviously going faster and would quickly be carried out of sight. There was a sharp bend in the river right in front of us. The downstream traffic came straight towards us, then turned and soon vanished to our right, into the bend, then slowly away from us, to disappear on another bend about one hundred metres away.

Our plan was to destroy a boat. We were not too interested in inflicting casualties. There had to be casualties to prevent return fire but the main firepower would be directed at the stern of the boat, just above the water line, hoping to destroy the propeller drive and hole the bottom of the boat, also destroy the engine.

To do this, the three other members of the patrol would concentrate all their firepower on the stern, while I would take out any possible retaliation. I would also watch for other problems. The patrol would be lying in their fire positions. I would stand slightly to one side, level with their feet to be able to see all around. Firing would commence as each reached his position and found the target. All shots would be well aimed, there was no rush. We would each fire twenty rounds into the target.

Mid afternoon came, and with it the rain. At first a gentle pattering, but distant thunder promised a heavier dose was on the way. My thoughts turned to the swamps. Heavy rain would spread the swamp area considerably, very likely making our exit much more difficult by narrowing that bottleneck. That's if we were still there the next morning.

The roar of the rain muffled the sound of the launch as it approached upstream. I was on almost continual watch, as the decision to attack had to be mine. Peering through the intervening greenery and the rain I saw a new sight on the river, a gleaming white launch with glinting brasswork. This was no ordinary run-of-the-mill river craft. It had to be something special. I could feel the tension of the patrol behind me, waiting for the signal. The launch was nearly upon us and my right hand was held out ready to turn the thumb, up or down. Then I saw the woman. She was standing on the bridge of the launch, between two men in uniform. One in Navy whites, the other an Army officer.

The target was perfect, just what we wanted. The launch was a good forty-five feet long, a nice boat, very naval or military in appearance, its Indonesian flag and other pennants flying proudly.

Neither I nor any man with whom I served in the British Army had ever intentionally made war upon women and children. I saw no reason to change. The thumb went down. I watched the people on the boat flash past. thirty or forty feet in front of me. They were laughing, enjoying a joke, the woman's black hair contrasting with her white dress, oblivious of a sudden death just a few metres away.

As the launch disappeared from view I heard someone mutter, 'What's he bloody waiting for? The frigging *Ark Royal*?'

The patrol had only been able to see the back of the launch as it turned and went away from us. When I told them there was a woman on the bridge, so very likely others as well as children on board, they were in full agreement with the decision not to attack.

Again we waited. The tempo of the rain increased. Thunder rolled and crashed all around. Lightning flickered and flashed in the dim light of the storm. Conditions were perfect, perhaps too perfect. I wondered if river traffic might call a halt until the storm passed.

I can't remember whether I first heard or saw the next launch. We were almost at the deadline for that day. I was beginning to think of tomorrow's luck when suddenly it was there. It was coming steadily upstream, a big one, at least forty feet long. Canvas drapes were rolled down at the sides, because of the rain, so I couldn't see the cargo. As it passed me I saw men in jungle green sitting as you often see troops in the back of Army lorries. The thumb went up, and the patrol hit their firing positions. I sprang to my fire position and took out the two men visible at the back of the boat, then put five shots into the cargo compartment to keep that happy.

The patrol was firing steadily, hitting the flat stern of the boat, centre of the water line. Pete was having trouble with that bloody rifle. I watched him go through the drills, trying to clear the problem, then I put another five shots into the boat to keep them busy, and turned to have a good look along the high ground behind us. Nothing showed, so I again turned my attention to the boat. Pete was still having problems, having to cock the rifle after each shot.

The boat slowed and lost way, smoke began to billow from the darkness under the canvas roof. I spaced six rounds across the middle of the target area, then changed the magazine. Only Pete was firing so I yelled 'Stop!' and that was it, we were on our way. Paddy and Kevin grabbed their packs and ran to the high ground, while we covered them. Then it was Pete and I who ran. But halfway up the bank I remembered my brand new water bag, of a type very hard to come by, so, begrudging its use by the opposition, I ran back to get it, followed by Pete, who thought I had seen something up ahead and was bugging-out in the wrong direction. He looked fit to bust as he watched me empty the water bag and stuff it in my shirt.

Then we were away. My last sight of the boat, it was dead in the water, beginning to turn as it drifted back, almost obscured by thick smoke. Something man-sized toppled like a log into the water from amidships. The boat had a list to starboard and the orange glow of fire was visible under the shadowy roof.

About a hundred metres into the jungle we stopped to check everything was OK. Everything was – except Pete's rifle. He was as savage as hell. We were all savage as hell come to that. It was bad enough having our firepower depleted in the river ambush, but it could be lethal for us if we had a head-on contact with the enemy while moving fast. Especially for me. I relied completely and with confidence on Pete to get me out of trouble if we hit anything. His fast reactions and ability with a weapon were crucial.

We agreed on adjustments to our contact drills which ensured we could do our best, come the crunch, and headed out fast. With any luck the uproar of the storm had covered the sound of the ambush, but it wasn't something we wanted to bet our necks on. The chances the enemy would be waiting for us were about 50–50 (much better than the 10–1 odds against us without the storm).

The advantages and disadvantages of slow or fast movement in different types of jungle have to be weighed against the requirement of the moment, the likely enemy situation and the type of jungle encoun-tered. A considerable amount of know-how and experience is required to get the right balance, in the right places and at the right time. An enemy lying in wait has everything going for him – except when! He's ready to blow you in half but never knows when you will appear, if ever.

Trying to move up silently on someone who is switched on and expecting you is one thing to avoid in the jungle. It is almost impossible.

Smashing through the sticks like a rampaging bull elephant gives ample warning of your approach, ensuring a hot reception.

We were now going to move as fast as possible, because we had to, but that didn't mean we were throwing caution to the winds, or making things easy for the opposition. To do it right, every member of the patrol has to be very good at his job to give the leading scout that hairbreadth of time afforded by surprise.

The leading scout has the job of finding the way through, as quietly as possible, while still navigating to maintain overall movement in the right direction. At the same time he has to be ready to react like lightning. The only way I could do it was to fix in my mind, 'The bastards are there – go get 'em!' To think that they will appear as surely as the hidden targets on the jungle range – and go for them. Confidence in your own abilities, training, experience and extremely fast reactions under pressure can help a lot. But you still know that if Lady Luck is not smiling upon you – the rest is rubbish.

Every patrol member must be just as switched on as the leading scout. Their extra problems are that their friends are probably between them and the enemy. They must be ready to bring instant fire to bear in the right places while being careful not to hit their own men.

They must keep their eyes open to left and right for any sign of problems, and make sure the man behind is still where he should be. They must keep in sight of the man in front but be far enough back not to be caught in the same burst of automatic fire, mine, or booby trap. In a contact with the enemy they must react instantly, guided by the actions of the man in front of them, or what happens to him. Complete, unwavering trust in each other is essential to any patrol on operations.

Lady Luck had smiled upon us in the ambush, with a thunderstorm at the right moment. She now continued to smile to the accompaniment of pouring rain which would cover the sounds of our movement. Nevertheless, fickle lady as she is, the rain could be switched off and a platoon of enemy could be waiting right in our path. She continued to smile.

The patrol had almost reached the point of greatest danger, the deployment track at the north end of the bottleneck, where our route lay nearest to the enemy base. I was moving swiftly up a short sharp slope when a movement ahead stopped me.

It was a snake, on the flat ground at the top of the slope. We saw each other at the same time, meeting head on, both in a hurry. The rifle was lined up on it before I knew what it was that moved. It stopped at the same time as I did, and reared up like I'd never seen before.

I had never seen one before, but I knew only too well I was facing a king cobra, at a range of about six or seven feet. It reared up to a height of at least four or five feet. As it was on slightly higher ground it looked enormous. We were eyeball to eyeball. The rifle had followed it up and was aimed at the centre of the hood, which swayed slightly but was almost still. I remained perfectly still, with my brain in overdrive. I dare not shoot except as a last resort. A shot would not only give us away to the enemy, but would put the patrol into its head-on contact drill. In other words create a small war on a snake, with a lot of ammunition being expended and possibly quite a delay to further progress in the right direction.

How far can the damn things reach when they strike? Is there any warning they are about to do so? How I wished I'd learnt more about snakes. We stood there, both poised to strike, not knowing each other's abilities, and, hopefully, neither wanting to start anything.

It seemed an age we froze like that, but was probably less than ten seconds, then, as quickly as it had risen, it dropped down and rushed away behind a log. Beautiful, sensible snake. I looked back at Pete, signalled 'snake', pointed to the log and moved on past it. The snake had vanished.

We rushed on, reached and dashed across the deployment tracks, then began to breathe easier. No sign of the opposition.

The rain, which had given us such good cover, both for the ambush and for the mad dash through the bottleneck, had slackened off by the time we took a five-minute break.

I checked back along the patrol. Reaching Kevin, he asked me what the sudden stop had been for. I told him, 'A snake'. For some reason Paddy hadn't told him at the time. Kevin looked past me at Paddy and whispered, 'You Irish bastard – I could have been bloody scoffed!' Kevin was not at all fond of snakes, unless they were curried.

Pushing on fast until almost last light we were well pleased with our progress by the time we looped and lay among some fallen trees, ambushing our back track. Then we heard the mortar firing from the enemy base. We listened with bated breath for the shells to land. They were a long way from us, and someone said, 'Thank Christ for that, they think we've gone further east.' I hated to spoil that peace of mind but had to say it. 'Why do you think they're not shelling this area?' There was a silence, then someone muttered, 'Shit!' After dark we cooked a good meal, then settled down for the night. We didn't all take off our boots and belts. It was a free choice, I took off mine and crawled thankfully into my sleeping bag.

Before first light in the morning we were ready to go, waiting for the first glimmer of light to give us enough to move. We had each drunk a cup of coffee, were ready for the day and anything it might bring.

Paddy was the only one with any weight on his back, as he was carrying the radio and would not let anyone else share the load. 'None of you bums could use it properly anyway,' was always his final argument.

Once we got under way again I kept check on Paddy as he had had some sort of 'bug' before the operation and wasn't as fit as he might have been.

We put in a distance to the east-north-east soon after starting the day's march, which quickly put us away from our original bearing and into Joe's 'good primary jungle', where we were able to move faster and quieter. Once or twice animals or birds gave me a start and stopped us dead in our tracks, but of the opposition there was no sign. Their tracks showed in a couple of places, but the freshest ones were days old.

Our next problem was finding and checking the LZ, a task which cannot be done in a hurry without risk of springing an ambush.

Base told us by radio there were no friendly forces in the area. I remember hoping they had it right this time, as we were travelling fast on a 'hair trigger'. I had already come within an ace of shooting a small deer, a bird and – would you believe – a falling leaf. At less than 1.000 metres from the LZ we stopped to give base our ETA (estimated time of arrival). I noticed Paddy was getting to look rough. He had almost stopped sweating, a bad sign under those conditions. He said he kept feeling dizzy, when Kevin accused him of 'walking like a drunk!'

I had to re-think the angles. We may yet have a 'war' on our hands. A sick man was something we could very well do without. There was another problem. None of the previous patrols to return through that particular LZ had been able to find it easily.

There was absolutely nothing between the river and the border which showed on the maps, except the spur, which was almost impossible to find on the ground due to the 'lumpy' nature of the whole area. We had nothing on which to check our position since leaving the river. With a very likely enemy 'follow-up' party, possibly (by my estimation) within an hour's march behind us, there was no time for errors. They could have been a matter of minutes behind us, and with that thought in my mind Kevin was way back on our back track, watching and listening, ready to slow them down a bit. I made a quick decision. A few minutes now could be well worth it later. We sent a signal requesting a helicopter to come. and hover over the LZ for fifteen seconds so we could get a definite fix on our approach. The request was granted almost at once and we were quickly on our way.

When I estimated we were about five hundred metres from the LZ a chopper came over, but instead of hovering over the LZ it circled around as if searching for us. I saw the chopper through a gap in the trees and could see the crewman leaning well out, looking down. I knew they were looking for us so took out my homing device and switched it on. The chopper came straight over us and the winch cable was lowered. It was too short to reach us, so went back up, then came down again with an extension on the end. This time it reached, so I told Pete to go first as he had the useless rifle. With the extension on, the winch couldn't be fully wound in, so Pete was dragged up through the trees and away, swinging and spinning under the chopper. His eyes were like chapel hat pegs.

The chopper went off a short distance then returned; it was Paddy's turn. But the winch-man leaned out and threw down an empty beer can with a note tied to it. The note said, 'Move 100 metres east.' This we did (and in so doing crossed our outward bound tracks on the way). The chopper had found a place it could get low enough to winch us up properly.

Paddy went first, then Kevin. I went last and expected the chopper to rush off. It didn't. The crewman looked at me and pointed down. He shouted, but the noise was too great to understand him. Then I realized he had lowered the winch again.

Suddenly all became clear. I was sat in the chopper with the homing device still switched on. The crew thought there was another man still to come. I sheepishly pulled out the offending instrument and switched it off, signalled the crewman there were no more to come, then we got out of there fast.

The LZ was about 300 metres away – full of a platoon of the Argyll and Sutherland Highlanders. I was glad to see so many friendly faces, but all I could think was, 'Shit!! they did it again!' We picked up Pete and were rushed straight to Lundu, where a Twin Pioneer was waiting to get us back to Kuching. A few more minutes and it would have been too dark for the aircraft to take off or land. So we only just made it in time to save ourselves a night at Lundu.

Years later I was told the Indonesian officer, whose life was spared by the presence of a lady, was Colonel Moerdani, of the Indonesian Parachute Regiment, who was then commanding the RPKAD, an elite para commando unit in the area. He later led the 'peace mission' which went to Kuala Lumpur and finally wound-up the hostilities in Borneo. Some years after that, Moerdani came to London as a general, and somehow Pete and Kevin got to meet him. Their opinion is he's quite a 'good lad'. Worth saving!

The patrol task to the Koemba was typical of the operations carried out by all of D Squadron's patrols on that trip to Borneo. Each patrol's work was made easier, often possible, by work done before by other patrols. Information fed back to our Operations Centre by previous patrols certainly made my job possible. We all looked upon our work as squadron, if not regiment, effort.

There was no brainwashing, or political rubbish involved in making men drive themselves to the point of collapse, risk horrific injuries and a lingering, screaming death in a war thousands of miles from home. We were defending a friendly nation from the military might of its neighbour. We had no doubt about whom was invading whom. The Commonwealth infantry units, who took the brunt of the war, were in a thin defensive line, in no way were they in a position to go on the offensive. There is no place like the front line to find out what is going on in a war.

The operations we carried out undoubtedly saved many lives on both sides. In my case, that one ambush, on what had been a secure supply line, caused the opposition to pull back troops from the front to guard it. Those troops still had to be supplied and a supply line can only cope with so much. The fact is, there were no more Indonesian attacks across the border in that area after we hit the supply line. It could no longer support enough troops at the sharp end. It had been proved vulnerable.

My patrol's efforts were an average minuscule part of the regiment's contribution in Borneo. We knew before we went in, whether we tried or not, whether we lived or died, the squadron, the regiment, the Army would go on – regardless. Commonwealth forces would achieve their aims in Borneo. So why bother?

In my case, the challenge. I considered myself an expert at my job, an expert with a big 'L' plate. No one knows it all about anything much, least of all about my trade. I always knew I would never learn it all but I had to keep learning, keep trying. Operations were to me like a great chess game, with the highest stakes. There was no greater thrill in life that to pit my wits and whatever expertise against a good opposition. Not so much to kill him as to outwit him. The more difficult the job, the greater the odds against me – the better I liked it.

There is no way I can speak for any other member of the regiment when trying to pin down what makes a man drive himself to the limits of danger, endurance or whatever. But, if there is one common factor, I would say it is that which is destroyed by putting drill and bullshit above real military training.[1]

---

1 Don Large. *One Man's SAS*. 1987.

The confrontation came to an end in 1966 as political turmoil in Indonesia undermined the politicians' will to continue the costly and ineffective campaign. Soekarno, the Indonesian President who had led the country to independence from the Netherlands, was toppled from power to be replaced by the far more pragmatic General Suharto. Negotiations began in May 1966 and concluded in August, after which incursions by Indonesian troops ceased. The part played by the SAS was, of course, relatively small but not insignificant. Their involvement in border surveillance and patrolling (including the raising and training of the Border Scouts, a unit of jungle tribesmen) was an important element in gathering intelligence for more conventional infantry operations, whilst their cross-border patrols (22 SAS were the first British unit authorized to cross the border) pointed the way for the later 'Claret' attacks on significant Indonesian installations. The Borneo campaign would not have been lost without the presence of the SAS, but it would certainly have dragged on much longer, and would have been a more costly and painful process for all concerned. As it was, 22 SAS suffered only three men killed in action throughout the campaign (three others died in a helicopter crash, an Australian SAS Lance-Corporal was gored to death by an elephant during a cross-border patrol and two Australians were also killed in a river crossing) out of a total of one hundred and fourteen British and Commonwealth deaths, and further cemented their growing reputation within the army as first-rate strategic reconnaissance troops.

Training for selection.

These exclusive photographs feature members of 21 and 22 SAS. They were taken by Adrian Weale between 1987 and 1992 during operations and exercises in Great Britain, Northern Ireland and other parts of Northern Europe.
All photographs are the copyright of Adrian Weale.

Above
Members of 21 SAS are instructed in methods of demolishing a vehicle using explosives.

Below
Demolitions training: preparing a 'ring main'.

Above
Placing charges.

Below
Demolitions training for members of 21 SAS.

SAS squadron on exercise in the UK, 1992.

Above

Fitness training is essential for maintaining the high standards of the
SAS. Sprinting from the start-line to the Land Rover . . .

Facing page, below

. . . pulling it back to the start-point . . .

Below

. . . and pushing it back again!

SAS recruit training for selection in the Brecon Beacons.

SAS patrol bergan rafting during an exercise in 1992.

Launching the raft.

SAS soldiers prepare a bergan raft for river crossing.

Maintaining all-round observation whilst crossing with the raft.

Above
Patrol signallers check comms
before deployment.

Below
SAS patrol members check kit prior
to deployment.

6. **Uniforms and Equipment**

Soldiers of the SAS have a distinctive, almost unmistakably functional look, which sets them apart from the rest of the army

In the early days of L Detachment, members wore the clothes and equipment they had brought with them from their previous units: mostly, of course, the Commando battalions of Layforce. In effect this meant standard issue British Army tropical 'khaki drills', teamed with the perfectly serviceable 1937-pattern webbing equipment (which was still to be seen in some backwaters of the British reserve and cadet forces as late as the early 1980s). Wearing standard uniforms was to have an unforeseen beneficial effect:

> We were all wearing khaki . . . and the lucky thing was that without wearing enemy uniform, which would have meant certain execution, just by wearing rather sketchy tropical uniform, you could get away with it behind enemy lines: there was not very much difference between Afrika Korps and Eighth Army.[1]

Badges for L Detachment were locally manufactured in Cairo in early 1942 by a tailor who misinterpreted David Stirling's sketch of a flaming sword to produce the famous 'winged dagger'. In fact Stirling had been expressly forbidden from issuing his men with special insignia by Middle East Headquarters – as a 'detachment'

---

1 Interview, Captain. L Detachment.

they were not entitled to them – but typically he ignored the order and managed to solicit General Auchinleck's informal approval for the cap-badge as well as specially designed parachute wings.

The winged dagger, an embroidered 'patch' rather than the more usual brass badge, was worn on the SAS men's normal headgear – side-hats and service dress caps – but men who had taken part in operations were given white berets and allowed to wear their wings above their left breast pocket rather than on their right sleeve. In fact the berets proved to be a magnet for derision and abuse from outsiders and were substituted with a rather more tactical sandy-beige coloured version, but the practise of wearing parachute wings on the chest was continued throughout the war and on into 21 and 22 SAS for World War II veterans (it was reinstated by the Rhodesian SAS Regiment in 1978).

With the formation of the SAS Brigade in 1944 and the return of 1 and 2 SAS to Britain for training for the Normandy landings, the uniform and equipment scales for the SAS regiments became more formalized. By this time the SAS had become an element, alongside the Parachute and Glider Pilot Regiments, of the 'Army Air Corps' and therefore newly joined members of the much expanded SAS were issued with maroon airborne berets, camouflaged 'Denison' pattern airborne smocks and the various other accoutrements of airborne units, whilst retaining their winged dagger badge and wings. These items were worn with the ubiquitous 'battledress' and this remained, in theory at least, the basic uniform pattern for SAS personnel until the late 1950s.

Nevertheless, SAS personnel of all ranks continued to interpret dress regulations fairly loosely. One of the most obvious examples, after 1944, was in the headdress worn by members of the Brigade. Members of 2 SAS, and the French and Belgian battalions, wore the regulation maroon airborne beret, but 1 SAS veterans of the Western Desert and Italy, led by their commanding officer, 'Paddy' Mayne, continued to wear their sandy berets, as well as other items acquired during the early operations.

This situation continued until the disbandment of the SAS Brigade in October 1945. But the formation of 21 SAS in 1947 brought slightly altered circumstances: the amalgamation with the Artists Rifles. This meant that the traditions of a relatively old regiment, formed in 1859, needed to be accorded some respect and, at first, the SAS winged dagger badge was discarded in favour of the Artists' Mars and Minerva insignia worn as a small silver-coloured badge on the maroon beret. The SAS badge was then temporarily relegated to a position on the upper right sleeve of the battledress below the parachute wings.

At the same time as this minor change in insignia was taking place, members of 21 SAS were being issued with the camouflaged 'windproof' combat suit which had been developed for use by specialist forces in extreme climates and designed to be worn over battledress. Although this was not exclusively given to members of the SAS it was sufficiently associated with them, both territorial and regular regiments, to become a 'signature' item, as distinctive as airborne forces' Denison smocks (which were also issued to the SAS).

The formation of 22 SAS in Malaya also brought about changes in the SAS style of dress and equipment. By 1949, 21 SAS had abandoned the Mars and Minerva cap-badge and reverted to the SAS winged dagger, and this style was followed by 22 SAS when the regiment was formally established in 1952 (the Malayan Scouts had a crest of a 'winged *kris*' but it wasn't made into a badge), but long-term operations in the jungle produced stresses and strains on combat uniforms and equipment that had a lasting impact. The standard uniform for patrolling in the jungle consisted of loose-fitting green cotton shirt and trousers, together with a green cotton 'sun-hat', and canvas and rubber jungle boots, and these were issued to and worn by the SAS, but the field equipment issued to British troops in the Far East, the 1944-pattern jungle webbing, was much less popular.

The reason for this was that the various pouches and straps associated with the equipment interfered with the carrying of the heavy rucksacks that were necessary for long jungle patrols; the belt consisted of three canvas parts as well as the buckles and hooks and was prone to fall apart; and the ammunition pouches sat high on the chest, preventing the wearer from lying prone:

The jungle kit issued in Malaya was simply ridiculous. If you wore the 'fighting order' on patrol you got blisters and weals across your back from the yoke where your rucksack rubbed and pressed it into your shoulders, but if you took the straps off and just wore the belt, it fell apart under the strain. What we did was 'borrow' cargo straps from the Crabs [Royal Air Force] and cut them into belt lengths, and the regiment got some ammunition and ration pouches run up locally; the water bottle pouch was OK . . . You could wear that lot below your bergan without it getting in the way.

This was the origin of SAS 'belt-kit', a system of webbing equipment that was originally unique to the regiment and which, until the recent advent of the modern PLCE (Personal Load Carrying Equipment) system, was issued to each man on a set pattern of:

- a 1958 pattern webbing belt
- a prismatic compass and webbing pouch
- an SAS ammunition pouch designed to hang low from the belt and hold four SLR or Armalite magazines
- an SAS ration pouch designed to hold a mess tin with rations and a small first-aid kit
- two 1944 pattern water bottles with aluminium mugs and pouches
- a large 'golock' machete
- two lightweight shoulder straps which could be attached directly to the belt.

The purpose of the belt-kit is to provide the SAS patrol member with sufficient ammunition, rations, water and other essentials to keep him going in the field when he is separated from his rucksack, which may be tactically inconvenient during certain phases of an operation or patrol and would thus be cached:

The key things you keep in your belt are bullets and water – lots of them. If there's any room left you put food, brew-kit and all the other shit in, but bullets and water is the main thing. Grenades, first-aid kit,

2 Interview, Corporal, 22 SAS.

compass – you keep 'em in your pockets – anything else, stick it in your bergan.[3]

Currently popular with SAS soldiers, as well as the wider army, are 'combat waistcoats', which fulfil much the same function as webbing belt-kit but which distribute the weight better, and which can generally hold more of the smaller items that might previously have been carried in the bergan rucksack.

The bergan itself is used to carry the many other items that are essential to the success of a long patrol or operation in the field. Apart from additional rations, ammunition, a few spare items of clothing, sleeping kit and so on, the bergan carries the equipment of the patrol specialists: the radio and signals kit, the medic pack, demolition stores; all packed in 'grab-bags' at the top of the rucksack so that if bergans have to be dumped for a quick getaway, the essential tools of the patrol can be rapidly rescued.

The everyday uniform for present-day members of 22 SAS consists of the DPM ('Disruptive Pattern Material' – the standard British Army camouflage cloth), camouflaged lightweight 'jungle' combat suit of loose-fitting trousers and shirt, worn with a blue regimental stable belt and beige beret in barracks (and with a standard military pullover during the winter). In the field, this uniform is varied by the addition of a hooded DPM windproof smock, and a variety of T-shirts, thermal clothing, fleece jackets and waterproofs according to the taste of the wearer, topped with either a GRP parachutist's pattern helmet or a soft military-style hat according to the wearer's taste (these include camouflaged peaked caps, jungle hats and wool skull caps: for security reasons the SAS beret, badge and wings are *never* worn in the field by members of the regiment).

Despite popular myth, the clothing and equipment issued to members of special forces for normal operations is not noticeably better than that given to soldiers of regular units. Even so, soldiers of the SAS have a distinctive, almost unmistakably functional look, which sets them apart from the rest of the army.

---

3 Interview, NCO, 22 SAS.

7. **Desert Disaster:**
Radfan, Aden, 1964

The plan was to insert an eight-man patrol into the area of the drop zone, which would then lie up for a period, observing enemy activity

22 SAS's second post-war entanglement in Arabia began in 1964, in the British Protectorate of Aden. The port city of Aden and its southern Arabian hinterland had been under British control since 1839, valuable as a refuelling and revictualling point on the route to British imperial possessions in India and the Far East. British policy in the colony, such as it was, had been to concentrate on the port, leaving the rural parts of the territory to the control of tribal leaders, whose loyalty was earned through treaties, bribery and occasional shows of force from the locally raised, but largely British-officered, Federal Regular Army (FRA). This policy had worked up until 1962 when, inspired by a heady cocktail of Nasser's pan-Arab nationalism and Soviet communism, the army of neighbouring Yemen had deposed their Imam, set up a left-wing government with Egyptian and Soviet backing, and begun to infiltrate weapons and guerrillas over the Radfan mountains into Adeni territory.

Little notice was taken of this growing insurgency for some time, with the result that a considerable deterioration in the situation had occurred by the time that a state of emergency was declared in December 1963. In an effort to halt, or at least slow down, the flow of weapons from Yemen, an ad hoc brigade of the FRA had moved into the Radfan in early 1964, but with little notion of how to proceed, the soldiers had simply occupied positions for a short period before withdrawing back to barracks. No effort was made at winning 'hearts and minds' or even realistically obtaining intelligence from the local population, and as soon as the FRA left, the rebels re-occupied their positions.

In the wake of the first attempts to deal with the Radfan problem a re-think ensued at Headquarters Middle East Land Forces and it was agreed to launch a second operation, this time involving several British units in addition to the FRA. Whilst this was in the planning stage, Major Peter de la Billière of 22 SAS was in Aden organizing a training exercise for A Squadron, which he was then commanding, and he got wind of the scheme. The plan involved using two battalions of the FRA together with 45 Commando Royal Marines (with B Company of 3 Para, then based in Bahrain, attached to them) to seize – initially – two hill objectives in rebel-held areas, one of which would be taken in an airborne assault by the Paras. De la Billière suggested that his squadron might be used to secure the Paras' drop zone.

A Squadron arrived in Aden on 22 April 1964 and, without taking time to acclimatize, moved forward to a base at the village of Thumier. The first task for the squadron was to begin patrolling in order to familiarize themselves with the ground and to find a suitable drop zone for the Paras. They were soon to find that it was extremely hard going:

In Aden – well, in all desert areas really – your big problem is water. There's very little lying about, and what is serves as a focus for humans and animals alike, making it difficult to use natural resources if you're trying to patrol covertly: and generally we are. So you're really stuck with what you can carry, which isn't a great deal because water is very heavy: maybe two or three two-pint bottles on your belt, and some more in your bergan. It wasn't really enough for one day in that heat, let alone four or five, which is what we had to do. The result was that at the end of each patrol you came in shattered – really shattered – and irritable and nasty with it. I've since been told that we were probably dangerously dehydrated, and we can't have been far off going down with kidney failure or some such nasty.[1]

---

1 Interview: NCO, 22 SAS.

After less than a week of patrolling, de la Billière was given orders for his main operation: sending a patrol to secure 3 Para's drop zone at the head of the Wadi Taym, inside rebel-held territory. The plan was to insert an eight-man patrol into the area of the drop zone, which would then lie up for a period, observing enemy activity, before emerging to clear and mark their target.

The operation started at last light on 29 April with a helicopter drop-off of the patrol, commanded by Capt Robin Edwards, 5,000 metres inside rebel-held territory. They began to move forwards towards their LUP when they hit their first problem: Trooper Nick Warburton, the patrol signaller, fell ill with suspected food poisoning. Although he managed to keep going he inevitably slowed the patrol down and it became evident they would not reach their objective before daybreak. This meant serious problems: an eight-man patrol, if spotted, would undoubtedly be outnumbered and possibly overwhelmed by rebels known to be in the area. They would be beyond artillery range and probably not strong enough to secure a helicopter landing site for helicopter extraction: all in all, a poor situation to find themselves in. Having selected an emergency lie-up, Edwards and his men settled down to wait it out.

Disaster struck during the late morning. A local goatherd appeared heading straight for the patrol's precarious position. Fearful that he would give their position away if they allowed him to escape, he was shot and killed.

The killing of the goatherd provoked an immediate reaction from armed tribesmen who were in the area. Although they did not at first realize who was responsible for the shooting, they soon started poking round to discover what had happened. Realizing that their position was now well and truly compromized, the patrol opened fire on the closest tribesmen, hoping to reduce the odds against them before a major contact developed. At the same time, Warburton reported the contact back to squadron HQ, from where Major de la Billière called up RAF close air support (CAS), based only eight minutes' flying time away in Khormaksar.

The remainder of the day was essentially a stalemate. Armed

tribesmen attempted to work their way close in to the SAS position, whilst the British soldiers sniped at any movement and directed RAF Hunter CAS bombers on to enemy positions. According to de la Billière, the RAF expended 127 rockets and over 7,000 rounds of ammunition during the course of the day in support of the patrol, and a Royal Horse Artillery battery gave supporting harassing fire on enemy approach routes, even though the SAS themselves were out of range. It was only when twilight came that the situation changed appreciably.

Darkness meant the end of close air support but it also gave the patrol the opportunity to make a break for it. By now the enemy snipers were closing on the SAS position, possibly within fifty metres, and as the patrol prepared to move, Warburton was shot in the head and killed. This setback was followed a few minutes later by the death of Edwards himself, killed as the patrol skirmished towards a wadi that would cover their retreat to safety. During the remainder of the night, the patrol fought their way back along the wadi, occasionally 'back-ambushing' their track to deter any follow-up by the rebels. By morning, the survivors were safely back in friendly territory:

The Edwards patrol was an out and out disaster, and it was made worse by the fact that the Arabs decapitated the two bodies and stuck the heads on poles back in the Yemen. All the guys who were on it, they'd only just got there from UK; the squadron had only been in the country about five days and they're stuck out on this important op. However good you are, it's difficult to adjust, to get acclimatized, in that short period.

What happened was the Paras cancelled their jump and marched in instead; and we hung around for another month or so, doing recce patrols, then fucked off back to Hereford and straight back out to Borneo.[2]

This initial deployment into the Radfan was, if not actually disastrous, certainly costly for A Squadron, and reflected the

2 Interview. NCO. 22 SAS.

hurried way in which they arrived in theatre and began operations. General de la Billière recounts in his autobiography that:

> . . . we finished our tour with the feeling that this had not been an ideal
> operation. As Mike Wingate Gray [second in command of 22 SAS at
> the time, and the overall commander of SAS troops in the Radfan]
> remarked in a letter to Woodhouse, written on 11 May, he thought that
> paratroops could do what we had been doing:
>
> > We are only operating in a super-infantry role of short-range penetra-
> > tion, and tough, well-trained troops could do it equally well. We are
> > only using part of our skills here.[3]

Which is somewhat disingenuous as de la Billière had originally
lobbied the C-in-C Middle East Land Forces personally in order
to obtain precisely that role for his squadron.

Over subsequent years there were several further deployments
of SAS into Aden, but little good came of it, not least because
Harold Wilson's Labour government made the horrendous mistake of announcing a deadline for total British evacuation of the
protectorate in 1967. Hitherto it had been intended that Aden
would remain Britain's military headquarters in the Middle East
even after it had achieved governmental independence, and the
hope of obtaining British military patronage had kept several
Adeni factions 'on side'. With the announcement of evacuation
it simply became every man for himself.

---

3 Sir Peter de la Billière. *Looking for Trouble* 1994, p. 224.

8. **Jungle Phantoms:**
Vietnam 1966–71

The Australian SAS Regiment probably earned the highest reputation amongst both their friends and their enemies: to the Viet Cong they had become the 'Phantoms of the Jungle'

The war in Vietnam is not one that is normally associated, in British minds at least, with the Special Air Service. In fact, SAS soldiers played an important and influential role in the conflict between June 1966, when the first SAS units arrived, and October 1971, when they were finally withdrawn. During that period they achieved 492 confirmed kills, 106 possible kills, 47 enemy wounded, 10 enemy possibly wounded and captured 11 prisoners, against losses of 2 killed by the enemy, 3 killed in accidents, 1 missing and 1 dead of illness; 28 other SAS soldiers were injured. The SAS men in question were members of the Australian SAS Regiment and the New Zealand SAS Squadron.[1]

The New Zealand SAS was directly formed to bolster 22 SAS for their campaign in Malaya, but the Australian SAS Regiment, as it became in August 1964, had slightly different roots. During World War II the Australian Army had formed 'Independent Companies' to operate in the Pacific theatre, successfully harrying

---

1 There have been persistent rumours that members of 22 SAS fought in Vietnam but there is little evidence, anecdotal or otherwise, to substantiate them. The only former member of 22 SAS to go to Vietnam was Capt Robin Letts, who won the Military Cross with 22 SAS in Borneo, before joining the Australian Army and going to Vietnam as a squadron 2ic with the Australian SAS Regiment. Lt Andrew Freemantle held a short service commission in the Royal Hampshire Regiment and served in Borneo before joining the Australian SAS Regiment for service in Vietnam: he subsequently returned to the British Army and rose to the rank of Brigadier. It is possible that some members of 22 SAS visited Vietnam officially as observers.

the Japanese rear areas on islands such as Borneo and New Guinea but, along with most special forces units of the Allies, these had not survived the general demobilization at the war's end. During the reorganization of Australia's armed forces in the late 1940s, there were no plans to incorporate any special forces capability and it wasn't until the early 1950s that pressure mounted to create an SAS-type unit.

In the immediate post-war era Australian defence policy was based on the concept of operating as part of a British Commonwealth command structure. With Japan defeated, there was no obvious threat to Australian security that could not be countered by using volunteer reserve-type formations, and Australian regular forces were to a large extent integrated into British-led operations, like the Commonwealth division that fought in Korea. Nevertheless, the rise of Nationalist and Communist resistance to the colonial powers of south-east Asia during the early 1950s, which saw the defeat of France in Indo-China, for example, as well as the Malayan Emergency, brought about a change in the strategic environment in which it became evident that Australia needed to be able to field formations independent of British or Commonwealth support, alongside existing defence commitments. Consequently, in October 1956, plans were announced to form a regular brigade group for service safeguarding Australia's immediate strategic interests in the Pacific/south-east Asian region, and that the brigade would include an SAS squadron.

The SAS unit was formed, initially as an independent company (1st Special Air Service Company, Royal Australian Infantry), towards the end of 1957, based in the Perth suburb of Swanbourne, Western Australia. Training was oriented towards raiding, harassment operations and surveillance patrols – the 'classic' capabilities developed by the SAS of World War II – but adapted to Australian/south-east Asian conditions.

Selection for the new SAS unit was initially made 'on paper' by the infantry postings branch, but experience on exercises made it clear that some form of aptitude course was essential in order to find the right soldiers to man the unit and, in November 1960, the 'Recondo' (reconnaissance-commando) course was introduced. This combined arduous physical selection with training in patrol and raiding techniques, operating in small teams, and had to be passed by all members of the unit.

The characteristics required by the Australian Army for their SAS soldiers were much the same as for their British counterparts:

> SAS training is tough and exacting. The role of the unit demands a particular type of soldier of outstanding personal qualities. These qualities and make-up count more than technical efficiency in his own arm or service. Technical efficiency can be taught, the personal qualities required for long-range, long-term operations in enemy territory however are part of a man's character and, although they may be developed over a period, they must be learnt in childhood. These qualities are: initiative, self-discipline, independence of mind, ability to work without supervision, stamina, patience and a sense of humour. The aim is to find the individualist with a sense of self-discipline rather than the man who is a good member of a team. The self-disciplined individualist will always fit well into a team when teamwork is required, but a man selected for teamwork is by no means always suitable for work outside the team.[2]

The physical and mental stress of the Recondo course can be judged from the following description of a typical incident:

> The patrol was required early that night to hold for several hours a feature overlooking a road junction. We had been on the move for four days, and I had had no more than a total of five hours' sleep. I finished my reserve water bottle that morning and I was limping badly from a large raw blister on my left heel. The enemy attacked our feature as we were ready to withdraw over the eight miles of sand dunes to the sea, for exfiltration at 0300 by DUKW. During the attack one of the patrol broke his leg, and the fourteen of us made a stretcher from bush timber and, four or six at a time, started to carry him back. My own rucksack and rifle weighed over sixty pounds, and I doubted I would ever reach the DUKW on my own, let alone sharing the carrying of a casualty –

---

2 Australian Army Selection Pamphlet, 1962.

and still remain alert for an enemy. My first turn at carrying was agony, and I doubted I would ever last until 0300. By 0200 it was obvious we would not reach the DUKWs in time, and we would be faced with a day of harassment by the enemy, and a twenty-mile walk back through the forward defensive localities next night. The pain in my foot, the thirst and the agony of heavy loads made me decide that by 0300 I would be able to go no further.

At 0400 I realized that my problems were probably no worse than those of my fellows, and we had developed a camaraderie to see the thing through. At 0630 dawn broke, and we could see ourselves one mile from the beach-head, and the DUKWs had gone. But I knew I could go on carrying that casualty forever, for I had already passed through all the physical and mental barriers in my mind I could foresee. I realized that obstacles are there to be negotiated, and, having crossed one, got less and less in stature.[3]

The first operational deployment for the Australian SAS was in Borneo (see page 99), where they operated under the command of 22 SAS conducting 'hearts and minds' operations with jungle tribes, undertaking long-term border surveillance patrols and attacking cross-border targets. Although this was a gruelling initiation for the Australians, in extremely arduous conditions, the unit suffered only three fatal casualties, none of which were the result of enemy action: one man was gored to death by an elephant, two others were drowned during a river crossing; even so, Borneo was to give the SAS an enormous advantage when they were finally deployed to Vietnam.

The first Australian SAS soldiers to reach Vietnam arrived as members of the Australian Army Training Team (AATTV) sent to assist the government of South Vietnam in 1962, but it wasn't until the middle of 1965 that a battalion-sized combat unit, the 1st Battalion Royal Australian Regiment (1 RAR), reached the war zone. 1 RAR operated initially under US command, but in 1966 the Australian Prime Minister, Harold Holt, announced that he was increasing the Australian commit-

---

3 Quoted in D. M. Morner. *Phantoms of the Jungle* Battay Press, 1989

ment to the war from the 1,400 men of the 1 RAR battalion group and the AATTV, to a 'task force' of 4,500, comprising two infantry battalions, support arms and services, an RAAF helicopter squadron and an SAS squadron, commanded by an Australian brigadier.

When the Australian SAS had been raised to Regimental status in 1964 work had started to increase its strength from one squadron to three. By the beginning of 1966 this was complete and it was decided that 3 Squadron would be the first to go to Vietnam. Before the deployment, there had been some misgivings about how the task force commander would employ his SAS troops, and it was particularly feared that he might allocate them to the infantry battalions as reinforcements to their reconnaissance capability. In the event this was not the case.

The Australian task force began to arrive in Vietnam in June 1966. They had been allocated a TAOR in Phuoc Tuy province to the south-east of Saigon, a rural area believed to contain at least seven Viet Cong (VC) battalions, which mainly operated in mountainous rainforest in the north of the province. It was the Australians' job to find and eliminate them.

The general principle governing the employment of the Australian SAS in Vietnam was simple, and not radically different from SAS tasks in Malaya and Borneo. They were inserted from their base at Nui Dat – usually by helicopter – into areas believed to contain enemy, which they patrolled until they found them, after which the Australian task force commander had the option to continue surveillance, to attack them using the SAS patrol on the ground (provided it was a small enemy force!), to bring in infantry, or to request an air strike from his American allies. The differences between the Australians' experience in Vietnam and that of the mainly British SAS operations in Malaya and Borneo were in the numbers of enemy that were being confronted and the sheer intensity of much of the fighting.

There were differences also in the conditions in which the Australians operated. In Borneo the shape of the terrain and the nature of the primary jungle effectively ruled out any prospect of night movement, but in Vietnam, which was much more densely populated and in which large swathes of the jungle had been cultivated at one time or another, this was not necessarily the case. This had several different effects on operations. In the first instance it ruled out the building of shelters, cooking and smoking at night, all of which had been possible, at least to some extent, during patrols in Borneo. This in turn led to more rapid physical deterioration during operations because it became impossible for patrol members to remain dry, which meant they spent a good proportion of each night cold, wet and shivering. The threat of VC movement at night also meant there was no question of removing boots, which meant that most SAS members suffered from severe fungal infections in their feet (and crotches too) which could become both painful and extremely distracting during operations. Other hazards remained much the same. The jungles of Vietnam contained the usual profusion of stinging and biting insects, together with potentially poisonous snakes, scorpions and spiders. The occasional tiger was also encountered.

The following example of a patrol that did not go entirely according to plan gives an excellent illustration of the risks run by the SAS in Vietnam:

The patrol was a reconnaissance and intelligence-gathering operation, the object being to get in, get the information and get back out again without the enemy knowing that we had been there. Consequently, we equipped ourselves for a seven- to ten-day patrol without resupply, and with a mainly defensive ordnance selection.

The five-man patrol was commanded by Sgt Mick Ruffin, the 2ic was LCpl Mick Honinger and Pte Brian 'Blue' Kennedy was the medic. These three were the experienced patrol members having been in-country for about ten months. Sgt Fred 'Bad News' Barclay from the NZ SAS troop was with us before he started to take his own all New Zealand patrol out. Fred got his 'Bad News' nickname following his participation in a series of patrols which all encountered fierce contacts, of which this was the first.

I was the new boy, and would perform the signalling tasks and carry the 25 set, a VHF voice communications radio. The 64 set, the mainstay of patrol communications, was with Mick Honinger; 'Blue'

Kennedy and Mick Ruffin had the URC10s, a handheld UHF emergency beacon and ground-to-air voice comms radio.

We were inserted by 9 Sqn RAAF slicks with 22 patrol at about 1430hrs on 30 December 1968. Both patrols moved east together for about an hour. until it was clear that the infiltration was successful. At about 1600hrs we separated, 23 patrol moving south into the grid squares assigned to us, and 22 patrol moved on to their area of operations. We patrolled routinely for about another hour, during which we kept the signal 'sched' using the 64 set, the only radio we carried capable of reaching our base at Nui Dat. This was my first use of the Morse key in operational conditions, but it was as routine as it had been in training.

We moved further south until we hit a line of craters from an old B52 strike and then doubled back parallel to our path and established an LUP for the night at about 1700hrs. The night was quiet with no activity by friendlies or the enemy.

The following day was equally uneventful as we patrolled about 2,000 metres of primary jungle that had been defoliated some time ago. Regrowth was well under way and the going was sometimes difficult as we encountered thick underbrush. We saw no sign of any enemy activity all day, and LUP'ed for the night in a thick growth of underbrush. I remember thinking about all the New Year Eve parties that would be under way in other places, but consoled myself with the thought that there would be a lot of heads feeling worse than mine the next morning. On New Year's Day 1969, we went through the usual patrol routine – awake before first light, alert as the day emerged then move a couple of hundred metres before breakfast (a brew and biscuits). Then we headed south-east continuing our search of likely watering spots for enemy signs.

Around 1400hrs we came upon a running creek not marked on the map, crossed it and commenced to climb up a gradual slope out of the creek bed in our normal patrol order of scout, commander, sig, medic and 2ic. As the slope levelled off about 200 metres above the creek we found our first enemy sign. A ceramic, three-gallon water jar with a black plastic sheet over the top of it stood against a tree. This was my first ever sight of anything even vaguely like enemy activity, and my concentration level went from 99.5 to 100.

Within a few more yards we came to the first bunker, and very cautiously reconnoitred the perimeter of what was a large enemy camp. Satisfied that it was unoccupied, we moved through the camp noting that there were six bunkers joined by well-formed communication trenches laid out in a perimeter capable of holding a company-sized group. The bunkers had not been used for a while but in the centre of the camp were several shelters made of bush cut from the jungle. These shelters contained shell scrapes and had been occupied within the last week.

As we moved out past the eastern perimeter of the camp Fred Barclay, who was scouting, came to a well-used track running north/south. He called the patrol commander up to inspect the track, leaving myself, 'Blue' and Mick Honinger about twenty metres to the rear covering them.

Being the furthest forward I was the first to see two VC moving north on the track about thirty metres to my right. They were about to stumble onto Fred and Mick Ruffin, who were hunched right down on the track's edge inspecting it. There was no time to attempt a covert warning, and a shout would assist the VC as much as it would help us. There was nothing for it but to engage them, which I did with a full magazine of 3–4 round bursts. 'Blue' joined me as he located the targets. Within five seconds the VC were clearly dead on the ground, and Mick Ruffin and Fred Barclay were moving towards them under the cover of our weapons to conduct a body search.

They didn't get there, however, as four more VC were coming up the track from the same direction. Mick Ruffin used his 'under and over' to lob an M79 round at them and signalled to us to withdraw. The VC were not intimidated by the M79 and opened up on us with small arms fire. Plenty of tracer, particularly green, came flying past us as the VC very aggressively advanced on us at the run.

The patrol swung into a smooth fire and movement routine as we returned fire and withdrew back towards the camp. These VC were very committed and charged onto us allowing Fred Barclay to kill one with three aimed single shots to the body and Mick Honinger to leave another on the ground for dead.

As soon as visual contact was broken we ceased fire and swung south to break the contact, moving relatively quickly to build up a buffer of space against the pursuit we expected would follow. Mick Ruffin kept us moving at a fast but sustainable and reasonably quiet pace for about ten minutes and then swung west, zigzagging away from the sounds of the follow-up that could be heard to the east.

All the time we were moving across multiple well-used tracks and then through another extensive enemy camp, which, although thankfully unoccupied, was obviously receiving considerable and current attention. The camp was bristling with bunkers and trenches, both new and under repair. Large trees had been felled and used to support substantial earthworks, and some of the bunkers had concrete structural components. From the state of the works and the wear on the tracks and the jungle floor it was clear that this was the base for a large enemy force who had been in occupation very recently and who would be reappearing at any time.

Try as we might we couldn't break out of the complex, which we were keen to do as it might have started spewing VC out of those bunkers at any moment. Our way to the east was blocked by the now occasional sounds of follow-up, we knew that the area to the north was more of the same and both southerly and westerly bearings kept us within the VC complex.

It was an anxious time, but finally we returned to primary jungle at around 1600hrs and after re-crossing the creek we could no longer hear any sounds of pursuit. Our patrol was now well and truly compromised and the time had come to get out while we hopefully still could.

We formed an LUP to establish comms, and I went to work setting up the 64 set to request extraction. I had just come back from running out the antenna when we again heard the enemy moving and talking to our east. Mick Ruffin told me to send our codeword for contact – M E L – Nui Dat acknowledged my initiating transmission, and I got away about ten MELs before the insistent signals for me to get ready to move got through to me. I abandoned the antenna (we carried a spare), closed up the pack and took my place in the patrol. The thickest bush was towards the south-west. so that's the way we headed. We hadn't waited for an acknowledgement from Nui Dat of our contact code so I didn't know if it had been received. It had!

At about 1700hrs the OC flew over in a light aircraft and we got voice communications with him via the 25 set I was carrying. Mick Ruffin gave him a sitrep and requested extraction. Unbeknown to us, our colleagues in other patrols were also in contact. As we had at least broken off our fight the OC decided to direct his available resources to those still in contact and said to Mick 'No extraction tonight – LUP'. What Mick heard was *'Extraction* tonight – LUP', a simple error which given the state of our stress levels and the noise of the aircraft was understandable. Mick acknowledged the transmission and closed down the 25 set. giving us the thumbs up to indicate the agreement to our extraction that evening.

We consulted the pictomap, identified a suitable LZ within walking distance to the north-west and headed off to what we thought was a helicopter ride back to Nui Dat. No sounds had been heard from the VC for some time and I was starting to feel quite pleased with the way things had gone. My baptism of fire had been faced and I thought I had acquitted myself quite professionally. We were out of a sticky situation and the slicks were probably already in the air to come and get us out.

We arrived at the chosen LZ at about 1745hrs, and hearing Hueys in the distance which we thought would be for us (in fact they were in support of our other patrols) moved onto the LZ to be ready for 'Albatross Leader'.

The LZ was an oval-shaped clearing about 500–600 metres across, covered in dry grass about 2–3 feet high. An old road, long since grassed over, ran north-west/south-east through it. We found an old dried-up mud wallow in which the grass was sparse and which formed a small depression in the ground about 3–4 metres across. At its deepest it was about a foot below the level of the surrounding ground. We settled into defensive positions ready with panel and smoke to signal the choppers.

Shortly before 1800hrs Fred Barclay picked up movement in the treeline, and then we could hear stealthy movements through the grass towards our position. M26 grenades were readied as we started to assess the difficult position we might be in if the choppers didn't appear soon. Of course they were never coming, but that thought hadn't yet entered our heads.

An enemy soldier raised himself immediately in front of Fred Barclay, apparently to orientate himself, and Fred shot him through the head with a single aimed shot. Two more appeared beside the dead VC, and one attempted to throw a grenade. However, they appeared to panic when they saw how close we were (about fifteen metres) and they dropped very quickly back to ground under our fire. The grenade exploded harmlessly closer to them than us. Two M26 grenades were thrown into the spot where they had gone to ground and as they leapt up to escape, the grenades exploded almost simultaneously throwing the two VC in opposite directions, the tail end of which 'Blue' and I saw as we raised ourselves to fire at anything still moving.

Unfortunately, there were still three of the enemy left untouched and they opened fire on the two of us kneeling up from a range of about fifteen metres. All of the rounds went high but we did get down onto the ground very quickly. Two more M26 grenades were thrown into the spot they were last seen but they were already up and running back to the treeline, under covering fire from a single enemy soldier within the trees. Mick Ruffin fired several M79s at the now re-united group without verifiable result.

The enemy then commenced a sporadic pattern of fire into our position. We had arranged our packs to provide some cover, but the fire passed harmlessly, if noisily, a foot or two overhead. They then became much more accurate with rounds impacting between us and kicking up dirt in the depression. To achieve this improved accuracy one had climbed a tree and had a clear view of our position. He was again engaged by M79, with which Mick was looking for a tree burst. This encouraged him to abandon his perch but in doing so he was exposed to our rifle fire and was hit, falling some five metres to the ground, where he was left by his companions.

Mick Ruffin told me to get on the 25 set to raise the choppers, because it was clear that they needed to arrive soon to catch the enemy on the ground. At this stage we were confident of defending our little dry mud wallow, believing that we only had to hang on until the gunships arrived to take out the remaining three VC with rocket and mini-gun fire. Although we could occasionally hear a Huey, I could not get any response to my VHF or UHF calls. even after about five minutes of trying.

Things then took a sudden turn for the worse when about fifty enemy emerged from the trees in an assault line about 130 metres to the south-east. As we moved around in the depression to face this new situation a large detonation occurred about twenty metres to our north, which peppered us with debris. Mick Ruffin told us forcefully to make sure we threw those M26s further out, but the puzzled expressions returned to him and a second explosion confirmed that it was in fact incoming mortar fire.

They kept up the mortar bombardment for about ten minutes, with occasional bursts of automatic rifle fire. We returned fire with both M79 and short bursts, although our ammunition supply was becoming a concern. The mortar fire was quite poorly directed, despite the best efforts of one of the enemy who was clearly the formation's com- mander. Just one round in our little depression would have settled the matter immediately, but between the packs and the slightly lower ground level we were untouched, if showered with dirt.

For our part, we were alternating between kneeling up to get off a few quick rounds at the assault line (and checking that they weren't any closer) and hugging the base of the depression. I was also working the 25 set to get any sort of an answer, and we had one of the URC10 beacons going – still with no response.

What to do?

As much as we would now have liked to 'bug out', it seemed most unlikely that we could all get away. The treeline was 150 metres away over open ground, which had to be covered under fire from fifty-plus enemy who obviously had the ordnance and the intention to make that option unlikely to succeed. On the other hand, the gunships could be appearing any moment (we thought) and the fire we were returning seemed to be ensuring that the enemy assault line did not advance. It seemed a question of what would happen first – reinforcements or an accurate mortar bomb, but we thought that defending our position was the best available option. We didn't exactly vote on it – Mick Ruffin put it forward as his intention and we all assented without question.

The situation then deteriorated further as the enemy group brought up a tripod-mounted medium machine-gun, with which they engaged us with long accurate bursts. We directed our fire at the MMG group with our M79 and aimed single shots, as this new threat was making things extremely unpleasant for us. I don't know if this upset their accuracy, but although the air seemed full of the crack of passing rounds, none of us was hit.

Kneeling up to fire at the MMG or assault line brought forth heavy automatic rifle fire and RPG rockets, and the mortar rounds continued to fall haphazardly. This all seemed a bit like Russian Roulette, but was essential to keep tabs on what they were doing and to discourage any advance.

We continued like this for another fifteen minutes, although it seemed very much longer. Our ammunition situation was becoming uncomfortable; the M16s with their last or second last magazine fitted, and the SLRs with less than sixty rounds each. All of the M79 rounds had now been expended, and we had two M26 and two white phosphorus grenades remaining.

We kept the radios working all of this time but still without response. The expectation of the arrival of the Albatross flight was turning more to hope (and in my case prayer – 'Blue' Kennedy and I both faithfully promised to attend church the next Sunday if we were still around). The one improving factor was that the light was beginning to fade. If the helos didn't arrive, and if the enemy didn't get lucky with a mortar or RPG round we may have been able to defend the depression until it was dark enough to slip away.

The VC may have had the same idea, because with a sudden intensity of small arms fire and much shouting and yelling they began their long-expected assault. The MMG now fired continuously and the mortar and RPG rounds arrived at 5–10 second intervals.

As we all faced the assault to try to break it up with return of fire, we saw two groups of about 10–15 enemy moving quickly down both flanks. Within a minute or so we would have been encircled, and the previously disregarded option of running the gauntlet of the open ground became marginally more attractive than staying put. We simply would not have survived if we had stayed.

Mick Ruffin told the others to leave their packs, but told me to take mine as it held the 25 set. As I lay down backwards onto it to get into the shoulder straps, a mortar round landed close to the lip of the depression and blew all the others over. They were up again immediately, heading off towards the treeline, with myself bringing up the rear.

I simply cannot describe the amount of ordnance directed at us. In the dusk, the volume of tracer going past me was simply continuous, all the way from knee height to ten feet overhead. And the noise of the passing rounds and the RPG and mortar impacts seemed like a massive string of immense fire-crackers. It seemed impossible at the time, and inconceivable now, that five men could cross 150 metres of open ground under such fire from so many weapons without one gunshot wound. Of course, one gunshot would have been all that was necessary, as we would not have left a man, wounded or dead, and returning to pick him up would without doubt have accounted for the rest of us.

I fell further behind as the heavy pack made movement more difficult, and as the first of my fellows reached a fallen tree on the edge of the clearing and turned to give covering fire, a mortar round impacted immediately behind me. I remember sailing through the air and landing heavily on my chest, winding me a bit. My companions thought the worst (they subsequently told me) but I was able to get up again. As I stood the left shoulder strap of my pack failed and it fell to the ground knocking my rifle from my hand. I had to bend to retrieve the pack, only to see the rear-facing section lacerated with rips, and water leaking from a holed container. I think Mick's insistence that I take the pack saved me from a similar fate. I abandoned the pack, attempting to fire a burst into it to destroy the radio, but only two rounds remained in my weapon and I think only one of those hit the pack.

I made the fallen tree where the rest of the patrol was intermittently firing single shots and shouting at me to 'come on, Mitch'. I'm not sure whether it was encouragement or abuse.

The enemy's barrage was now less fierce, and we quickly moved into the treeline on a bearing directly away from the main group. A large amount of dressed timber was hidden just inside the trees, and we had to negotiate a course around it. Under the canopy the light was fading fast and although firing continued in our general direction none now came near and it gradually diminished.

We continued to move until midnight, quickly at first but then into a normal patrol pace. At the night stop we redistributed the remaining ammunition and tried to assess the damage. Fred Barclay had a head wound from shrapnel, as did both Micks. I had a bit of a peppering around the back of the neck, but none of these were serious or debilitating.

The next morning saw us moving about 200 metres before a light helo out looking for us responded to our URC10 call. In about half an hour we were on an LZ and the slick was on its way in to extract us. We arrived back at Nui Dat just a bit too late for breakfast.[4]

On the other hand, the boot could be on the other foot. Some SAS patrols were specifically tasked to take offensive action, including assaulting through potentially large Viet Cong bases:

The assault was great fun . . . We killed about six-plus VC in the first round and grenaded all bunkers on the western perimeter. From the noises in the bunkers they were definitely occupied. Dennis Cullen pushed forward about ten metres in front and was held by about four VC firing on the assault party with M1 carbines and M3 SMGs. This confused us initially as I thought the support might have mistaken us for VC. We grenaded this trench then neutralized the area behind with M79 rounds. The results were unknown so I decided we had better find the radio before a counter-attack was organized. Lobb and Kerkez kept fire up to our line of advance. From the sounds further down the spur line it seemed that a flanking party was setting out.

---

4 Quoted in D. M. Morner. *Phantoms of the Jungle* 1989, pp. 280–88

I stumbled across the radio roughly in the centre of the camp. It was sitting on a rough table under a camouflage of hessian and undergrowth. Fortunately Lobb and Kerkez had missed seeing it otherwise there would have been little to pick up. I grabbed the radio under one arm and stuffed all the documents I could find down my tunic. Fire was now coming from across the valley. Yellow tracer usually signified an RPD in the vicinity so I ordered withdrawal. Several of the more agitated VC were now moving towards us but they were dealt with by Cullen . . . The only bodies we claimed were the ones we had shot again to ensure they did not come to life behind us during the assault.[5]

But despite the evident success of the Australian SAS in Vietnam (together with the NZSAS, the New Zealanders provided an SAS Troop from December 1968 to February 1971) their operations were the subject of criticism from both inside and outside the regiment. Brigadier 'Sandy' Pearson commanded the Australian Task Force from October 1968 until September 1969 and later wrote:

In Vietnam, some of their operations appeared to be successful. That is, they provided information and greatly contributed to harassment and attrition. But we were never successful in contacting enemy – based on that information – by normal infantry. What happened, too, was that the time spent on the ground between insertion and extraction of SAS patrols got progressively shorter. In fact, they were requesting almost immediate extraction – in some cases minutes only – which made the whole operation farcical and expensive in helicopter hours . . .[6]

SAS officers accept the validity of some of Pearson's criticisms, but the reality is that the SAS were being used in a medium reconnaissance role, which, although easily within their capabilities, was not entirely appropriate for the level of operational support and effort that an SAS patrol requires. Pearson evidently did not want to tie up resources by inserting small patrols that could not effectively defend themselves against the type of forces

---

5 Quoted in D. M. Morner. *Phantom of the Jungle* 1989, p. 259
6 Ibid., p. 278

he was expecting – and hoping – that they would meet, but as that was inevitable in the role in which he was using them, it was clearly a vicious circle. The only solution would be to insert larger, more aggressively armed patrols, thus losing the advantage of stealth that the SAS clearly possessed.

Strategic special forces operations undoubtedly took place throughout the Vietnam War but the Australian troop commitment – in effect a brigade – essentially ruled out any but the most peripheral SAS commitment. The fact that the US government was prepared to conceal 'illegal' strategic cross-border operations from the US Congress made it highly unlikely that they would involve an ally in them. As a result, Australian SAS operations outside Phuoc Tuy province were limited to training South Vietnamese soldiers in SAS skills, and giving advice and assistance to their American Special Forces colleagues.

The Australian SAS left Vietnam in October 1971 after five years of hard jungle operations and with many lessons learned. Of the many SF/Commando/LRRP units that took part in the Vietnam War, the Australian SAS Regiment probably earned the highest reputation amongst both their friends and their enemies: to the Viet Cong they had become the 'Phantoms of the Jungle'.

9. **Weapons**

The lightweight Armalite series rifles have become the most popular amongst British SAS members

SAS operations have always required a considerable degree of flexibility on the part of those taking part. This has allowed soldiers access to a greater range of weapons and given them far more choice in selecting weapons than is given to other soldiers.

When I joined the SAS in 1942 I was given a tommy gun – the old Thompson – which was a dreadful old thing: very heavy even though it could shoot quite straight. But as a sub-machine gun it wasn't much use because it was almost as big and heavy as a rifle but the range wasn't any more than a hundred yards or so. I 'lost' it as soon as I could and picked up a German Schmeisser which was considerably better: it was small and light and the stock folded up so it was easy to carry and store in a handy place in the jeep. I also had an old Smith & Wesson .38 which looked like it had belonged to someone's father on the Western Front, but I didn't ever use it.

On the jeeps we had Vickers machine guns which came out of planes, I was told, which were most impressive. They were mounted side by side and fired at a tremendous rate out to several hundred yards and really used to get the Eyeties heads down – we kept those all through the war.

But when we came back to England for D-Day, we were re-equipped with Brens and Stens and the American carbine. Now the Bren gun was excellent, very accurate and quite light for what it was, but the Sten – that must be one of the worst weapons ever made! Even when they were new they looked like they were going to fall apart, and you never knew whether they would fire or not. In the desert they got full of sand so quickly they were worse than useless, and you couldn't hit a barn door at fifty paces with it. Absolutely dreadful! I should think that at least half of us used German weapons when we could get them.[1]

Malaya:

In the jungle we used a lot of different weapons, but the one thing you weren't worried about was long range because when you had a contact it was never more than twenty or thirty yards' range if that. A lot of the lads carried shotguns, some would carry sub-machine guns like the Australian Owen or the Patchett, some had the M1 and some had the Lee-Enfield 'Jungle Carbine', which was a standard Lee-Enfield No. 4 with a shorter barrel. Later we had the FN, which was the same as the SLR but could fire bursts . . .

The first time I was in a contact, I saw this shape moving above my rifle sight, maybe twenty yards away, and I squeezed the trigger as we'd always practised, released the shot, followed through, and then realized that I couldn't see the chap I'd fired at. By this stage there was a good deal of commotion and shooting going on around me, so I fired another five or six rounds in the direction of the chap I'd seen, thinking that if I hadn't got him the first time, then perhaps I might get him as he took shelter. I fired low because I'd seen in Korea how people always shoot high when they're panicking . . .

Afterwards we cleared forwards and found a body. I don't know if it was the chap that I'd shot at but I suppose it was; he'd been hit by five or six rounds, I should think, and was very dead . . . He was quite a young chap, in his early twenties I should imagine . . . and I did feel very sorry for him: he was in one bloody hell of a mess.[2]

---

1 Interview. NCO. 1 SAS.
2 Interview. NCO. 22 SAS.

The introduction of the FN/SLR to the British Army in the late 1950s/early 1960s led to a short period when SAS weaponry was more or less standardized with the rest of the Army:

> The SLR was – still is – a very fine rifle. If you look after it properly it will always work and the 7.62mm bullet is lethal at very long ranges. There are only two drawbacks: the first is that it's a bit on the long side, particularly if you're operating in the jungle, for example; the second is that it loses the zero when it's broken open for cleaning. The fact that it doesn't fire automatic is a bonus, in my book, because an automatic weapon uses more ammunition, and if you want to use it, you've got to carry it.[3]

This opinion is echoed by an NZSAS veteran of Vietnam:

> We basically had a choice of using the SLR or the Armalite 'under and over' [M203] but about half still went for the SLR because of the stopping power. With the Armalite you could hit somebody and they'd still come at you, even though they were dying maybe, but the SLR: that fucking pole-axed the bastards.
>
> To make it more suitable for the jungle, we found you could take the last few inches off the barrel, so it wasn't so long, but there was a danger of it splitting or bursting, so we got the armourers to put a stainless steel nut around the end when they'd been sawn off . . .[4]

Since the 1960s the lightweight Armalite series rifles have become the most popular amongst British SAS members for 'Green' (uniformed) operations because of their light weight, relatively compact size, trouble free maintenance and reliability. The original comparatively feeble 5.56mm round introduced with the rifle in the US Army has been upgraded to a heavier, higher velocity design with a tendency to tumble after impact, causing it to give up more kinetic energy into its target and thus cause enormously more damage. In fact, the British Army was one of

---

3 Interview. Officer. 21 SAS.
4 Interview. NCO. NZSAS.

the first to recognize the potential of the AR-15, as the rifle was originally known, and obtained a number for use in jungle training and operations as early as 1965, before it was adopted for use by the US Army. The attachable 40mm grenade launcher which was introduced for Vietnam has also become a more or less standard feature for SAS Armalites, creating a weapon that:

Doesn't fuck up, gives you accurate aimed single shots, controllable bursts and HE [high explosive] fragmentation for luck. What more could you ask for?[5]

For other tasks there are more esoteric weapons available:

The first time I used a Welrod was a real eye-opener. On TV when someone uses a silencer it's this big tube that gets stuck on the end of a pistol and you hear a little '*phut!*' and that's it. But actually that kind of silencer rarely works very well because it doesn't stop the bullet going through the sound barrier, which makes a loud '*crack*', and it does nothing to control the noise of the working parts clanking around. The Welrod was developed for SOE during World War II and it's basically one big silencer attached to a pistol grip which comes off for reloading. It doesn't make hardly any noise at all because it fires single shots – so the working parts stay quiet – and it uses low-powered ammunition which doesn't break the sound barrier. If you didn't see it, you'd never know that someone was shooting at you – until they hit you, that is![6]

Anti-terrorist and 'Black' (hostage rescue) operations demand a largely different armoury. Together with requirements for accuracy, reliability and portability comes a need, in some cases, for concealment as well. Even for assaulters in a relatively straightforward and overt hostage rescue scenario, compactness is a prime requirement in selecting weaponry because in the cramped confines of an airliner, for example, a long or awkwardly shaped weapon might not be easily brought to bear on any potential

---

5 Interview, NCO, 22 SAS.
6 Ibid.

target. For this reason, the SAS has largely settled on the Heckler & Koch family of assault rifles and sub-machine guns:

> When they first started the team they went for the Ingram, a really tiny 9mm sub-machine gun, but it's like the MP5K – impossible to be really accurate – and if you're clearing a room full of terrorists and hostages, you really can't afford to be spraying bullets around all over the place. The standard MP5, on the other hand, is very accurate because it fires off a closed bolt, and it's comfortable and natural to hold for instinctive shooting as well.

> Over the water though, the Troop generally use the HK53 and G3. The '53 fires a 5.56 round and the G3 fires 7.62. The G3 was brought in because in one contact the lads opened up on a carload of Provos with their '53s but they all got away. When they found the car they found that the laminated glass in the windows had disintegrated most of the rounds, it had stripped the copper jackets off them as they went through, and so they had virtually no effect. The 7.62 has a bit more punch for going through car doors and that and makes one fucking hell of a racket when it does it; we call it 'the Barking Dog'.[7]

Specifically designed for counter-terrorist operations is the stun grenade:

> It's a handy bit of kit because it gives you a nice big comfortable edge without killing any of your hostages. You lob it into a room and you get a big magnesium flash and a huge bang, and everyone in there's going 'Fucking Nora! What the fuck was that?', and while they're doing that, we stroll in and nail the bad guys.[8]

---

7 Ibid.
8 Ibid.

10. **Civil Aid:**
Dhofar, Oman, 1970–76

The battle of Mirbat in July 1972 has gone down in legend as a supreme example of the courage and tactical acumen of 22 SAS

Operation Storm, the counter-insurgency campaign that took place in the Dhofar province of southern Oman between 1970 and 1976 was in many ways a classic of its kind. A relatively small security forces contingent – approximately 12,000 regular soldiers (10,000 members of the Sultan's Armed Forces, a battalion of Jordanians, a battalion group of Iranians, together with the British contribution) – successfully defeated a well-organized, well-armed, communist-backed insurgency (calling itself the Peoples Front for the Liberation of the Occupied Arabian Gulf and subsequently the Peoples Front for the Liberation of Oman), which enjoyed the support of a contiguous safe-haven country. 22 SAS, which had at least a squadron in Oman throughout the conflict, was to play an important role.

The roots of the rebellion lay in several different areas of Omani life. The Sultan, Sai'id bin Taimur (the same man who was ruling the country during the Jebel Akhdar revolt), was a feudal and autocratic despot. Although by all accounts a charming and kindly individual, he evidently had little understanding of the modern world and was fearful of its intrusion into his fiefdom. Although oil had been discovered in Oman in the early 1960s, and the country was potentially very wealthy, Sultan Sai'id refused to borrow development funds against future oil revenue and the infrastructure of the country was essentially medieval. This situation was compounded by Sai'id's belief that by preventing modernization he would be able to maintain control of the country. Fearful that modern education – even modern techniques of agriculture – might serve as a focus of dissent, he ruthlessly used his armed forces, which were largely composed of British officers on loan and 'contract' (i.e. mercenary) service, and Baluchi mercenaries from Pakistan, to suppress any signs of development, even going to the extent of concreting over newly dug wells and destroying crops.

Not unnaturally this caused some resentment amongst people who were perfectly capable of finding out how the world was changing outside their own borders, and who were, in fact, being subjected to a stream of propaganda from the communist Peoples Democratic Republic of Yemen, as the Aden protectorate had become after British withdrawal in 1967, as well as from Cairo, Baghdad and other centres of Arab nationalism. In any case, although the Sultan was, theoretically, an absolute monarch, in practise his freedom of action had always been partly circumscribed by the tribal chiefs of the interior, who traditionally regarded him as an effete plainsman. Not surprising, then, that rebellion was breaking out throughout Oman within two years of the SAS's victory on the Jebel Akhdar and that despite the best efforts of the Sultan's Armed Forces (SAF), it was growing stronger all the time.

Nevertheless, the discontent of traditionally rebellious mountain tribesmen in a feudal backwater of the Arabian peninsula would have been of little interest were it not for the strategically vital position of Oman at the mouth of the Persian Gulf. Oil from Kuwait, Iraq, Iran and Saudi Arabia was transported in vast quantities through the narrow Straits of Hormuz, which divide Oman from Iran, and an unfriendly government would theoretically possess a stranglehold on a considerable proportion of the world's oil supply. Not surprisingly, there were a number of parties with a strong interest in the outcome of the Dhofari rebellion and it is believed that both Soviet and Chinese aid was making its way to the rebel factions in the mountains.

22 SAS's renewed interest in the Oman was aroused in early 1970 when the Regiment's then commanding officer, Lt-Col

John Watts, made a covert tour of the Gulf travelling as 'Mr Smith'. From his visit to Oman and from his previous knowledge of the country (he had commanded D Squadron during the Jebel Akhdar campaign), Watts recognized that a number of urgent measures needed to be taken in order for the increasingly beleaguered Sultan's Armed Forces to get a grip on the situation. Principal amongst these was a need to begin to win over the 'hearts and minds' of the Dhofaris rather than just punishing them, which remained the Sultan's policy, although implemented by the British-led SAF. Watts' ideas, however, were to no avail in the face of the intransigence of the Sultan, and he returned to the UK.

Just four months after Watts' quiet visit to Oman – and possibly partly as a result of it – the situation changed drastically. On 23 July 1970 Sultan Sai'id was deposed in a *coup d'état*, almost certainly engineered by MI6, and replaced by his son Qaboos, who had been partly educated in Britain, had been trained at Sandhurst, served in a British Army regiment but who had been under virtual house arrest after returning to Oman. The way was now clear for a radical policy change.

One of the earliest priorities was to ensure there were no further sudden changes of government, and shortly after the coup the first organized SAS group, a team of bodyguards under an SAS Warrant Officer, arrived to begin round the clock protection of Qaboos. This was followed in September by the arrival of fifteen more men under the command of Capt Keith Farnes, who later commanded 21 SAS, who were sent to the Dhofari coastal town of Mirbat to explore ways to defend the coastal plain, by then becoming increasingly hostile, and re-occupy the Jebel.

However, the first operation mounted by the SAS in the Oman actually took place in the far north of the country where the Musandam Peninsula stretches north into the Straits of Hormuz. Here there was some evidence that Iraqi forces had carried out a small-scale landing or incursion with the intention of subverting a supposedly 'primitive' tribe who lived there. In response to this, the SAS, in conjunction with the SAF's Trucial Oman Scouts mounted a heli- and seaborne landing in conjunction with an operational free-fall parachute insertion by G Squadron's air troop – the first of its kind by 22 SAS. The operation proved somewhat farcical. Although there were some signs that troops had possibly been there, the Iraqis themselves were no longer in evidence; but the original beach landing by boat and helicopter had originally taken place several miles from the intended site as the result of a map-reading error; and the free-fall jump was hit by tragedy.

Free-fall parachuting was apparently conceived as an operational technique by Peter de la Billiere when he was Adjutant of the territorial 21 SAS regiment in 1960–62. De la Billière recognized that at typical free-fall heights above 10,000 feet or so, aircraft were less immediately identifiable and did not present the 'signature' that normal paratroop-dropping planes would have. At the same time, free-fall parachutists are normally, by delaying the opening of their canopy, much more precise and accurate in hitting their intended drop zone than paratroops jumping in 'sticks' with static-line parachutes. The Musandam jump, on 12 December 1970, involved a free-fall from 11,000 feet into the Wadi Rawdah, a depression formed by a bowl of mountains which was itself 4,000 feet above sea level. All went well until one of the SAS men, LCpl Paul 'Rip' Reddy, deployed his canopy. It is not entirely clear what happened next, but it is believed that Reddy's overloaded bergan caused his fall to become unstable and he tangled in his parachute as it opened. He plunged into the ground before he could deploy his reserve.

Meanwhile, in the south of Oman, the more important problem of the Dhofar rebellion was being addressed. To a very large extent the principal cause of Dhofari unrest had been removed by the coup and a considerable number of the more traditionalist rebels began to drift back to areas under the new Sultan's control in the months which followed. This actually served to highlight a division amongst the rebels between a hard-core of communists and more traditionally minded tribesmen who had simply balked at the Sultan's repressive regime: some Dhofaris were now beginning to suffer at the hands of the anti-Islamic communists who behaved in a high-handed arrogant way in the areas under their control. Nevertheless, there were many areas of policy in which rapid changes had to be made if the whole of the province was not going to fall under communist domination. Watts came up with a five-point plan with which he hoped the SAS might contribute to bringing the situation under control. He argued that the regiment should provide or facilitate:

1 An intelligence cell
2 An information team
3 A medical officer supported by SAS medics
4 A veterinary officer
5 When possible, the raising of Dhofari soldiers to fight for the Sultan.[1]

The provision of an intelligence cell was organized by 22 SAS's Intelligence Officer, who arranged to staff it with several junior Intelligence Corps NCOs (this was to prove something of a precedent for 22 SAS, which subsequently acquired a permanent Intelligence Corps section[2] at Hereford, and whose intelligence officers are now professionals supplied by the Corps). In the wake of the coup they gained access to a number of former dissidents who had returned from the hills and who were in a good position to supply information on the rebels strength and organization.

Psychological operations – euphemistically known as 'information services' – were handled by a small team organized by an SAS corporal, who proved to have a natural talent for the task. A field surgical team came from the Royal Army Medical Corps; a vet from the Royal Army Veterinary Corps. The role of 22 SAS, now in squadron strength and using the cover name British Army Training Team (BATT), could now start in earnest.

The first task was to establish outposts from which Civil Action Teams could begin providing aid for the community. The permanent basis of the teams were medically trained SAS NCOs, living amongst the Dhofaris, providing them with healthcare and arranging other aid as appropriate:

1 AFS Jeapes, *SAS: Operation Oman* 1980, p. 21.
2 Generally referred to as the 'Green Slime' because of the Intelligence Corps' usual cypress green beret. although they actually wear the SAS beige beret when serving with the Regiment.

We were told 'go out there and win their hearts and minds. If you can show them that the government is trying to help them then you've won half the battle without a shot being fired.' So there we were in Mirbat in our nice little house, surrounded by potentially hostile Arabs. I was glad I wasn't in one of the first teams out there because it was very tense and they were literally sleeping with their rifles!

As a medic my job was to hold a sort of sick parade for the locals in the town and to patrol out to outlying areas to do the same thing there, treating them when I could or referring them to the doctor if it was too complicated or serious. The biggest problem they had was with hygiene . . . if they had boiled their water and cooked their food properly it would have halved my workload, and malaria was chronic as well. At first when the BATT medics moved in they didn't have a lot of success because the locals were coming to them as a last resort and often it was too late, but by and by as more people who would have been seriously ill were treated and cured, our reputation built up and we became an accepted part of the scene. Their priorities were children, men, animals and then women! But it took a long time for them to allow us to go anywhere near their womenfolk.[3]

As this fundamental and crucial work was getting under way, the second major facet of 22 SAS's work was also beginning, the raising of the Dhofari militias:

We started off with a few guys who'd come down from the Jebel of their own accord. We gave them uniforms, we gave them food and medical attention, we gave them new weapons – FN rifles – and started training them, but most importantly we started paying them. Now these 'Firks'[4] were aggressive little buggers, like all the Dhofaris, and they liked a scrap; but at the same time they didn't necessarily want to rough it too much out on the Jebel if they could avoid it. So as word got about that the Firqats were starting up, more and more of them were coming down to join in, and bringing their weapons with them,

---

3 Letter, NCO, 22 SAS.
4 Short for *Firqats*, an Arabic word meaning a 'company of men' in the military sense. It was the name used to describe the Dhofari militia units raised by the BATT.

which they got a big fuck-off reward for. After a while, most of them were SEPs⁵ which was great: they didn't need so much training!⁶

The original intention was to make the Firqats non-tribal in the hope that it would decrease friction within the units and make them less independent and easier to control; in practise this didn't work out: the first non-tribal unit, the Firqat Salahadin, suffered badly from tribal strife and thereafter Firqats were tribally based. For their SAS mentors – the BATTs – serving with the Dhofaris could be something of a culture shock:

'All the news is good,' I whispered. 'We will get the automatic rifles for your Firqat but the *geysh* [army] are short of equipment. We will have to buy it in Salalah. By the way, I have a present for you.'

I felt under my shirt and produced a brand new Smith & Wesson .357 magnum, fully loaded. The pistol gleamed blue-black in my hand, accentuating the whiteness of its ivory handle.

'It is too big,' he said. 'I want one smaller, an automatic.'

I was staggered. It was a beautiful and expensive pistol which I had gone to much trouble to get for him. I had thought he would be delighted with it, or if not, would have had the courtesy to pretend to be . . .

It took BATT some time to understand that no such sentiment as gratitude exists in the average Dhofari's character. Since all things come from God anyway, and the giver is merely doing the will of God, he cannot help himself, so what is the point of being grateful to him?⁷

This experience was echoed by others:

It would have been easy to treat them as primitives or kids – they could really be mind-bendingly childish at times – but at the same time they were sly and cunning; and they were arrogant as well. Apart from

---

5 Surrendered Enemy Personnel – defectors from the rebels.
6 Interview, NCO, 22 SAS.
7 AFS Jeapes, *SAS: Operation Oman* 1980, p. 51.

observing normal *Jebali* customs when you dealt with them, you
needed a good idea about their religion, and you needed to remember
their pride. These guys were still running vendettas down from ten
generations ago, they weren't going to forget an insult from some
arrogant BATT lance-jack who'd only been in their country for ten
minutes and they weren't going to thank us for updating their techniques for bumping-off people they'd been bumping-off for centuries![8]

The military advantage of the Firqats was not in the firepower
they provided but in their detailed knowledge of the ground they
were fighting over and the tactics of the rebels; and their
psychological impact on the *adoo* (enemy) was enormous: having
forsaken religion and traditions for communism, the rebels were
shaken to see individuals that they knew and respected going
back into the government fold – and being welcomed. They were
not much use in set-piece battles where the superior discipline
and battle drills of the SAF were very evident, but in intelligence
collection and reconnaissance patrolling they came into their
own and became an invaluable and indispensable part of the war
effort, despite the suspicions of the SAF establishment towards
them.

In addition to civil aid projects and raising the Firqats, 22
SAS were involved in wider military operations and also took
part in the most significant single battle of the campaign, at
Mirbat on 19 July 1972.

The first major operation was Operation Jaguar, launched in
October 1971 and designed to regain a permanent presence on
the Jebel for the SAF. This involved two complete squadrons of
SAS (B and G); two companies of SAF; a pioneer platoon, some
Askars and five separate Firqats; the force adding up to some 750
men under the command of Lt-Col Watts, CO of 22 SAS. This
succeeded in seizing the strategically important airstrip at
Lympne as well as subsequently allowing the Sultan's forces to
capture the rebel village of Jibjat, thus firmly establishing an
operational toehold on what had, hitherto, been the heart of
rebel territory. It also accounted for the first SAS soldier killed

8 Interview, NCO, 22 SAS.

by enemy action in Oman – Sgt Steve Moores – since the Jebel Akhdar campaign. For the men of B Squadron who took part, the most memorable aspect of the operation was the initial approach march to Lympne with each man carrying loads well in excess of 120lbs across miles of broken, rocky terrain:

> On and up, up and on. I began to see rocks as phantom *adoo* [enemy]. Everything in me was so parched that I wished the monsoon would come back, and for the first time I could properly imagine the horror stories of the Korean War when men, crazy with thirst, would open up the radiators of trucks and drink the contents, a cocktail of rust and anti-freeze. Then I began to spot things on the track: hexamine blocks (used for cooking), rations, a tube of condensed milk, but this was no hallucination; this was the *firqats* unloading, on the point of jacking in and giving up. It was the best sight of the night, that condensed milk. It gave me strength. I'm fucked if I'm jacking.[9]

The battle of Mirbat in July 1972 has gone down in legend as a supreme example of the courage and tactical acumen of 22 SAS. It resulted from the success that the Sultan's forces, including the SAS, were enjoying in their counter-insurgency campaign and the fear, on the part of the rebel leaders, that they were losing their grip on the population of Dhofar. In consequence, it appears the rebels decided to mount a large-scale attack against the town of Mirbat to demonstrate their continued ascendancy over the SAF.

At first light on 19 July, more than 250 guerrillas of the Dhofar Liberation Front (the combatant arm of the PFLOAG) began to move towards Mirbat, covered by fire from both mortars and recoilless artillery. Their opposition consisted of approximately thirty Askars armed with .303 Lee-Enfield rifles, twenty-five members of the Dhofar Gendarmerie (DG) armed with FNs and a light machine-gun, and nine members of 22 SAS under Capt Mike Kealy; eight from B Squadron, one from G Squadron, there to do a stores check before his squadron took over responsibility for the town later that day. The three groups of defenders were

---

9 Jack Ramsey, *SAS: the Soldiers' Story* 1996, p. 111.

all occupying different locations: the Askars were in the town Wali's fort; the gendarmes were in their own fort; the SAS were in their two-storey BATT-house.

Alerted by the incoming mortar fire, the SAS team stood to, expecting that it was no more than the usual 'dawn chorus' of harassing fire from the Jebel. Instead, they soon realized that they were being subjected to a sustained attack. After sending a contact report, the SAS men began responding using their own support weapons: an 81mm mortar and a .50 Browning heavy machine-gun; whilst a Fijian SAS Corporal, Labalaba,[10] made his way across 500 metres of open ground to the DG fort to operate a 25-pounder field gun.

The rebel attack was concentrated on the DG fort, probably with the aim of capturing the field gun. After Labalaba reported that he had been 'chinned' by a bullet he was joined by Takesavi, who helped him for a short period before he too was hit. By now the rebels were very close to the gun-pit and Labalaba was using the artillery piece as a direct fire weapon, aiming over open sights at the enemy only a few hundred yards away.

At this point Labalaba decided to give up on the field gun and use a 66mm mortar which was nearby. As he made his way towards it, he was shot in the neck: he died almost immediately. Takesavi was now on his own, wounded, and firing his SLR one handed from the gun-pit at the enemy less than a hundred metres away.

In the BATT-house, Capt Kealy decided to take the team medic, Trooper Tobin, to the DG fort. They covered each other across the open ground but as they arrived at the gun-pit, Tobin was mortally wounded by shots to the face. Taking cover in a nearby trench, Kealy was now able to talk to Takesavi, but they appeared to be in an impossible situation, virtually overrun by the guerrillas attacking the fort. It was now that salvation arrived in the form of Strikemaster ground attack aircraft of the Sultan's Air Force, which made repeated bombing and strafing runs at the

---

10 The British Army recruited a number of Fijians during the 1950s and 1960s, several of whom gravitated towards the SAS. A second Fijian, Takesavi, was also present at Mirbat and went on to become one of the most highly decorated soldiers in the British Army.

guerrillas, despite heavy ground fire. As the momentum of the rebel attack faltered, members of G Squadron, under Major Alistair Morrison, arrived to reinforce the position.

It was a complete coincidence that there were two SAS squadrons in Dhofar at the time of the Mirbat battle, and even more fortunate that one of them had just completed its build-up training and was literally about to take over from the first, providing an entirely fortuitous but extremely effective quick reaction force. In the face of the stiff resistance of the Mirbat garrison, close air support and unexpected reinforcements, the enemy had no option but to withdraw, leaving behind thirty-eight bodies. In contrast the defenders suffered nine dead, including Labalaba and Tobin.

As well as being a stiff military defeat, the battle of Mirbat was a major symbolic blow to the rebels, demonstrating that even in strength they were unable to overwhelm a well-organized garrison of the Sultan's forces. Although it would be incorrect to ascribe the victory at Mirbat entirely to the BATT, the action of Labalaba, Takesavi and Kealy at the gun-pit, supported by the mortar and machine-guns at the BATT-house, probably delayed the enemy enough to ensure that they had not achieved any of their objectives by the time that air support (delayed by low cloud) arrived. Both the DG and the Askars in the Wali's fort fought well and deserve their share of the credit for resisting the attack.

Mirbat marked a watershed in the SAS involvement in Oman. General de la Billière later wrote:

> Now that the Sultan's Armed Forces had been built up into an effective, self-contained means of defence, properly trained and equipped, the SAS was able to step back into a supporting role . . . we concentrated on rehabilitating the Firqats on their own territory up the mountain, helping to rebuild their villages and set agriculture in motion again.[11]

The Dhofar campaign, Operation Storm, proved beyond all doubt that victory is only achieved in counter-insurgency

---

11 Sir Peter de la Billière, *Looking for Trouble* 1994, p. 278.

campaigns when the hearts and minds of the population are won over. It also illustrated what can be achieved by a well-trained special forces unit without necessarily resorting to the violence of which they are undoubtedly capable. The SAS took part in a good deal of combat in the Oman – twelve members of the Regiment died there – but there is little doubt that their most important role was in providing and organizing civil aid for the Dhofaris, and in training and organizing the Firqats to fight their own battles for their own territory. It is a lesson that, even now, many governments and many armed forces remain unable, or unwilling, to learn.

11. **Medic Training**

Many SAS operations and a good deal of training takes place far beyond the reach of normal medical help. As a consequence SAS patrol medics, in both the regular and territorial regiments, are trained to a very high standard in techniques of advanced first aid, basic field surgery and casualty management:

It's funny really, but I think if you went round the Regiment asking the guys which aspect of their training was most important to them, the most valuable if you like, I suspect that you would get a solid majority for the medic course. And I think that would be a surprise to most people outside the Regiment who'd maybe think that we're all obsessed with unarmed combat or silent killing or whatever. If you think about it though, it's probably the most intellectually demanding training that we do – learning to recognize and treat a range of tropical diseases, for example, as well as sorting out gunshot wounds – and the end result is very satisfying.

I was pleased to get put on the medic cadre, it was a course I wanted to do, and the hospital attachment was a real eye-opener. I was working in this casualty department in Birmingham, watching the more complicated procedures and then getting hands-on under supervision, and the casualty rate on your average Saturday night was appalling! You had traffic accidents, fights, bottlings, knifings: the whole works. I never saw a shooting, but other guys have on their attachments.

The Real SAS

I'm from a small village in Scotland. I joined the army when I was sixteen and I'd never taken any interest in school or exams. If you told me thirty years ago that I'd be able to stabilize a casualty with multiple shrapnel wounds and blast injuries, or treat a village full of kids with bilharzia, I'd have thought you were taking the piss. So yes, that's probably the skill that I'm proudest to have gained during my time in the Regiment.[1]

---

1 Interview, NCO, 22 SAS.

12. **Winning the Firefight:**
Counter-Terrorism 1970s–80s

**The successful conclusion to the Iranian Embassy
siege caused a worldwide ripple of admiration for
the capabilities of the SAS**

By 1972, 22 SAS had spent the best part of twenty years fighting insurgents of one description or another in various parts of the former British Empire, but the role of the SAS in combating terrorism in Britain had yet to be defined. In that year, the new commanding officer, Lt-Col de la Billière, commissioned a young troop commander, Capt Andy Massey, to make a study of possible SAS roles in counter-terrorism. Massey came up with the concept of the 'team', a self-contained assault force on permanent short-notice standby for deployment in case of hijackings, hostage takings and so forth, and this idea was 'staffed' through to the Ministry of Defence: there it was shelved.

It was a source of considerable concern at that time, when strikes and other industrial upheavals were commonplace, that the military should not be seen to be taking on any of the functions normally reserved for the police. 22 SAS had a clear role to play in fighting counter-insurgency campaigns, but it was much less obvious that there was a need for some form of domestic assault force and, at that time, mainland Britain had remained largely free from the kind of violence that might be countered by a military, or paramilitary, anti-terrorist force.

Massey's ideas were resurrected and revived in September of the same year by events at the Munich Olympics. A group of Palestinian terrorists, from the so-called Black September group, attacked the Israeli team in their accommodation in the Olympic village, killing two and taking nine others hostage. The German authorities, utterly unprepared for such a situation (the same would have been true of any other country), attempted to negotiate and then launched an ambush at Furstenwald airport, from which the terrorists and their hostages were about to be flown. In the chaos that followed, four Arab terrorists, one German policeman and all the Israeli hostages were killed: the operation was an unmitigated disaster.

The shockwaves from Munich reverberated around the entire western world. It was evident that very few, if any, domestic police forces were equipped, trained or psychologically prepared to deal with groups of well-organized terrorists armed with military weapons. In Britain, which already had a domestic counter-insurgency situation in Northern Ireland, Prime Minister Edward Heath's government turned to the Director of Military Operations for a solution. The DMO was immediately able to produce Massey's paper and authorization was granted to form a counter-terrorist team under the code-name Pagoda.

The original Pagoda unit was, over succeeding years, to develop into the Special Projects (SP) team that eventually hit the Iranian Embassy, London, in May 1980. By then it was drawn from a squadron of 22 SAS on permanent standby for counter-terrorist duties at the Regiment's Hereford base.

The counter-terrorist squadron provides manpower for three distinct units in the fight against terrorism: the Red and Blue SP teams, identically manned and equipped units which would, in extremis, be able to deal with at least two major incidents at the same time; and the Northern Ireland troop, based in Ulster, where they are the focus of the Regiment's part in the ongoing campaign to contain Republican terrorism. The SP teams are the subject of much scrutiny and imitation by Britain's allies: both the Australian and New Zealand SAS have added a very similar capability to their armoury of operational techniques, whilst the United States created Delta Force (Special Forces Operational Detachment Delta) in direct and conscious imitation of 22 SAS, under Col Charlie Beckwith, a hugely experienced Vietnam veteran who had served in 22 SAS in the 1960s. It is an acknowledged fact that counter-terrorist techniques are willingly shared between the democracies in order to maximize their chances of defeating this menace, and the western world has become an enormously more hostile environment for terrorists since 1972.

The most famous SAS counter-terrorist operation remains the assault on the Iranian Embassy in Princes Gate, London, on 5 May 1980. Six days before, on 30 April, a group of six Iraqi-sponsored terrorists had entered the embassy and seized twenty-six hostages, including an armed Metropolitan Policeman, Trevor Lock. The terrorists were ethnic Arabs from the oil-rich Iranian province of Khuzestan (also called Arabistan). Khuzestan had been annexed by Iran in 1926 and the mainly Arabic population were undoubtedly the victims of persecution by the ethnically Persian authorities put in place above them. Nevertheless, it is most likely that the terrorists were agents of Iraqi intelligence, intent on causing trouble for the unstable Islamic government of Iran.

The SAS were initially alerted to the incident by PC 'Dusty' Gray, an ex-corporal from the Regiment who was now working as a police dog-handler, and the SP team actually began its move to London before a formal request had been made for SAS assistance. After a brief stopover at the Army's language school in Beaconsfield, Red Team were deployed into a building close by the Embassy in the early hours of 1 May and set to work on an Immediate Action (IA) option, a rough and ready plan for use in the event that the terrorists started killing their hostages before a deliberate assault plan could be developed.

As the siege dragged on, Red Team were relieved by Blue at the Embassy and headed for Regent's Park Barracks, where a mock-up of the Embassy had been constructed by the Irish Guards Pioneer section, from which they were able to work out their plans for a deliberate assault. According to General de la Billière, who was then the Director SAS in the rank of Brigadier:

> . . . the aim was to attack every floor of the building simultaneously, and to break in so fast on all levels that the gunmen would not have time to execute anyone. Success depended on every SAS man

knowing his task precisely: the soldiers had to pick out the terrorist, recognize every hostage (from memorizing photographs), and keep within pre-set boundaries so there was no risk of shooting each other.[1]

The crisis came to a head shortly after mid-day on 5 May. The terrorists had been assured by their controllers that they would be flying out of Britain with their hostages within 24–48 hours and were not psychologically prepared for a long siege. By day six they were extremely edgy and anxious: at 12.40pm their leader warned the police negotiators that he would start killing hostages in two hours time, but the first shots were heard from inside just fifteen minutes later.

It seemed evident to the police and the SAS assault team that a hostage had been shot, but a decision had been made at ministerial level that the SAS assault could only begin when *two* hostages had been killed. This was based on the principle that a single killing might have been an accident but that a second was much less likely to be so (in reality, it smacks of the futile condition-setting beloved of politicians and civil servants at all levels in order to establish their authority and place in the pecking order). In any event it meant a further delay whilst the Home Secretary was briefed on the current military assessment by de la Billière, who needed permission to bring the assault team to immediate 'notice to move' (i.e., ready to go as soon as the order was given). This order was given (by the police commander at Princes Gate) at about 3.50pm, and the assault team were declared ready at 5.00pm, nearly an hour ahead of schedule. Thereafter it was a question of waiting for developments. These were swift in coming.

At 6.20pm, the police deployed a priest from Regents Park Mosque to talk to the terrorist leader, but whilst the conversation was in progress further shots were heard and shortly afterwards a body was dumped on the steps of the Embassy. After permission had been given to remove it, a quick autopsy was carried out which swiftly established that the body (of Abbas Lavasani, the Embassy's press officer) had been dead for some hours. The logic

---

1 Sir Peter de la Billière, *Looking for Trouble* 1994, p. 326.

of this discovery was that it was now possible, if not probable, that the required two hostages were dead. The police sought a decision from the Home Secretary, who in turn consulted Prime Minister Margaret Thatcher, and permission was given to send the SAS in on the orders of Assistant Commissioner John Dellow, who was in command of the incident.

Once the decision had been made to use the military option, the aim of the negotiators shifted somewhat. At least part of their task now became to lull the terrorists into a false sense of security, and they sought to do this by agreeing to the terrorists' demand that they bring a bus to transport the terrorists and hostages to Heathrow Airport. In reality, as this was happening, the assault team was moving into position for the attack. The surviving recording of the negotiator talking to the terrorist leader culminates in the following sequence:

Salim (terrorist leader): We are listening to some suspicion . . . er . . . movements.

Negotiator: There are no suspicious movements.

Salim: There is suspicion, OK. Just a minute . . . I'll come back again . . . I'm going to check.

The sounds that Salim had heard were members of Red Team on the roof, preparing to abseil down the rear of the building, and a 'pair' from Blue Team placing a frame charge on the front window prior to scurrying back into cover. As Salim left the phone, the assault commander, Major Hector Gullan, gave the order 'Go! Go! Go!', and a large stun charge in the Embassy's lightwell was detonated. The explosion was audible half way across London, but even so the tape clearly shows the negotiator repeating *after the detonation*: 'Salim, there are no suspicious movements'!

It is not technically difficult to storm a single building like the Iranian Embassy, but it is enormously difficult to storm such a building *and* rescue all or most of the hostages within, and it was here that the enormous skill and long months of training paid off for the SAS assault force. In the first few seconds of the assault, one of the terrorists did open fire on the hostages, killing one of them, but very shortly afterwards the assault force had killed four of the terrorists and a fifth was shot by a sniper stationed in Hyde Park.

The sixth survived because the soldiers were unable to positively identify him within the building:

> Then we found that one of the baddies had got past us and got ready to take him back inside to finish him off. As he was being dragged back in, one of the women hostages put her arms tight round his legs and begged us, 'No, no, no, please don't. He was really good to us.' I guess she had formed some kind of bond with her captor. Other people were now watching and he was kept alive. That's the only reason there was a survivor.[2]

Only two of the hostages died.

The successful conclusion to the Iranian Embassy siege caused a worldwide ripple of admiration for the capabilities of the SAS as a hostage rescue force and caused a shudder of fear amongst terrorists, and since May 1980, Great Britain has seen very little international (as opposed to Irish Republican) terrorism. Despite this, the hostage rescue training has not been in vain and the SP teams have been sent into action several times to less public events including, for example, the rescue of a prison officer held hostage by inmates at Peterhead prison, Scotland, in the late 1980s.

The main counter-terrorist campaign with which 22 SAS has been involved is in Northern Ireland. The first SAS deployment took place in 1969, when D Squadron were sent in overtly with the task of searching for and preventing Loyalist arms shipments into the province, but this was a short-lived venture into the campaign and the Regiment had more pressing tasks to attend to, on Operation Storm in the Oman and elsewhere. In fact, the Regiment was not formally and permanently committed to the campaign until 1976.

Even so, there was a peripheral SAS involvement in counter-

---

2 'Mack', quoted in Jack Ramsey, *SAS: The Soldiers' Story* 1996, p. 161

terrorism in Ulster before D Squadron were sent there in 1976. In 1970 Brig Frank Kitson, who was in command of the Army's 39 Brigade, in Belfast and north-east Ulster, received permission to create a small covert anti-terrorist unit with which he hoped to apply some of the counter-terrorism measures that he had used successfully in Kenya and elsewhere. This unit, which came to be called the Mobile Reconnaissance Force (MRF), consisted of volunteers from various units based in Ulster, who used basic surveillance techniques together with 'turned' terrorists as spotters, in an attempt to mount ambushes on PIRA operations and arrest members of the IRA command structure. As time went on, the MRF mounted more sophisticated operations, which included the setting up of a bugged massage parlour and a door-to-door laundry service, which allowed the Army to analyse clothing for explosives traces. Security in the unit was rudimentary, to say the least, and a series of compromises took place which eventually led to the disbandment of the MRF in 1973.

Despite the failure of the MRF, there was a recognition that some elements of the concept had been sound and it was decided to create a new unit to conduct surveillance against terrorist targets in Ulster. The job was initially offered to the Intelligence Corps, who maintained a pool of surveillance expertise, as well as a small operational surveillance unit for specialist tasks in Germany, but the Corps' manpower was stretched so thinly by the demands of operations in Ulster that they were only able to offer instructors for the new unit. Instead, it came under the auspices of the Director SAS, the bulk of the original manpower came from B Squadron of 22 SAS and has, until very recently, been commanded by SAS officers.

The role of the new unit, now widely known in the army as 14 Intelligence Company – although this is one of a number of cover names that it has had – was, and is, to provide the capability to mount airborne (i.e. from helicopters), mobile and foot surveillance, and to use static observation posts to gather intelligence about terrorist targets. Its personnel are selected from throughout the armed forces and go through a rigorous selection process similar, but not identical, to that of 22 SAS. It became operational in 1974 and, despite IRA propaganda and smears, represented the only actual commitment of SAS troops (who initially formed about half of the unit) between 1970 and 1976.

The immediate cause of the deployment of D Squadron in 1976 was an escalating series of sectarian killings that were taking place in south Armagh, a rugged and rural area which borders the Irish Republic. The population of south Armagh, by an anomaly of the partition in 1922, was of largely Catholic/Nationalist orientation and this, together with the difficult terrain and ease of escape into the relative safety of the Republic, had created a uniquely difficult area of operations for the security forces. The various IRA units in the area were, for a time in the mid-1970s, able to achieve a measure of equilibrium with the security forces: neither side was in a position to dominate the situation. During the six months leading up to January 1976, sectarian death squads had murdered twenty-four civilians from the Nationalist and Loyalist sections of the population, culminating in the appalling massacre of eleven protestant workmen in a revenge attack for five Catholics previously murdered by Loyalists. The press had by now given south Armagh the nickname 'Bandit Country' and there was a widely held perception that the area was getting out of control. The response from the government of Harold Wilson was to publicly announce that he was sending in the SAS.

The very public arrival of the SAS in south Armagh had a massive psychological impact on terrorists and the Nationalist community in the area. Although the IRA/Sinn Fein propaganda machine had been claiming the presence of SAS soldiers in the province for several years, the news that they were actually there caused a dramatic reduction in terrorism in south Armagh. D Squadron was based in Bessbrook, a small, largely Protestant village surrounded by Catholic communities, and placed under command of the CO of the Armagh Roulement Battalion (ARB), although in practice he would be guided in their use by higher authority. Their role, according to one Army officer quoted at the time, was to: 'Kill terrorists.'

In fact, the SAS were being provided with the best intelligence available to the security forces and being sent out to act on it, using their tactical skills to establish observation posts and ambushes:

> We were inserted to do an OP – an observation post – way down south in a bit of countryside between Newry and Forkhill; in other words, right there in what the press were calling 'Bandit Country'. The idea was that we would occupy this OP during darkness because some arms were supposedly going to be collected or dropped – I forget which – and then lie up in our FRV during the day, and the plan was that we would be there for about four days.

> The insert went fine. We went in with a patrol of infantry out of Bessbrook Mill one night. They did an overt patrol, stopping vehicles, questioning pedestrians and that sort of thing, and we cut away to an RV to lie up. In the morning, the heli came in and lifted them out and, as far as the locals were concerned, the army had fucked off out of the area.

> In reality of course, there were still four of us there, lying in these bushes waiting to go. We were on hard routine which means no talking, no hot food or drinks and no smoking; you don't cut through bushes or thorns, you piss into a bottle and you crap into a plastic bag and roll it up like a cigar; basically everything goes with you, you leave no mark that you've been there, because you might want to mount a further operation there or exploit the position again or something. If your OP's full of old compo tins, or even buried squaddy turds, some farmer's dog is going to come along and dig the fuckers up and it's compromised.

> On the second night there was a bit of a commotion a few hundred metres away which seemed to be some guys with torches searching around some farm buildings that were there. Probably they were rabbiting or ratting or something like that, but the fear-level just imperceptibly ratchets up, like you're thinking, 'Maybe they're looking for us? What if they get the drop on us?' This was not that long after the Regiment had been deployed for the first time, and it was the squadron's first tour, so we were a bit fired up by the experience, though, thinking about it, I can't see why because most of us had done several tours there before we joined the Regiment.

Anyway, the next day came and there's still nothing happening and no change in the neighbourhood, not to speak of anyway, and we'd pulled back into our lie-up. But around mid-morning this crappy blue Datsun pulls up near the barn and the driver is this big local player, a serious hood who we know is up to his neck in all kinds of dodgy stuff. Anyway, he doesn't go anywhere near where the weapons are cached but just stands around, having a smoke, like he's waiting for someone.

Sure enough, about ten minutes later, the farmer comes rocking up and they're talking away about something and the farmer is pointing with a stick at something, and me and D are thinking, 'What's going on? What's he pointing at? Like, is it us?' After about twenty minutes of this, [the suspect] gets back into his car and drives off.

Well, I don't know about the rest of the boys but I was a bit spooked by this, 'cause I'm thinking that something is definitely going to go down. We had a bit of a Chinese parliament, in whispers, and we decided not to call in the cavalry but sit it out and see what happens.

Anyway, it got dark again and D and me moved back into the OP and settled down to wait. Fuck all happened for about five hours, and the lights went out in the farmhouse, and it was all quiet; and we're just lying there with no sound except for the odd car going past on the road. Then, at about two in the morning, I suddenly got this feeling that there was someone coming up behind us; I don't know what it is, but when you're on operations a lot you get a kind of sixth sense, or maybe you're just listening harder, but the old hairs were standing up on the back of my neck and I'm definitely thinking, 'There's fucking someone there!'

I gave D a dig in the ribs and signed to him that there was someone behind us, and he started listening as well and, sure enough, you could hear someone moving about. There was a stand of weeds and nettles and things behind us, about six or seven foot high, and whoever it was was moving carefully through this.

I was in a bit of a state of controlled panic by now because anyone going into the nettles should've been seen by the other two and taken out, so I was thinking that they'd maybe got the others first. Our little problem was that we were facing the wrong way to open fire and we had to move very carefully to bring the weapons to bear. I had an SLR, which I've always thought was a great rifle, and it had a round up the spout but the safety was on, so that was going to make a bit of a racket as well. Anyway, I very, very slowly rolled over onto my back and eased my rifle round, brought it up into the aim and waited while D did the same. He had an M-16 I think.

Anyway, this rustling is getting closer and closer and I've got the safety off and first pressure on the trigger and were ready to go when suddenly this fox jumps out into a little area of grass and stands there. I fucking nearly shat myself! The fox is about two metres away, he has a sniff, smells us and fucks off back into the bushes. It took me the rest of the night, and a big whack from D's flask before I calmed down.

The others nearly pissed themselves laughing when we told them how close we'd come to taking out the leading Provo fox in Forkhill.[3]

The SAS's first year in Ulster generated the kind of controversy that has remained with them ever since. In March 1976 Sean McKenna, a local IRA commander, was snatched from his home in the Irish Republic by armed men who took him north and delivered him to an Army patrol: who promptly arrested him. Two months later, Peter Cleary, another Provo wanted by the security forces in the north, was arrested by a four-man SAS team that had staked out his fiancée's house for some time. They moved him to a nearby field and called in a helicopter to take him back to Bessbrook, but, as three of the exhausted soldiers marked out the helicopter landing site, Cleary attacked the fourth man who had been left to guard him and, in the struggle, was shot and killed.

The first two incidents were successes, if controversial, but the third was a disaster. On the night of 5 May 1976, an unmarked car containing three heavily armed plainclothes SAS men was detained by a member of the Garda a short way south of border crossing point 'Hotel One Alpha' south of Newry. A little later,

---

3 Interview, NCO, 22 SAS.

two more SAS cars appeared and were arrested by the same officer. In total, eight SAS men were under arrest in the Irish Republic having crossed the border illegally.

The soldiers' explanation was that they were on a reconnaissance operation and had made a map-reading error, but it was easy enough for Republicans to make propaganda about SAS 'hit squads' operating in the south. In fact, the cock-up explanation is the most likely: the road that crosses the border at that point is narrow and twisting, and is painted in one place with misleading markings several hundred metres north of the actual border. Even so, the wide publicity that the error received can only have undermined the reputation of the Regiment whilst hinting at nefarious cross-border activities.

During the early stages of the campaign, the task of liaising and 'deconflicting' between the various security agencies, and particularly between police and army covert operations, such as they were, had been handled by Military Intelligence Officers (MIOs) who were members of the Army's Special Military Intelligence Unit (SMIU[NI]). But with the arrival of the SAS in south Armagh, it was decided that they would need their own liaison officer to ensure that SAS operations were cleared with local police and army commanders, and to liaise with the Police Special Branch and army intelligence to ensure that the SAS received the best possible briefing for their operations. Accordingly, an officer with good local knowledge was appointed to the staff of 3 Brigade, based in Armagh, with the specific title 'SAS LO': this was Capt Robert Nairac of the Grenadier Guards.

Nairac knew the area well having served as second-in-command of a detachment of 14 Company (then using the cover-name 4 Field Survey Troop) operating around Armagh and was well known through this connection to a number of SAS officers, although he was not, in fact, a member of the SAS. His local knowledge was invaluable to the SAS when they first arrived in the area as a paper he circulated to SAS soldiers, and to other army units, suggests:

TALKING TO PEOPLE IN SOUTH ARMAGH

INTRODUCTION

1 Just as it is reasonable to regard everyone with serious suspicion it is also important to regard any local as a possible source of information. Most people (possibly 80%) are sick of the violence and would like to see the troubles end. Some would go as far as to do something about it if approached in the right way. Amongst fringe PIRA or even active terrorists there are those who might be 'turned' by the right approach. Generally speaking four factors prevent this:

    a Fear of the PIRA

    b Fear and mistrust of the Army

    c Genuine sympathy for the 'Republican' cause

    d Tradition

Most of the points made in this paper are applicable to the RC communities throughout NI.

AIM

2 The aim of this paper is to suggest how best to overcome these four difficulties.

FEAR

3 Fear is the most important factor in keeping people's mouths shut. They look on everyone – fathers, mothers, sons, neighbours as possible dangers. To have been seen talking to soldiers may often mean a 'visit' and some sharp questioning. All too often a friendly nod from a local has resulted in uniformed soldiers openly visiting or greeting them. If this goes on a beating or a knee or head job is the end result. Therefore, if you wish to talk to someone, follow these points carefully:

a Do not single them out for attention. If you visit their home, visit at least four or five others, before and after – to try to make your visit to your subject as normal as possible.

b Make sure that your subject realizes that he/she is not being singled out, even if they are.

c Give them an excuse for your visit. They will certainly be asked why the 'Brits' visited. Find a plausible excuse to tell them straight away, e.g. 'We are calling on all the houses around here because . . .' Obviously use the same story for all the visits on the operation.

d If, after the interview, they appear at all friendly, give them the opportunity to ask you back, e.g. 'We often check the houses round here so we will see you again if that is OK?' This gives them the chance to say how they would like you to come, e.g. 'Fine, but come after dark', or 'When the kids are out'. If you get this you have got a contact.

4 If you can convince your subject that you are totally discreet and will not put them on the spot, many people will help.

DISTRUST OF THE ARMY

5 Many innocent people fear and mistrust the Army. Some, no doubt, have excellent reasons to do so. The

Army is, inevitably, a 'Brit' instrument, and harmless people suffer inconvenience or worse, after the incident. Furthermore we are seen as outsiders and interlopers. When faced with sincere complaints, blind denial is worse than useless. One is merely calling your plaintiff a liar! They may well be, but a far better line is to switch to the attack, e.g. 'I agree it is bad, but when you have seen your friends blown to bits . . .' Also try the 'young eighteen-year-old soldier' line. Any soldier who has been killed must be either eighteen years old, fresh out of home, or married with a new baby. It is possible to gain sympathy and genuine emotion from these very emotional people. Nonetheless, the best way is obviously to avoid giving useless offence. Admittedly if a totally committed Provo gets a beating it may not do any harm. However it creates a bad impression. In any case it is very difficult to tell who are the Provos, and many totally innocent people have traces. It is always worth remembering that some who are openly anti SF in public, are probably putting on an act to impress the real terrorists.

GENUINE REPUBLICANISM

6 At heart all Catholic men and women in south Armagh have some sympathy for the Provo cause. It is a complete waste of time and totally unproductive to heap abuse and pour scorn upon the PIRA. Remember that you as an outsider are probably talking about their son, neighbour, etc. 'Misguided and misled' is a much better line of attack than 'foul bastards'. Then once again attack their sympathy. Try the 'young soldier' line. Be wary of using accidents – south Armagh PIRA have a good record of not causing civilian casualties. If that does not succeed move on

to 'Kingsmills' or the 'Tullyvallen Orange Hall Massacre'. You could suggest to them that these two incidents were unlikely to win over the Protestants to the idea of a 32 counties. It is useful to use three lines of attack for different age groups:

a **The Youth (14–25 years)** These days this age group is very well up in history – so know your facts. The best line of approach is to try to shake their convictions. Attack PIRA propaganda and use all the Provo nastiness you can think of. Some of them have consciences, if so they will have some doubts. One good line from you could shake them out of their attitudes. Try and get them to argue politics with you. The hard facts of Protestant determination and military power always shake them. E.g. 'If we pull out do you think anyone can control the Prot paramilitaries?' or again, 'If 20,000 British soldiers are pushed to defeat the Provos who the hell is going to control 20,000 UVF men?' Ask them for their solutions – but know your facts, they will know theirs.

b **The 26–38 year olds.** All the above arguments can work well for this age group. If they are newly married or have young kids try, 'Is this a fit place to bring up kids?' Also this age-group is very financially aware: the advantages of British Social Security etc, should be used: be careful not to patronize. Try talking very much 'man to man', or indeed 'man to woman'. You will often get a favourable reaction by talking about 'wild tearaway kids'.

c **The Parents (40s . . .)** In this age group you probably have the greatest chance of success. Undoubtedly the emotional 'eighteen-year-old soldier – just like your Danny', line can work well. Also try the 'evil men leading young lads astray' line. Above all with this generation play on their parental worries: use the picture of sinister, hard men pushing young Republicans into getting irretrievably caught up in violence.

TRADITION

7 South Armagh is traditionally a lawless and independent-minded area. It is resentful of authority of any kind. Furthermore, certain things are taboo. It is said that if you raped your next door neighbour it would soon be forgotten; if your grandfather had been an INFORMER you would soon be an outcast. It follows that there are certain deep-rooted traditions that will shut people up like a clam. Never ever use the words INFORM, INFORMATION, WITNESS or INTIMIDATE. Never write anything down; it smacks of police work. Never offer money for INFORMATION. (It may come to that after months of cultivation but to offer it is fatal.) There are ways round these taboos: 'May I call for a chat?' 'Can you help?' Avoid the direct question: hint, suggest and work round the subject. If you wish to say, 'It is high time the bad men were locked up,' try to get them to say it for you. Ask their advice, opinion in very general terms.

SECURITY

8 Finally, be very wary of giving away more than you get. Always consult 'Int' to see whose name you may mention. Do not ever use information from MISRs or 'P' Cards directly. You could be talking to the local PIRA IO!

USEFUL EUPHEMISMS

9 NO	YES
'Can you give me any information?'	'Perhaps you might be able to help?'
'The Provos are stupid murderers.'	'Some of the boys have gone too far.'
'Your son is a terrorist.'	'Your son is taking up with a bad crowd.'
'Did you see that shooting/bombing?'	'Terrible business that bomb, it must have given you a fright.'
'Will our visit lead to intimidation?'	'We don't want to embarrass you.'
'We have come to see you.'	'We are calling on all the houses round here because . . .'
'We want to ask you some questions.'	'We have just come for a chat.'
'How can we see you without fingering you?'	'We'll call again but we don't want to embarrass you.'

USEFUL LINES TO TAKE

10 a 'That young soldier that was killed – only eighteen – just arrived – left a mother and/baby, etc.'

b 'There are some evil men working on the young lads and leading them on, etc.'

c The WOMEN FOR PEACE. 'How can the Provos claim support of the people? 25,000 marchers attended the peace march in Belfast – 400 people were at the Provo rally in Camlough.'

d 'Every bomb that goes off, and every shot that is fired puts a 32 counties 10 years further off.' Or '. . . means more troops/searches/VCPs.'

e 'The Provos are the worst Republicans we have ever seen.'

f The Easter proclamation: 'Let no *rapine cowardice* or *inhumanity* dishonour our cause.'

g Cite various Provo murders of policemen off duty in front of their wives/kids, etc.

h When genuine complaints are made: 'Well I agree, but when you have seen a young boy (like that soldier, etc) blown apart . . .' 'What if it was your Danny/ Pat/etc.'

SOME ANSWERS

11 *Question*
'Who are the Army protecting in XMG?'

Answers
'Well I agree, but face it: if the boys stopped shooting and bombing we could go.'
OR
'I agree, but shooting and bombing for six years has only meant more soldiers/SAS/searches/VCPs.'
OR
'Yes, but do you want those Provo boys running your lives?'
OR
'Yes, but how long would an unarmed village policeman last in XMG – you must have some law.'

CONCLUSION

12 Throughout south Armagh there are many people who
   have vital bits of information. With skill and professionalism it is possible to extract lifesaving
   tit-bits. If approached the right way the
   fence-sitters (probably 60% of the community) will
   come down to our side. When that happens we have won.

R L NAIRAC

Captain

SAS LO

Nairac took his responsibility for collecting intelligence seriously:
to the extent that he took it upon himself to visit bars and pubs
in plainclothes hoping to be able to pick up tit-bits of raw
intelligence useful to the squadron. In Crossmaglen he was well
known as a member of the armed forces, and treated with great
suspicion and circumspection by the locals (who nicknamed him
'Danny Boy'), but in the smaller villages he felt able to try out
his pose as a Belfast Republican, called Danny MacErlean. This
was to prove his undoing.

On 14 May 1977, Nairac called in at the Three Steps Inn in
the small village of Drumintee to have a few drinks and to listen
to an Irish folk group. There is no reason to believe that he was
visiting for any specific 'intelligence collection' purpose: more
that he was simply there to 'sniff the air' and see if he could pick
up any gossip. He stayed for several hours, drinking and chatting
with the locals, relying on his fake Belfast accent, singing along
to the band. Although he was confident in his disguise, he was
actually creating intense suspicion amongst local Republicans
who were present, and who were making efforts to find out who
he was. As the evening came to an end and Nairac left the bar,
he was confronted by a group of local Republicans, beaten up
and driven off to a field to meet an IRA executioner who had
been summoned, drunk, from a pub in Dundalk, across the
border. After a violent and vicious torture/interrogation, during
which Nairac clung to his cover story, the drunken gunman –

Liam Townson, the son of an English civil servant, who was OTR (on the run) from his home in Meigh, near Newry – made several attempts to shoot him with a faulty revolver before finally succeeding. Nairac was buried in an unmarked grave and his body has never been found.

Nairac's horrific murder was a salutary lesson to the SAS and other covert forces operating in Northern Ireland. Despite the fictional image pushed by thriller writers and in television dramas, it is virtually impossible for an outsider to mimic the accents and attitudes of a group to the extent that he will become accepted by them, even during the space of a couple of hours of casual conversation in a pub. It is also believed that Nairac had become careless in his operational drills. Although he had told the SAS squadron's duty officer at Bessbrook Mill that he would return to base at 11.30 that night, the officer didn't actually raise the alarm for a further thirty-five minutes, essentially because Nairac had slipped into a habit of checking-in late. Finally, it is believed that Nairac had not taken his personal weapon, a Browning Hi-Power 9mm pistol, into the pub but had left it in his car. During the fight in the pub car-park, when Nairac was first confronted, he made great efforts to retrieve the weapon, but by then it was too late. The lesson that the SAS have learned over many years is that it is only by getting the basics right that successful operations can be built.

The pattern for SAS operations in Northern Ireland has remained essentially the same since D Squadron first arrived in the province, although the system for tasking them has become hugely more sophisticated and the actual SAS presence has been considerably pared down. In theory at least, SAS soldiers are only sent on operations based on the hardest intelligence available with the intention of using their superior tactical skills to arrest or, if necessary, kill terrorists in the act of committing their crimes. In 1980, a reorganization took place of Ulster-based special forces, leading to the creation of what is called 'the Group', short for Intelligence and Security Group (Northern Ireland). The Group consisted of a troop of SAS (at that time drawn solely from the Hereford-based counter-terrorism squadron and known colloquially as 'the Troop'), together with the various components of 14 Intelligence Company (usually referred to as 'the Det'), a specialist intelligence collation team ('the Spooks' or 'Green Slime'), and a variety of technical and administrative specialists in support, all co-located together at one of the Army's permanent garrison bases and commanded by an SAS lieutenant-colonel. Tasking for this new grouping, as well as parallel RUC anti-terrorist units and infantry battalion Close Observation Platoons, was to be centrally handled by Tasking and Co-ordination Groups (TCGs), which comprised representatives of police, Special Branch, military intelligence, special forces and MI5.

The best example of joint SAS/14 Company operations was the ambush mounted at Loughgall RUC station in May 1987. 14 Company and E4A (a police surveillance team) units had watched an eight-man ASU (active service unit) of PIRA's so-called Tyrone Brigade developing and preparing an attack against the part-time RUC station at Loughgall, County Armagh. With a reasonably accurate idea of when the attack was going to take place, the Troop, reinforcements brought in from G Squadron in Hereford and some members of 14 Company set up an ambush in and around the target and waited for developments.

The IRA gang, led by a hard-core terrorist, Jim Lynagh, planned to crash a stolen JCB excavator through the perimeter of the police station, and then detonate a large bomb held in the scoop, designed to demolish the building. The security forces, backed up by massive firepower (at least two 7.62mm GPMGs were deployed into the quiet Ulster village) had set up the main 'killer group' within the police station together with 'cut-offs' on all likely escape routes.

Just after 7.20pm on 8 May 1987, a blue Toyota Hiace van containing five members of Lynagh's gang pulled up outside Loughgall Police Station. The IRA men got out, lined up and opened fire with a selection of automatic rifles, possibly with the intention of giving covering fire to the JCB, which now headed towards the fence carrying another three members of the gang. The JCB crashed through and stopped close to the building and the three terrorists leapt off and ran back for cover, but as they did so, the waiting soldiers opened fire. Almost simultaneously, the bomb in the JCB detonated, flattening the end of the police station and wounding several members of the security forces.

Three terrorists, Seamus Donnelly, Patrick McKearney and Jim Lynagh, were killed in the Toyota as they tried to shelter from the hail of SAS bullets; one, Patrick Kelly, was killed as he stood by the driver's door, whilst Eugene Kelly and Declan Arthurs died as they pathetically tried to find shelter behind the van. Meanwhile, Tony Gormley and Gerard O'Callaghan were running for their lives. They both reached the cut-offs and died there.

But along with the terrorists, an entirely innocent local man, Anthony Hughes, who was driving past with his brother Oliver, was also targetted by the soldiers. Both were hit several times, and while Oliver Hughes survived, Anthony Hughes did not.

A second dimension to SAS operations against the IRA can be observed in actions outside the UK, the most obvious example of which has been Operation Flavius, the attempted arrest of the Gibraltar bombers in March 1988.

The IRA's plan to detonate a car bomb during the changing of the guard outside the Governor's residence in Gibraltar was, it seems, in some respects an attempt by the IRA to retaliate against the British Army for the Loughgall incident. Had it succeeded it would undoubtedly have caused a great deal of injury and loss of life, although whether it would have been much of a 'propaganda coup', as some writers have claimed, is open to question. Attacks on 'soft targets' – military or civilian – have never aroused much sympathy from anyone, even Republican apologists.

It appears that the IRA team chosen for the attack were the victims of their own notoriety. All were known to the security forces as members of the IRA and routine surveillance picked up the fact that they weren't around their usual haunts. When they were spotted by Spanish police on the Costa del Sol (Danny McCann and Sean Savage were, in fact, returning to Ireland, travelling on false passports), it was evident that there was a possibility of an attack against a British military target in Gibraltar (equally, the terrorists may have intended to attack a British target in Spain) and whilst the Spanish police kept watch for their return, an MI5 and Special Branch team moved to Gibraltar to work with the local police and await events.

Surveillance operations during February 1988 had shown that an Irishwoman, travelling on a stolen passport, was appearing in Gibraltar on Tuesdays, the day on which the resident infantry battalion normally mounted a full-dress changing of the guard ceremony. In fact the ceremony had been temporarily suspended, but when it resumed, on 23 February, and a week later, on 1 March, the woman was seen to take a close interest in the route that the soldiers followed. On this evidence, an SP team moved to Gibraltar on 3 March to make preparations for an arrest operation.

As it happens, the IRA team left Belfast the next day and rendezvoused at Málaga Airport, where, by chance, they managed to 'lose' the Spanish surveillance. During the next twenty-four hours it is evident that the IRA gang were involved in some quite detailed preparation. A bomb consisting of 141lbs of Semtex plastic explosive had been manufactured and smuggled into Spain for them, and they were also busy obtaining vehicles to conceal it and bring it into Gibraltar. Whilst the IRA team were making their preparations, so were the security forces, with a senior MI5 officer briefing the soldiers about their opposition:

The briefing I gave was as follows – that there was reason to believe that the Provisional IRA was going to carry out an attack in Gibraltar, the target being the changing of the guard ceremony on 8 March.

It was believed that a three-man active service unit, as the IRA calls it, was despatched to carry out this operation, and that they were intending to kill as many soldiers as possible using a bomb detonated by remote control. We believed that it would be brought across the border in a vehicle and that the bomb itself would remain hidden inside that vehicle.

The ASU would comprise three members – two of whom were known to be Danny McCann and Sean Savage, and the third was later identified as Mairead Farrell. It was known that Savage and McCann were active, extremely dangerous terrorists. More was known about McCann than Savage. They were believed to be dangerous terrorists who would almost certainly be armed, and if confronted by security forces personnel, would be likely to use their weapons and it was further believed that if the method of detonation of the device was indeed a radio-control device, they might seek, if confronted, to detonate that device.

Radio control would be much the safest way to explode a device from the terrorists' point of view: they would be away from the bomb when it went off. We also considered the possibility of them using a timing device – a bomb with some form of clock in it, but we considered that highly unlikely. Very recently there had been the explosion in Enniskillen where a large number of innocent civilian bystanders had been killed and we assessed that they would not be likely to use a timing device. It seemed to us far more likely it would be a remote-control device. We believed they would probably drive it in some time before the parade, either Monday night or Tuesday morning.[4]

With the intelligence aspects of their briefing covered, the soldiers were given detailed orders by their overall commander, the squadron OC. Broadly speaking, it would seem that the team were split up into two-man groups with the intention of providing armed back-up to an MI5 surveillance team who were there to keep tabs on the terrorists; and with the capability to make 'hard arrests' at the appropriate moment, on the instructions of the police commissioner. 'Soldier F' takes up the story:

I was the senior military advisor to the Police Commissioner of Gibraltar during the operation which took place in early March. In that capacity I was a permanent member of the advisory group which had been established to run the operation against an IRA active service unit. The purpose of the military force in Gibraltar at that time was to assist the police in arresting the IRA unit. It was clear to us that we were subject to the instructions of the Police Commissioner.

We were mindful of the priorities which he had laid down himself, and that the execution of that plan was to follow the sequence that he had

---

4 Evidence, Gibraltar Inquest.

requested. We were to arrest the offenders, detain them and defuse the bomb.

We had been told that the Provisional IRA were under pressure to produce what they, in their terms, describe as a 'spectacular'. In other words, some obscene act against the security forces. We were told that it was going to be a button job – that it would be detonated at the press of a button.

At 2.30pm on 6 March, in the joint operations room, we received a message on the radio of a possible sighting of Farrell and McCann entering Gibraltar on foot. At the same time there was a possible sighting of Savage in the town.

At about 2.50pm McCann and Farrell, with a second man, were identified in the assembly area: looking at it, walking through it and paying particular attention to one of the cars parked there. The second man was then identified as Savage, and almost simultaneously information was passed that it was Savage who had been seen parking the car at 12.15pm and fiddling with something in the front for several minutes before leaving it. The presence of these three in the band's assembly area was a clear indication that they were about to launch their attack. Our preferred option was to arrest them whilst they were on foot in the area, but we knew from the briefing that they were dedicated and ruthless terrorists and, if compromised, would be likely to resort to the force of arms to carry out their operation.

On the day of the operation, the terrorists were kept under surveillance and at 3.25pm were seen to return to the assembly area and examine it and the car once again before heading towards the border. At 3.40pm the Police Commissioner finally handed control over in a signed form to me. By this stage, the ATO (Bomb Disposal Officer) had examined the car and was convinced that it contained an IED (Improvised Explosive Device).

From this point, I could hear the tactical commander on the ground moving his soldiers into position and checking with the Gibraltar police officers assisting them. At about 4.00pm we received reports over the radio that the terrorists had been apprehended and that shooting had taken place. Once we received reports that the scene on the ground had returned to Gibraltar police control and that the soldiers had been removed from the scene, I formally returned control to the Police Commissioner.[5]

Events had, in fact, moved much faster than anticipated by the police and Army team. The soldiers and surveillance team believed that the car brought in by the terrorists and parked in the assembly area for the ceremony contained the bomb and that it might well be primed and ready for detonation. The decision was made to go for the arrests and effective control passed to the soldiers on the ground. 'Soldier A':

I saw that all three terrorists were together, talking and smiling. They were looking back up the road in the general direction of us. I decided I would then move down the right-hand side of the road to effect the arrests as all three were together, and I knew that C and D were nearby.

As I was moving up, Savage moved away and started walking south towards us. I wasn't expecting the split. As he moved past, Soldier B was about to turn round to arrest Savage, but I stopped him and said we should keep moving and arrest Farrell and McCann: I was told over the radio that C and D would effect the arrest of Savage.

Farrell and McCann then started moving off again towards the border and I was about ten metres behind them when McCann turned round. He had a smile on his face and he looked over his shoulder, and he looked right at me. We had eye to eye contact. We looked directly at each other. The smile went off his face. It is hard to describe how he looked. He had a look that he knew who I was, a look of alertness that I was a threat.

At that stage I was going to shout a warning to stop. At the same time I was getting out my pistol. I went to shout 'Stop': I don't know if it came out . . . I honestly don't know. He looked at me, his right elbow moved across the front of his body . . . At that stage, I thought he was

---

5 Evidence, Gibraltar Inquest.

going for a button: for me the whole thing was the bomb in the band area.

I fired at him, one round into his back from about three metres. I caught out of the corner of my eye some form of movement by Farrell. She had a bag under her arm and she was going for it. I thought she was also going for a button so I also shot Farrell in the back once. I fired a further three rounds at McCann: one to the body, two to the head.

McCann was down on the ground and so was Farrell, and their arms were away from their bodies. I then turned round to see if Savage was behind them, but I couldn't see him.[6]

As two SAS men fired at Farrell and McCann, another two were approaching Sean Savage:

Before I could get any closer I heard the sound of gunfire. [Soldier C] shouted 'Stop'. Savage spun round, he didn't stop, and his hand went towards the pocket in his hip area.

Uppermost in my mind at that point was that a bomb had been left in the Ince's Hall car park. I believed Savage had a detonator and was going to detonate that device. I had to make a decision. There were gunshots to my left rear: a threat to people around me; and to C and me. I had milliseconds to make a decision.

I had to move a woman away with my left hand, draw my pistol with my other hand and engage Savage. I fired nine rounds. The last two rounds were aimed at his head. He was possibly just inches away from the ground. I kept firing until he was on the ground and his hands were away from his body because at any time he could press a button and detonate the bomb which I had been told was in Ince's Hall car park.

In the course of approximately four seconds, Farrell was hit three times, twice by Soldier B and once by Soldier A; McCann was hit nine times, four shots from Soldier A, five from Soldier B; Savage was hit fifteen times, six rounds from Soldier C, nine from Soldier D. It is a tribute to the enormous skill of the soldiers

---

6 Evidence, Gibraltar Inquest.

that in this cataclysmic explosion of violence, no bullets missed their targets and no civilians were hit. As the noise died away and the soldiers were sure that the terrorists posed no further threat, control was handed back to the police on the scene. It was then that it was discovered that the terrorists were unarmed and none of them was in possession of a remote control device. Investigations later that afternoon were to show that the car left by the terrorists in Ince's Hall car park did not contain a bomb and that it was actually a 'blocking car', left to keep the parking space for the actual bomb (which was later found in a car park across the border in Marbella). What had, at first, appeared to be a triumphant success for the SAS was now clouded with doubt as to whether they should have opened fire at all.

The debate over the Gibraltar operation encapsulates the problem of using a military force like the SAS in what is, fundamentally, a policing role. SAS men are trained, first and foremost, to react as soldiers, using firepower, aggression and their tactical skill to resolve combat situations: to 'win the firefight', as military jargon puts it. But in counter-terrorist operations the law constrains the security forces to use minimal levels of firepower and aggression, and most people would accept that gunfights and killing are best avoided when enforcing the law in a democratic society. There is a good argument for saying that the ruthless, split-second decision-making skills developed by SAS soldiers are not necessarily appropriate for individuals ostensibly being sent to make arrests in the interests of justice. After all, whatever the significance of the movements made by Farrell, Savage and McCann were, they were neither 'going for a button' nor a weapon: they were unarmed.

Criminal law, which covers the activities of terrorists, rests to a large extent on what has been called the 'stable door' principle: that it is just and proper to impose punishment for wrongdoing, but that punishment is imposed after the event and as a reaction to it. Thus we wait until the horse has bolted before we punish the person responsible for leaving the stable door open. Ascertaining that individuals may have the intention of committing a terrorist crime in a certain place at a certain time, and using that knowledge to mount an ambush on them in the knowledge that they will most probably be killed, is sailing very close to the wind from a legal point of view. If we tell highly trained, well-armed SAS soldiers that they are to attempt to arrest heavily armed terrorists involved in committing a major atrocity, we must expect the soldiers to be prepared to use lethal force if they believe the threat warrants it, but when we turn out to be wrong, as in Gibraltar, we are placing those soldiers in real danger of legal punishment themselves.

The SAS are called upon to perform a variety of anti-terrorist tasks. Few would doubt their ability to perform them with great skill and dedication, and most of those tasks are perfectly proper for the Regiment to be involved in: the SAS's ability to provide long-term surveillance cover in difficult conditions has been proven over many years, whilst the need for decisive violence in hostage rescue situations is self-evident; but there must be a question mark, in a democracy, over an apparent policy of using soldiers in what are, effectively, pre-emptive strikes against citizens, no matter how disaffected and despicable they are.

13. **Helicopters**

Since the mid-1950s, the helicopter has been recognized as the most useful insertion option for the SAS. Flown by the RAF's Special Forces Flight, Chinooks, Pumas and Wessexes have become a mainstay of SAS operations:

I don't mind flying in planes, and I don't mind parachuting, but I hate helicopters. It's the noise, the smell . . . and particularly that awful lurching about that they do in the air. I feel sick almost as soon as I take off.

On this particular exercise we were going in by helicopter. We had to fly from somewhere down in the south of England . . . in Hampshire . . . via a civvy airport in the Midlands, all the way up to the Scottish border near Carlisle. We were going in a Chinook, which is a big steady, stable beast normally . . . but on this occasion the pilot was under orders to fly tactically . . . using ground cover and so on, and I guessed it was going to be pretty bad.

After a day spent planning, rehearsing, eating and resting, the pick-up was at about eight o'clock. My patrol was meant to be the first on the ground so we'd missed the last hot meal because we had to get down to the HLS early. We were loaded up to the eyeballs with food and water for about four days, along with ammunition, smoke grenades, radio batteries, helmets, some spare clothes and all the hundred-and-one other bits of crap that you carry because it 'might come in handy'. I guess my bergan must have weighed about fifty or sixty pounds – mainly because of the batteries and the water.

Anyway, when we'd got down to the landing site we were told there was a delay and that we would have about forty minutes to sit about waiting. I took the opportunity to eat a can of compo bacon grill that I had in my pocket – I'm not sure why, it's like spam from hell – and we settled down to wait. When we'd been there for about twenty minutes there was a rain shower and we all got soaked and then, roughly on time, this Chinook painted in desert camouflage turned up and we all piled in.

The Chinook was carrying a whole bunch of people – several patrols and some guys from RHQ – and space was very tight inside; I was right at the back, sitting on the guy behind's bergan with my own in front of me on the tail ramp, completely unable to do more than turn my head because of the crush. We took off and, sure enough, after a few minutes I began to feel queasy.

At first, it wasn't so bad because even though it was completely blacked out inside, the chopper was going along, straight and level, to an airport in the Midlands to refuel. We arrived there and the tail was dropped and we got some fresh air and that was great. But when we took off again it all turned horribly wrong. By now it was completely dark outside as well and I'd totally lost my horizon. I guess the pilot was flying at two hundred feet or less but the Chinook was bouncing about like a bucking bronco. Maybe ten minutes into the second leg of the flight I knew I was going to start puking – and soon – and I began to fumble around helplessly for something to do it into.

Special Forces Flight helicopters don't seem to carry sick-bags, I didn't have anything and so there was no alternative – straight in front of myself over my legs and bergan. After struggling for a while, I managed to get my rifle out of the way and, seconds later, whoosh! – out it all came; made even more horrific by the scent of bacon grill that was mixed into it.

I felt better for a few minutes but I was bloody embarrassed – as if I'd let down the squadron by throwing up in front of the RAF loadie – but the chopper continued to lurch about and, sure enough, I puked again, and again, and again.

We were in the air for about another hour after my first heave and, by the time we got to our HLS, I'd thrown up about five times; completely covering my bergan and my windproofs. But the truth was that, apart from the embarrassment aspect I didn't care, all I wanted to do was get out of that fucking helicopter and get down on the ground where I could breathe clean air.

Suddenly, after another stomach-heaving lurch, word came down from the front that we were approaching our target and should get ready to go. At the same time, someone opened a window at the front, and a wave of icy air came through the fuselage – but it was scented with the heaviest smell of vomit I've ever come across and I thought: thank god! It wasn't just me.

The Chinook touched down, the ramp opened and the four of us ran out, carrying our bergans in one hand and our rifles in the other, and got down into all round defence while the chopper left. It was pissing down with rain and freezing cold but my sense of relief was . . . profound I suppose.

We cleared the HLS and moved off to an LUP whilst we waited for a reaction to our insertion, but there wasn't one. Next morning, even though the rain had been washing us down for six hours or more, when there was enough light we could see that every last one of us was absolutely covered in sick. We stayed out for about six days, in pouring rain most of the time, and, at the end, I could still smell bacon grill on my clothes, my belt kit and my bergan.[1]

---

1 Interview, Officer, 21 SAS.

14. **A Short War:**
The Falklands Conflict 1982

**Members of the Regiment were saddled with a
reputation as military supermen that they mostly
neither liked nor wanted**

It was as much of a surprise to 22 SAS Regiment as it was to the
rest of the British military and intelligence establishment when,
on 1 April 1982, information was received that Argentina was in
the process of launching an invasion of the Falkland Islands, a
rocky windswept outpost of the British Empire in the far South
Atlantic. In the confusion that followed, as the Task Force was
hastily assembled, there was no clear thinking on how special
forces might be employed and how many would be required, and
it was at the initiative of the CO of 22 SAS, Lt-Col Michael
Rose, that D Squadron, under Major Cedric Delves, were despatched to the forward mounting base at Ascension Island, close
to the Equator, on 4 April.

Rose joined D Squadron the next day, bringing with him an
SAS headquarters element, and soon linked up with Brig Julian
Thompson, Commander of 3 Commando Brigade (which was
then the Task Force's principal land element). As a member of
Thompson's planning staff, Rose was able to develop a special
forces strategy which envisaged using D Squadron in a raiding or
OA (offensive action) role, together with G Squadron in the IR
(information reporting) role. In addition to the two SAS squad-
rons, the special forces effort was bolstered by the presence of the
Royal Marines' Special Boat Squadron, as well as the Arctic and
Mountain Warfare Cadre, a Royal Marines training unit whose

specialized fieldcraft skills suited them for use as an additional source of IR patrols.

Although it is a principle of special forces operations that they should be commanded at the strategic level – that is, by the overall commander in any particular 'theatre' – Operation Corporate, as the campaign to regain the Falklands was codenamed, was a Naval-led operation controlled by the Headquarters of the Commander-in-Chief of the Fleet (HQ Cincfleet) at Northwood in Middlesex, in a bombproof bunker deep below ground. However, as we have seen, Lt-Col Rose had decided to take himself and his regimental tactical headquarters to Ascension Island, where, for better or for worse, together with D and, shortly afterwards, G Squadrons, they became de facto components of 3 Commando Brigade under Brig Thompson. This posed certain problems.

The first difficulty to be overcome stemmed from the unfamiliarity of the Naval hierarchy with the potential scope and the degree of support required for SAS operations. This was solved comparatively easily by establishing an SAS liaison cell within HQ Cincfleet, and by the personal intervention of Brig de la Billière, still the Director SAS in 1982, who ensured that the C-in-C, Admiral Fieldhouse, was fully briefed on SAS capabilities. The second difficulty was less tangible but, anecdotally at least, considerably more problematic: the chain of command and reporting. The full extent of the confusion over who was responsible for tasking special forces patrols at each stage in the campaign, and how the intelligence they acquired should be disseminated within the force never seems to have been completely resolved. The whole picture has also been crowded by inter-unit rivalries and jealousy which has tended to obscure facts in relation to some aspects of SAS operations.

The first operations in which the SAS were involved were moves to recapture the island of South Georgia, 800 miles to the south-east of the Falklands group, which was held by a small force of Argentine commandos. South Georgia is a little over 105 miles long and approximately 18 miles wide at its widest point, but its mountainous terrain and relative proximity to the Antarctic make it geographically and climatically a very different proposition to the Falklands, being icy and bleak, and buffeted by severe 'katabatic' winds carrying ice and snow particles at up to 100 miles an hour. For practical purposes, the island is uninhabited, apart from a small scientific team from the British Antarctic Survey, whose leader doubles as the island's magistrate and immigration chief. It had been occupied by the Argentines on 3 April after a brief skirmish with a small party of Royal Marines detached from the Falklands garrison at short notice, and landed from HMS *Endurance*, the Royal Naval Antarctic survey ship which eluded the Argentines and continued to lurk in the area.

The plan, developed in London, was to send a Royal Marines company (M Company of 42 Commando) together with an SBS section and a troop of SAS in a small task group consisting of the destroyer *Antrim*, the frigate *Plymouth*, and two auxiliaries, *Fort Austin* and *Tidespring*. The idea was that the special forces would mount OPs providing information for the Marines, who would then capture the enemy garrison with the assistance of naval gunfire support. The Argentine garrison was believed to be no more than about sixty strong, to be based solely in the two tiny settlements of Grytviken and Leith (both former whaling stations) and to be well out of range of land-based air cover, although a serious threat to the task group was present in the form of a submarine that was believed to be cruising the area.

The South Georgia task group left Ascension Island on 9 April for the voyage south with most of D Squadron embarked on the *Fort Austin* – the squadron commander, Major Delves, felt that none of them would want to 'miss a scrap' – and making intense preparations for their forthcoming operation.

The commander of the land element of the South Georgia task group was Major Guy Sheridan, the second-in-command of 42 Commando, but the SAS were placed under the command of the captain of *Antrim*, who was the overall task group commander. In reality, this meant that the SAS commander could act as his own boss – few Naval officers would have sufficient experience or knowledge of special operations to question his decisions – but it led to the SAS attempting an operation that came close to disaster: a helicopter insert onto the Fortuna glacier.

The SAS scheme to land on the glacier and then move along the coast to positions overlooking Leith was strongly opposed by several members of the crew of *Endurance*, onto which the SAS had moved as the last step before landing on the islands, and by Major Sheridan, who was a highly experienced Arctic and mountain warfare specialist. They argued that the weather would be too severe. Despite this, the SAS team, from 19 (Mountain) Troop under Capt John Hamilton, decided to go ahead. During the afternoon of 21 April, and after two abortive attempts, the troop bundled out of their helicopter and onto the glacier; the first British forces to return to the islands.

They soon realized that they had been wrong. The glacier was being buffeted by 50mph winds that blew ice particles into their equipment and weapons and was criss-crossed by dangerous crevasses. Having covered about 500 metres in the first five hours' march, they were obliged to seek shelter in a crevasse for the night, having decided to request evacuation the next morning. This came in the form of three Wessex helicopters:

The helicopters lifted off, the Mark 3 Wessex with navigational equipment leading and the two Mark 5s following. I was in the first Mark 5. The flight plan was to follow the glaciers down to a landfall and then out to the ships. The Mark 3 put in a shallow right-hand turn, height probably about 200–300 feet, the first Mark 5 started the turn but was hit by a sudden whiteout in which the pilot lost all his horizons and we crashed into the ice. The pilot managed to pull the nose up before impact so that the tail rotor hit first and the helicopter rolled over on its left-hand side. The main door being uppermost, everyone got out quickly, the only injury being Cpl Bunker, who hurt his back.

The remaining Mark 5 and Mark 3 then landed and we transferred to them . . . the two helicopters lifted off again and exactly the same thing happened, whiteout followed by crash. This time the Mark 5 rested on its right-hand side. The Mark 3, unable to return because of extra payload, then flew back to *Antrim*. I and the other passengers were taken to the wardroom where an emergency medical room had been set up. After refuelling, the Mark 3, with the same crew still aboard, returned to the area of the second crash, but was unable to land because of the weather. It returned to the ship, having contacted the troops on the glacier, who had no serious injuries. They had in fact managed to erect a survival tent carried by the helicopter and had also retrieved equipment from the first crash.

The Mark 3 then returned to the second crash, and this time picked everyone up and returned to *Antrim*. It had seventeen passengers, very much overloaded, and the pilot had to fly the helicopter straight onto the flight deck as he was unable to hover and approach normally . . . [1]

For this, and other examples of superb flying during the campaign, the pilot, Lt-Cmdr Ian Stanley, was awarded a DSO.

A second attempt to land SAS soldiers was then made using the Boat Troop's Gemini inflatable motor-boats into Stromness Bay. This was similarly unsuccessful: three of the inflatables failed to start and had to be towed behind the two which would. Caught in a sudden squall, two of the unpowered boats broke free from their tows and were carried away: the crews of both were fortunate to be retrieved some time later.

As it turned out, the special forces OPs (the SBS managed to get some men ashore as well) were virtually irrelevant to the final outcome of Operation Paraquat. This was precipitated by the sighting, on 25 April, of the Argentinian submarine *Santa Fe* on the surface approximately five miles from Grytviken. Attacked by anti-submarine helicopters from the task group it was severely damaged and forced to put in to the harbour. With the main threat to the operation neutralized, Major Sheridan requested and received permission to attack Grytviken without delay:

All SAS troops were helicoptered ashore, landing on an area of flat ground known as the Hesterleten, two kilometres south-east of the BAS. The troop formed up in all-round defence to await the arrival of some thirty men from M Company, 42 Commando, and the commander of the operation, Major Sheridan, Royal Marines. Prior to our insertion a Forward Observation Officer and party had inserted to control the naval gun support. Having shaken out for an advance to

---

1 NCO. 22 SAS. Strawson. *History of the SAS Regiment* 1984, p. 229.

contact, we engaged likely enemy positions, and by this time naval gunfire was supporting our advance.

In the area where the Brown Mountain ridge line joined the coast we saw what appeared to be men in brown balaclavas among the tussock grass. They were engaged by GPMG fire from approximately 800 metres and by naval gunfire. Capt Hamilton and I also engaged a possible enemy position on the top of Brown Mountain with Milan. Advancing across open ground towards the ridge line we discovered that the balaclava'd enemy were in fact seven or eight elephant seals, which were now somewhat the worse for wear! The enemy position on Brown Mountain had been a piece of angle iron on which we had scored a direct hit.[2]

Unnerved by the naval gunfire, the Argentines were now busy stringing up white sheets to hang out of the windows of the BAS station, and the SAS troop, led by Major Delves and Capt Hamilton, and covered by the Marines on the ridgeline, moved through the whaling station to take the Argentine surrender. On the next day, 26 April, the small Argentine garrison at Leith surrendered without a shot being fired.

The next phase of SAS operations was the insertion of the G Squadron IR patrols, which started on 1 May. In all, ten teams were inserted by naval Sea King helicopter into strategically important areas around the islands, together with six SBS patrols tasked to examine possible beach landing sites. Locations covered by the SAS at this stage included Port Stanley, Darwin/Goose Green, Fitzroy, Bluff Cove, Fox Bay and Port Howard, whilst the SBS appear to have concentrated on the San Carlos area and amongst the inlets and natural harbours along the north coast of East Falkland. In the meantime, an offensive action target had been located for D Squadron: the Argentine airstrip at Pebble Island off the north coast of West Falkland.

Pebble Island, known to the Argentines as Isla de Borbon, was home to an Argentine Navy Turbo-Mentor attack squadron of four aircraft. It had been located by a patrolling British Harrier,

---

2 NCO, 22 SAS, Strawson, *History of the SAS* 1984, p. 230.

which had picked up emissions from the base's air-traffic control and early warning radars. D Squadron's Boat Troop, under Capt Tim Burls, were tasked to recce the area and inserted during the night of 10 May. They evidently reported favourably because the rest of D Squadron followed on 14 May:

45-minute flight by three Sea Kings onto LS secured by 17 Troop. Capt Burls then briefed the Squadron and Troop officers on the ground. Distance from LS to base – six kilometres. The moon was bright and very little cover was afforded by the ground. Each man carried two 81mm mortar bombs, which were dropped at the base-plate. 16 and 19 Troops were led to their respective targets by scouts from 17 Troop.

Base-plate to forward RV four kilometres. Capt Burls led 19 Troop onto airstrip via the forward RV manned by Capt West and Sgt Major Gallagher. Once on the edge of the airstrip we began to engage visible aircraft with small arms and 66mm rockets. By this time naval gunfire and illumination was being produced by HMS *Glamorgan* and our mortars were also firing some illuminating rounds. We were aware of some incoming enemy small arms fire, but it was totally ineffective.

I was a member of Staff Sergeant Currass's patrol and was the extreme right-hand man. I was hit in the lower left leg by shrapnel at about 0700 hours. Staff Sergeant Currass helped me put a shell dressing on the wound. The Troop moved onto the airstrip and started systematically to destroy the aircraft with standard charges and 66mm. Capt Hamilton covered Trooper Armstrong, who went forward to destroy the last aircraft. The Troop then shook out and started to fall back off the airstrip. A land mine was then detonated in the middle of the Troop, Cpl Bunker being blown some ten feet backwards.

I was beginning to feel faint from loss of blood and consequently was told to head back towards the forward RV with two others. Just off the airstrip we heard Spanish voices, at least four or five, shouting some fifty metres towards the settlement. I opened fire with M-203 and put down some sixty rounds in the direction of the voices. Two very pained screams were the only reply. The Troop came down behind us and we moved back through the forward RV at about 0745 hours. During the

move back I was helped over various obstacles and so was Cpl
Bunker. The helicopter pick-up was on time at 0930, and the flight
back to *Hermes* lasted about one hour twenty minutes. Cpl Bunker and
I went directly to the sick-bay where we were looked after admirably.[3]

With great good fortune, D Squadron's attack came on a night
when six Pucara ground attack aircraft had been dispersed to
Pebble Island from the Goose Green airstrip to avoid Harrier
attacks, and they, the four Turbo-Mentors and an Argentine
Coastguard Skyvan were all rendered inoperable by the attack.
The airstrip had been guarded by a platoon of Marine conscripts,
but it appears that the majority of them were ill and only a
skeleton guard had been mounted. Although a relatively easy
and uncomplicated operation which wouldn't have been beyond
the capacity of a well-trained infantry or Marine company, the
Pebble Island raid was of genuinely strategic impact. For the loss
of two men lightly wounded (there were no fatal casualties on
either side), D Squadron knocked out ten of the thirty-four
Falklands-based ground-attack aircraft being operated by the
Argentine Air Force and Navy, in what was a virtual re-
enactment of the desert airfield raids of 1941 and 1942. If
properly employed by the Argentines (although Argentine military incompetence was almost mind-boggling), these aircraft
could have had a significant impact on the ability of the British
to move troops about the islands and might even have threatened
the main landings, which took place a week later. As it was, the
aircraft crews were deployed on hilltops with radios to act as
early warning observers.

Unfortunately for the SAS, the great success of Pebble Island
was followed by the tragedy of the Sea King crash of 19 May in
which eighteen members of the Regiment, mostly from 19 Troop
but including D and G Squadron Sergeant Majors, a Forward Air
Controller and his signaller, members of 264 SAS Signals Squadron, and some non-Sabre personnel were killed during a routine
cross-decking flight. Although this was clearly a serious blow it

---

3 NCO. 22 SAS, Strawson, *History of the SAS* 1984, pp. 231–2.

did not, in the short term, critically affect the Regiment's ability to conduct operations in the Falklands.

The main landing of 3 Commando Brigade was scheduled to take place at San Carlos during the morning of 21 May. By this stage SBS recce had established that there was a small detachment (of slightly less than company strength) of Argentines in the area, occupying Fanning Head and Port San Carlos and a rather confused attempt was made to neutralize them using naval gunfire and persuasion by a Spanish-speaking Royal Marines captain. Simultaneously, D Squadron were sent to Darwin/Goose Green to mount a diversionary raid.

Goose Green contained a small Argentine Air Force base equipped with a number of Pucara ground-attack aircraft together with a battalion of conscript infantry, forming the largest concentration of Argentine forces outside the Port Stanley area (there were approximately 1,100 Argentines there). The D Squadron group, numbering about forty and led by Major Delves, were carrying an average of 80lbs in weight per man, mostly consisting of ammunition and other ordnance, and were presumably guided by the IR patrol that had been in the Goose Green area for sixteen days. Their intention was to persuade the Argentine garrison that they were under attack by about a battalion in the hope that this would prevent any move from Goose Green in the direction of the landings; to reinforce this impression they were to be supported by the guns of HMS *Ardent*.

In the event, the raid did not work out quite as planned. An NGFO who was tasked to direct the *Ardent*'s gunfire found that his codes were now out of date and the ship was unable to open fire during the night; and the considerable amount of firepower of the SAS did not actually hit the main Argentine positions. The SAS's shooting was reported to Port Stanley by Lt-Col Piaggi, the Argentine commander, but more out of puzzlement than fear; still unaware of the landings to the north, he placed his garrison on alert. Far more effective, psychologically at least, was *Ardent*'s bombardment, which finally arrived after daylight and which was concentrated around the north side of the grass airstrip. Although it caused no casualties, a 20mm anti-aircraft gun was damaged and widespread fear was engendered.

Far more crucial to the success of the landings was an oppor-
tunistic air strike called in by a G Squadron IR patrol in the hills
above Port Stanley. His team had noted the existence of a
helicopter hide area east of Mount Kent and, after several
abortive attempts, succeeded in directing in a Sea Harrier attack
on 21 May which destroyed four enemy troop-carrying helicopters. In fact these aircraft were earmarked to provide lift for the
Argentine strategic reserve (Agrupacion de Ejercito Malvinas
Reserva Z), which was therefore stranded well away from the
landings and was not committed against them (probably just as
well for its members: the Argentine reserve consisted of a single
conscript infantry company).

In the period immediately after the landings, the contribution
of the SAS – and other special forces – was less obviously useful
than before the arrival of main force troops of 3 Commando
Brigade. The three 'commandos' (in effect battalions) and two
airborne battalions brought with them their own highly trained
reconnaissance sub-units (the Patrols Companies of 2 and 3 Para,
it is worth remembering, are the direct descendants of the
Parachute Squadrons of 22 SAS from Malaya and Borneo) and
the Brigade also had the Mountain and Arctic Warfare Cadre as
a brigade recce asset. As a result the No Man's Land between the
main Argentine position around Stanley and the British beachhead became somewhat crowded. A distinguished SAS officer,
serving at that time with a Parachute battalion, recalls:

One of the problems with the Falklands was that there were too many
guys out front wandering around recce-ing in an area that is normally
reserved for battalion patrol units. You had our own patrol company,
you had the SAS, you had the Arctic Warfare Cadre, you had SBS
patrolling a bit, you had neighbouring units also doing their bit. The
companies had great difficulty doing their own recces. Everyone was
trying to get in on the act: they should have said, 'Right, one lot will do
it'. You had strategic troops operating alongside tactical troops, which
is not the best way of doing it.[4]

---

4 Interview, Officer, 22 SAS.

Whilst General de la Billière has noted that:

> After the war criticisms were made that the intelligence which they [the G Squadron IR patrols] produced was never passed on far enough down the chain to be of practical use; I think this was true, but the fault lay with the system, not with the men on the ground.[5]

But although these two critiques of the SAS are valid for the special forces role in the campaign as a whole, they do not apply to the battle which has prompted most criticism of the Regiment: Goose Green.

The Goose Green action was prompted, above all, by increasing disquiet amongst Margaret Thatcher's war cabinet at the lack of action and mounting *matériel* losses. It seems that there was concern that Britain might be perceived to be losing the war and it was decided that action was needed to quell this impression. On 25 May the container ship *Atlantic Conveyor* was sunk by an Exocet missile, destroying a number of support helicopters that were earmarked to provide the land force's heavy lift capability. As Brig Thompson and his staff tried to think their way through the problems this posed, Thompson was ordered, from London, to provide a major success. His only realistic option was to launch 2 Para at Goose Green.

The criticism that is levelled at 22 SAS regarding Goose Green is that they gave Lt-Col 'H' Jones, 2 Para's CO, a misleading impression of what he should expect to face when he arrived there with his battalion. Brig Julian Thompson, in his account of the campaign, remarks that: 'Jones went on board the *Intrepid* to see the SAS Squadron that had attacked Darwin on D-Day and they told him that, in their opinion, the whole isthmus was held by about one company.' But this statement is contradicted by the 2 Para 'O' Group for the attack, which took place the next day (27 May), during which Jones's intelligence officer informed the assembled company commanders and attachments that there were 'a minimum of three companies' in the area. The intelligence officer, Capt Allan Coulson, was right: as

---

5 Sir Peter de la Billière, *Looking for Trouble* 1994, p. 345.

we have seen, there was a battalion of Argentine infantry at Goose Green, and after their epic observation of the area, it is difficult to believe that the SAS can have had a false impression of what was there. The reality of Goose Green is bound up in a combination of understandable euphoria at 2 Para's eventual victory and unsurprising military ignorance on the part of media representatives who were present.

When Goose Green was eventually captured, 2 Para took approximately 1,000 prisoners and there were about fifty dead Argentines scattered around. The battle had proved to be much harder fought than expected for the simple reason that the British had an unrealistically low expectation of the poor quality of the Argentine soldiers and had relied on a battle-plan that was over-complicated and over-optimistic. Six-figure grid references given out for Argentine company positions turn out to have been wrongly transcribed at some stage, and, amongst other things, Jones had told his officers that: 'All previous evidence suggests that if the enemy is hit hard he will crumble'. A comment that had no basis in reality for the simple reason that the only ground combat, at that point, had been the retaking of South Georgia and the 'scrap' between an SAS squadron and the sick, frightened, conscript guards at Pebble Island airstrip. The battle for Goose Green lasted as long as it did because the Argentine garrison did not roll over and put its hands up as soon as the British appeared.

Whatever briefing Jones received from 22 SAS, it is evident that he based his plan on facing approximately a battalion of fighting troops – which is precisely what 2 Para were up against. In the euphoria of victory, the numbers of prisoners taken became exaggerated and the inexperienced journalists with the Task Force did not fully understand the difference between the five hundred or so Argentine infantry who were captured and the similar number of air force personnel who took no part in the fighting. The rumour that 2 Para defeated a vastly superior enemy has now passed into military myth, so much so that a recent book confidently states that 2 Para were outnumbered ten to one! The debate on this subject does tend to ignore the reality that it was a considerable feat for 2 Para to defeat an equally strong enemy in prepared positions.

For the remainder of the conflict both squadrons continued to operate but the increasingly restricted real estate available for special forces tended to marginalize their efforts. Even so, their contribution included seizing the important high ground at Mount Kent after a D Squadron patrol had discovered it to be unoccupied (a large part of D Squadron, together with elements of 42 Commando were flown forward to take possession) and maintaining observation on the Argentine garrison on West Falkland. It was there, on 10 June, that a D Squadron IR patrol was finally discovered by a four-man Argentine special forces patrol (from Compania de Commando 601) outside Port Howard.

In a sharp firefight, the patrol commander, Capt John Hamilton, was wounded in the back but ordered his signaller to attempt to make a break whilst he gave covering fire. Shortly afterwards he was killed and, although the signaller was captured, two members of the patrol did get clean away. The signaller then used a novel form of resistance to interrogation:

> Yeah, poor old Roy 'the Fonz' got nabbed, but he got away with it. He's a bit swarthy is Roy, and he persuaded the Argies that he was John's servant. They had no problem believing that, and so they didn't bother with much of an interrogation, they thought he was the cook or something.[6]

It was also during this period (in fact on 2 June) that a clash took place between a G Squadron patrol and an SBS patrol, led by Sgt 'Kiwi' Hunt, near Teal Inlet. Hunt's patrol had been dropped off by helicopter in the wrong position and they were making their way to their correct target area when they were spotted by an SAS patrol commanded by an officer. The SAS set up a hasty ambush, and when Hunt and his men were about ten metres from it, the SAS officer challenged them in English. Hunt and two others stopped and behaved correctly, but the rear man in the patrol attempted to creep away and an SAS machine gunner opened fire, killing Hunt.

This tragic 'blue on blue' incident, of a sort inevitable in war,

---

6 Interview. NCO. 22 SAS.

was perhaps made worse because it occurred between two small units whose tasks mean that they must often work closely together. Although blame per se cannot be directed squarely at anyone involved, the death of 'Kiwi' Hunt did serve to poison the atmosphere between the SAS and the SBS for some time, and the alleged reaction of several SAS men, that 'Hunt had strayed into "their" area and got what he deserved',[7] did not help to calm matters.

The final offensive operation of the war by the SAS was a diversionary attack launched during the night of 13/14 June by a combined force from D and G Squadrons (together with six SBS members and a handful of Marine coxswains from 3 Commando Brigade's Raiding Squadron) against Cortley Hill Ridge, a feature that formed the northern arm of Port Stanley harbour and which housed several fuel storage tanks. The force travelled in four Royal Marines Rigid Raider craft from a lie-up in Berkeley Sound, but as they approached land they were spotted by a crew member aboard the Argentine hospital ship anchored in the harbour who alerted the nearest ground unit, an anti-aircraft battery (this was technically a breach of the hospital ship's neutrality but it is virtually unimaginable that the crewman would have acted differently, Argentine or British), which was positioned, unsuspected, nearby. The anti-aircraft battery brought fire to bear on the raiding party, who soon realized that they were in real trouble as large splinters and cannon rounds began to tear into their craft. Whilst this was happening, the major battalion assaults against Wireless Ridge and Mount Tumbledown were taking place and were naturally receiving priority for artillery and naval gunfire support, but this made it difficult to bring down fire to support the raiders' now essential withdrawal. Nevertheless, after a somewhat fraught period, a short barrage from the guns of 29 Commando Regiment RA allowed the SAS to make their excuses and leave, having suffered three minor casualties and with their Rigid Raiders looking somewhat the worse for wear.

The Stanley Harbour raid was an operation that was widely

---

7 Hugh McManners, *Scars of War* 1994, p. 231.

criticized after the war for having been more of a diversion to the British than the Argentines. Confusion about where the SAS were going to be and what they were going to be doing led 2 Para on Wireless Ridge to impose a restrictive boundary to their west which was to prove a constraint to the easy manoeuvring of at least one rifle company, whilst the use of limited artillery resources to get them out of trouble in the middle of a planned shoot on other targets was also a disruption to the main effort. As far as can be judged, the anti-aircraft battery was the only Argentine unit to be involved in the action (with the exception of the hospital ship) and so it cannot easily be said that the raid diverted Argentine resources. With hindsight it can be argued that launching a diversionary raid within an operation taking place in such a comparatively small area was never likely to achieve all that much impact, the Argentine leadership in the Falklands was of such a low standard that they had little concept of using reserves at all, let alone diverting them from the more important battles taking place to the south and east, and they were only ever likely to attempt to deal with the raid in a piecemeal, positionalist way: the Argentines were fortunate that the nearest unit happened to have sufficient firepower to utterly overwhelm the relatively lightly armed SAS force.

Argentine resistance in the Falklands collapsed the day after the Stanley Harbour raid: with 3rd Commando and 5th Infantry Brigades dominating the high ground around Port Stanley, poised to sweep into the capital for the last battle, the Argentine commanders had no realistic option, although Lt-Col Rose, the SAS commander, helped them along to this decision in a nicely judged negotiation. Thus it was that the most interesting special forces operation planned for the Falklands campaign never actually took place.

On 4 May the British type-42 destroyer HMS *Sheffield* was struck amidships by a French-built Exocet missile fired from a Super Etendard bomber of the Argentine naval air arm. In the ensuing explosion and fire, twenty members of the crew died and many more were injured. The ship was abandoned and sank whilst under tow six days later.

The loss of the *Sheffield* had a galvanizing effect on both the

Task Force and the War Cabinet. The Chiefs of Staff had informed the Cabinet that an amphibious landing, if it was to take place, needed to happen before 30 May, when the onset of the southern winter was likely to have made the weather too unpredictable, but the Super Etendard/Exocet threat appeared to be a potential war-loser even though the Argentines were known to have only a limited number of them. If an Exocet was to destroy one of the aircraft carriers or a troopship it might prevent the landings taking place at all. Some means, therefore, needed to be found to neutralize the Exocets.

Whilst various ideas were considered, and then rejected, at government level, it would appear that the Director SAS and his staff developed a plan for a 'target attack' against the Rio Grande naval airbase on Tierra del Fuego, the rugged island off southern Argentina, from where the Super Etendards with their deadly payload were believed to be operating. In essence, the concept was simple: two C-130 aircraft carrying B Squadron would take off from Ascension Island and fly, courtesy of air-to-air refuelling, across the South Atlantic ocean to Rio Grande, where they would land and be abandoned. Once on the ground, B Squadron would fan out across the base, destroying as many Super Etendards and Exocet missiles as they could find and killing any Argentine aircrew that happened to be there. With the attack completed, B Squadron and their RAF aircrew would tactically evade across country, making for RVs on the other side of the border with Chile.

Amazingly, this audacious option was accepted by the military and political leadership and B Squadron began specific training and rehearsals in the second week of May. However, it soon began to emerge that there were considerable reservations in the squadron about the operation, not least from the squadron commander and some of his most senior NCOs, who apparently believed that it would lead to the destruction of the entire squadron. One NCO has been quoted as saying that B Squadron were: '...all going to die to fulfil an old man's fantasies',[8] the old man in question being Brigadier de la Billière.

---

8 Harry McCallion, *Killing Zone* 1995, p. 176.

With hindsight it is hard to believe that it was seriously intended to launch such an attack on Rio Grande. The problems facing the assault force were enormous and the plan, in so far as details are known, seems to ignore many of the earliest lessons learned by the SAS in 1941 and 1942.

The first of these is that the entry phase of any special forces operation needs to be as secure – and flexible – as possible. The first operation against the airfields at Gazala and Tmimi in November 1941 failed because the parachute entry chosen was a 'one-shot' succeed or fail method which offered no real prospect of a rethink: on the day that the operation was launched conditions were known to be wrong but there was a great deal of pressure on Stirling and his men to succeed; they went ahead and the parachutists ended up scattered, captured and killed; they didn't achieve their aim. Flying two C-130s over a great distance would invite any number of things to go wrong, all of which might cause the mission to abort or, if it continued, to fail. These include: mechanical failure in either or both of the aircraft; failure to reach a refuelling RV; illness amongst the flight crew; detection by the enemy; navigational errors, and so on. Although these things may seem obvious, they do happen – the SAS had the example of the failed US attempt to rescue hostages in Iran two years before to go by – and there is no easy way to avoid them. Stirling's airfield attacks in the desert began to succeed because he switched to a method of entry – jeep convoys across the desert – that could within reason be relied on and which was flexible enough to accommodate the unexpected. The final approach and landing at Rio Grande would also have been problematic: even if the Argentines had not detected the British approach sufficiently early to respond aggressively it is possible that the aircraft would have had to land on an unfamiliar airfield without the normal aids to navigation and landing, and with the prospect of finding other aircraft blocking their approach.

But even if B Squadron had reached their target successfully, there was still no outright guarantee of success. One problem that Stirling and his men never resolved was what to do if their quarry was not there. On a number of occasions, the early SAS successfully penetrated airfield defences only to find that the aircraft were absent; apart from shooting up empty hangars and blowing up storage facilities, there was nothing they could do about it except wait for the next opportunity to present itself: this would not have been the case at Rio Grande: there could be no second bite at the cherry. Even with top-class intelligence resources there would be no certainty of all the aircraft, all the missiles or all the pilots being present on one airfield nor even, given that the squadron would have limited 'time on target', that they would be able to find them all even if they were there. In any case, although it is fair to argue that the SAS would have had an enormous edge over any defenders present at the airfield, there is an enormous difference between carefully penetrating an airfield from the outside before launching an attack and landing two enormous Hercules aircraft in the middle of it before starting: one alert GPMG gunner in the wrong place might have wiped out half of the squadron before the assault could begin.

The final worry for the squadron was the exfiltration. However incompetent and inexperienced the Argentines were in conventional war, their forces certainly had good knowledge of counter-insurgency and internal security procedures, developed during the ruthless 'Dirty War' against left-wing guerrillas in the 1970s. The follow-up after a raid on Argentine soil would probably have been enormous and it is likely that a proportion of those who had survived the assault would have been caught as they made their way to Chile; it is difficult to predict what would have happened to them. Despite these objections and others, the operation was to go ahead.

The first phase was to land a small party near the airbase to conduct reconnaissance prior to the arrival of the main force and, on 17 May, a Sea King helicopter left HMS *Hermes* carrying three aircrew, nine members of 22 SAS commanded by B Squadron's Boat Troop commander, and a huge extra fuel load. They reached their landing site apparently undetected but, as they prepared to unload, they saw a flare being fired over the sea and came to the conclusion that they were compromised. The commander then made the decision to abort and the helicopter took off again, now heading for Chile, where the SAS men were to be dropped off before the crew took the helicopter further and simulated a crash landing, after which they burned the aircraft. A few of the SAS men in the Sea King had briefly set foot on Argentine soil but it seems that they were the only ones to do so.

Despite aborting the reconnaissance, the main operation remained 'on' for some time, but during this period the squadron apparently became polarized between those who felt the operation should be cancelled and those who wanted to continue. This came to a head on the night before the squadron flew out to Ascension when the Boat Troop Staff Sergeant – one of the most senior members of B Squadron – voluntarily resigned from the SAS, believing it to be a 'suicide mission', and the B Squadron commander was sacked by Brigadier de la Billière, who replaced him with the Regiment's second in command.

The operation was finally halted with B Squadron sitting in aircraft with the engines running, ready to go. By now it had been discovered that the Argentines had established a radar guardship off Tierra del Fuego and were likely to have considerable advance warning of the SAS's arrival. Instead, B Squadron flew down to the islands, parachuting into the sea, to replace the exhausted IR patrols of G Squadron. They did not see any action before the surrender.

The Falklands campaign was not an unqualified success for the SAS although, on balance, they did make a significant and worthwhile contribution. Part of the problem was that less than two years after the Iranian Embassy assault, members of the Regiment were saddled with a reputation as military supermen that they mostly neither liked nor wanted. This reputation was current amongst the media covering the campaign, amongst politicians and civil servants, and to some extent amongst the military as well. As a result, expectations were high and, in combination with a command hierarchy that was largely navalled – and thus unfamiliar with special operations – there was a degree of overemphasis on offensive action tasks coupled with an unrealistic expectation of what might be achieved by them.

At the same time, the SAS hierarchy was anxious that the Regiment should benefit from the experience of taking part in the campaign and this may have led to the acceptance of roles that were not necessarily entirely appropriate for strategic troops. The reality was that the Royal Marines and Parachute Regiment battalions which made up the bulk of the infantry strength on Operation Corporate were units trained to work with a higher degree of autonomy and flexibility than their 'line' counterparts, and it would not be too outrageous to suggest that a well-led Marines or Para Company would have been just as capable of conducting the Pebble Island raid as D Squadron were.

As always there were a lot of lessons to be learned, both at the strategic level and at the tactical, personal, level:

In a sense we came back down to earth a bit in the Falklands because a lot of it was just pure, hard soldiering. We were up against real soldiers, even if they were crap, and a lot of firepower. You had to be on your toes the whole time because it wasn't like Ireland, where if you get a compromise you just get lifted out, it was for real. If they spotted you, they came after you, like they did with Hamilton, and they had mortars, artillery, the lot. So, yeah, we were on our toes . . .

The other big thing was the amount of gear we were humping around. I'd done exercises in Europe and the States where the weather wasn't so great, but because you know there's a finite limit on your deployment, and you know that it's not going to get *so* bad, you can always leave out some of your warm kit, some of your rations, and you have a much more manageable load. But down there, if you didn't take it all, you'd go down with exposure for sure. When I came back in off the first OP, I reckon I was in quite a bad way. I'd lost a lot of weight, my legs were shaky, I was getting bad headaches, and I was feeling dizzy all the time. I didn't tell anyone because I didn't want to seem like a wanker, and I felt a lot better after some decent food and proper rest. My bergan on that one must have been 120–140 pounds, easily. We had all the OP kit, we had first-aid gear, batteries, ammunition, rations, water; and we had all the warm clothing, but we fucking needed it, no two ways.

Yeah, so it was back to real soldiering.[9]

---

9 Interview, NCO, 22 SAS.

15. **Discipline**

A lot of people think that we're slack somehow, or even sloppy, because we don't all have ultra-short hair and we tend to wear a variety of gear when we're in the field. They get hung up on the sneaky-beaky aspects of what we do and they forget that 22 SAS is just as much a military unit as, I don't know, 3 Para. There isn't a lot of shouting and yelling because there doesn't need to be: almost all the guys are NCOs in their parent units and they know the deal, they know how to behave without a lot of imposed discipline. But if you fuck about, you do get gripped and they don't mess around. At the end of the day, RTU [return to unit] is the ultimate threat: everybody has worked their arse off to get to Hereford and you really don't want to get binned for some pathetic disciplinary cock-up.[1]

---

1 Interview, NCO, 22 SAS.

16. **Selection**

Out of the approximately 150 officers and other ranks that start selection, it is unusual for more than twenty to pass, and often considerably fewer get through

It has long been recognized within the special forces community that no SF unit can exceed the sum of its component parts: the men. But this is particularly true within the SAS. From the earliest days of the Regiment, it was clear that for the types of operation envisaged by David Stirling and the other 'founding fathers', the SAS required soldiers of the very highest quality. Since then, several different ways have been tried to obtain them.

The origins of the SAS lay with the army Commandos. As the Dunkirk disaster was unfolding at the end of May and beginning of June 1940, leaving the major part of the British Army stripped of heavy weapons and unlikely to be able to go on the offensive for some time, Lt-Col Dudley Clarke, the Military Assistant to the Chief of the Imperial General Staff, was pondering ways in which Britain could hit back at the German Army. The situation was that, having captured Norway, Denmark, Poland, Belgium and the Netherlands, and being on the verge of defeating France, the German Army was about to find itself in possession of a coastline stretching from the Arctic to the Pyrenees. Clarke understood that this meant that any large-scale opposed landings in Europe were well beyond the resources available to Britain, but he also realized that this immensely long coastline presented the Germans with a security problem: they couldn't realistically hope to secure every last yard of it. Would it be possible to harass the Germans using small-scale forces of highly trained soldiers, hitting their targets from the sea and then clearing out quickly before serious opposition could be mounted? Clarke thought that it would.

Clarke briefed his superior, General Sir John Dill, about his idea on 5 June 1940, the day after the fall of Dunkirk. In turn, Dill briefed the newly installed Prime Minister, Winston Churchill, on 6 June. On 8 June 1940, formal authority was given and the 'Commandos' were born, named after the Boer guerrilla units that had defied the 250,000 British and Imperial troops in South Africa for two years, after the defeat of the regular Boer forces in 1899.

Soldiers for the Commandos were obtained from two sources: volunteers were solicited from army units now back in Britain after the Dunkirk débâcle, and a nucleus of officers and men came from the 'independent companies' that had been formed to attack the German lines of communication in Norway, but had actually wound up taking part in heavy fighting as conventional infantry. The criteria laid down for selection for what was described as 'special service' were that volunteers should be: '. . . young, absolutely fit, able to drive motor vehicles and unable to be sea- or airsick'. No details of the kind of work expected of the soldiers was given – that would come later. Thus, at this stage in the formation of what were, in effect, special forces, selection for further training was by interview and recommendation. Provided the individual soldier met the basic criteria, he was in.

This relatively informal selection process continued after the establishment of L Detachment of the SAS Brigade in July 1941. The original members of the unit were mostly guardsmen, former members of the now disbanded 8 Commando who were waiting to rejoin their units. After David Stirling had received authority to begin recruiting, they were the first men he turned to. Others were recruited through personal contacts:

I decided that I wasn't going to hang about any more and that I would like to go back to the second battalion of the Camerons who were in the desert at the time. I was literally on my way to do this when I met

David Stirling in the street – at an important moment in my life – and he said, 'I'm starting up something called the SAS, which isn't really a regiment – it isn't really anything yet – and would you like to join?', and I thought, this sounds like fun, and I joined . . . So rather light-heartedly I got on a truck a couple of days later and went down to Kabrit.[1]

This method of selection – in a slightly more formal version – remained in force throughout the war. In essence, selection was implicit in the training: it was assumed that a soldier who could keep up with the training would be suitable for operations. It was a system that usually worked but sometimes didn't: one of only two British officers who committed treason during the war by changing sides and joining forces with the enemy – in fact the *Waffen-SS* – Douglas Berneville-Claye, alias 'Lord Charlesworth', served in A Squadron of 1 SAS.

It was not until the post-war resurrection of the SAS to fight terrorism in the Malayan jungle that the 'selection' process began to emerge in the form in which it is still recognizable. Although 22 SAS in its entirety was based in Malaya, selection was carried out from a base at Dering Lines army camp in Brecon:

It was basically a shoestring operation. The camp was pretty basic and all you were given was a rucksack and a few odds and ends: nothing at all fancy. I don't really know what I was expecting: I suppose something a bit more glamorous and 'James Bond', but what we got was a lot of doubling about on the assault course, and long, long marches in the hills.

What worried me when we were doing these walks wasn't whether I could go fast enough – I mean, I'd been in the Parachute Regiment for four years and I was reasonably fit – but I was worried about finding the RVs. You got taught map-reading and such as a paratrooper, but when it came to it on exercises and training, it was the officers and sergeants who did it and we just followed along, thumb up bum, mind in neutral. Like I say, I could read a map, but I wasn't confident about it. All through selection there was that big worry that I would get badly lost,

---

miss an RV. get RTU and wind up back in the battalion getting double the bullshit 'cause I'd failed.

It got to the end, to the endurance march, and I was doing OK. The map-reading was working out and I was making good time with about five miles to go, and then I slipped and fell. I was going up a very small incline at the top of this re-entrant and I put my foot on a flat rock and it just slipped off. I landed on my arse but I'd twisted my knee going over, and when I tried to get up, the pain was shooting up my leg and the knee was coming up like a football. The last five miles were the most painful thing I've done, ever. When I got to the last RV, I was literally crying with pain and my jaws were aching from gritting my teeth. I was about halfway down the field: not the first back but certainly not the last, and I had time for a brew and a rest before we were taken back to Brecon. When we got there, we were taken into the office one by one to be told if we'd passed or not. I went in and was told, 'Well done, you've passed, take the weekend off,' and I limped out, back to my hut and didn't move for about twenty-four hours![2]

By the 1980s, selection had evolved into roughly the form that it takes today, although changes continue to be made. Two selection courses are held every year, midwinter and midsummer, and approximately 150 personnel turn up for each, assembling on a Sunday afternoon:

On the actual selection there were about 130 blokes and about twenty-five officers, all the way across the spectrum of the Army from logistics through to teeth arm units. There were blokes who were Commando trained, Para trained and . . . er . . . ceremonial trained like me.[3]

Almost all will have put themselves through a very arduous period of preparation which they normally have to fit in with their normal military duties:

I had a bit of a problem 'cos I'd knackered my knees. I was keen as mustard when I went to my battalion, but I was very bored there as well

2 Interview. NCO, 22 SAS.
3 Interview, Officer. 22 SAS.

so I used to run carrying packs of varying weights, and not too surprisingly this started to damage my knees, so I didn't manage to do any running at all at Warminster on my platoon commanders battle-course. Then I went to NI and just patrolled and patrolled – no running – put on a lot of weight, came back and just started cycling and doing leg raises to try and get the strength back in my thighs. So how long was it before I started training specifically? I suppose I'd always had it in mind ever since I joined the Army, but I specifically started training for it after I got back from NI which would be March or April of the year that I went to do selection – the summer course.[4]

Choice between the winter and summer courses can be crucial:

Summer selection has a few advantages over and above the winter months: that the weather is generally more congenial; you don't get so many sleet storms coming straight into your face which is very depress-ing; you get a generally more pleasant run. But the downside is that the surface isn't easy to cover up in the hills because all the growth is up: all the plants are up, the grass is much longer and the 'babies' heads' are in full flow – one mate of mine actually dug up a baby's head and brought it back with him 'cause they're such nasty little buggers – they're little wavy tufts which ensure that you destroy your ankles with consummate ease.[5]

The first item on the agenda after the initial kit-issue and a briefing was the Army's Combat Fitness Test (CFT), a nine-mile run-walk in combat kit wearing webbing and carrying a weapon, an additional load of about 35lbs. The CFT is common to all parts of the Army, from cooks through to paratroopers, and is not especially difficult for a normally fit person to pass:

The first day, yeah, you get your kit and you also do the CFT which a surprising number of people fail – nine failures on ours – which considering it's supposed to be the basic fitness test for the British Army – you've really got to ask yourself . . . I mean it's just nine miles

---

4 Ibid.
5 Ibid.

with a pack on your back: absolutely bog standard, no-bullshit CFT, and nine people jacked and a couple were in serious problems with heat-stroke and that kind of thing . . . you've got to ask yourself what these guys are doing and who they are trying to kid turning up there . . . You can only assume that they had an attitude problem and either didn't understand what they were doing there or they didn't really understand what it was all about – which is an easy trap to fall into.[6]

Those that survived the CFT were now able to settle in to selection proper:

The first real test is 'Fan Dance' which is a beast – really hard work. No matter how fit you are it's hard work, and anybody who says it isn't is full of shit. In theory you've got to follow your DS, and if you stay with him then you're guaranteed to be one of the fittest guys there because the instructors are very fit and they're not carrying very much kit: they're not carrying a rifle, just a pack. It's basically a run up Pen y Fan: up the hill. down the other side, back up Fan and back down it again, and at the end of that, your legs feel like bloody jelly!

And against that there are those who turn up who simply don't want to be there, they've decided they've made a big mistake and they jack before they even start, and you see them sitting by the side of the path as you go to the hill . . . As soon as you start off and you go up the Fan, you're starting off in big bunches and you've got guys already sitting there at the side of the track, just jacked and giving it yawn, yawn, yawn.

I set a pretty good pace. Me and one other guy kept up with the instructor, and we did well, we set a good time. I found it very hard work but then I was going for a slightly different target: I didn't just want to pass it, I wanted to do well on it – as I did on the whole thing – and so I set quite a beaster of a pace. I tried to keep up with the instructor, and by and large I succeeded. As I say, my legs felt like bloody jelly when I finally got back down the other side and got back in the truck – but it felt good to pass it.[7]

6 Interview, Officer, 22 SAS.
7 Ibid.

The 'Fan Dance' has a significant place on selection simply because it is the first major test designed to get rid of volunteers who lack the motivation and/or foresight to prepare themselves properly. The survivors now begin a phase which is regarded by the Training Wing DS as preparation for test week:

By the time we'd formed up again after the Fan and had another briefing before we went on the hills again, we were probably down to half the course: so we'd got through half the people and this was day two of the course. Half the people simply didn't make the grade on the 'Fan Dance'. Logistically they have to do it – they simply can't feed and transport that many people around – so there is a practical reason, but also, frankly, if they can't pass the Fan they won't be able to do the rest of it.

The DS are brutal about it, they can set the times how they like and they don't have to give any reason – it's just 'Fuck off, you failed!' The whole thing is about this big F for fucking failure.

But then the intensity picks up! If you get an injury at any stage you're pretty much fucked. You have to keep tabbing through it, because you can only take one day off, like playing your joker. One day off to rest an injury isn't much and if it's getting tricky, you're fucked. So already people who turned up with injuries are running into problems, because they will have beasted it on the Fan, and people collect injuries on the Fan as well, so things are beginning to get a bit hairy.

You're also doing some training. Working on the proviso that people with little infanteering skill have got to be given as even a chance as regular infanteers, they start you off with basic map-reading, basic navigation, and you're still going round in groups so you're not yet going round independently.

So you've done a bit of navigation work and then, at the end of that week, you have a beaster on the tennis court – there's just a little bit of bullshit going on. The tennis court is all about pissing people off, there's a lot of: 'Fucking get up! Get down! You just keep on going 'til you get it right! You're still too slow!' and all that kind of thing, and people 'jack' on that. In fact I saw a couple of officers jack on that, which was pretty lame, I thought.

It's all very impersonal at this stage, you're all still basically cannon fodder but it's not like being back at boot-camp, it's just that you're expected to perform and if you don't, you're out! Apart from the tennis court there's very little swearing and shouting – they don't rift you, you just perform or you're fucked.[8]

At the end of the first week the walks become more serious and volunteers are expected to be able to navigate themselves about:

The next big sorter – or certainly beaster any way – is quite a nasty run: the 'Gilbert Gut-Buster'. Which is just that: a run. Some of the bigger lads who are good at carrying bergans find it quite tiring. It's around Hereford or down at the training area. I'm not sure if people specifically get binned after that or if it's just generally to add to the exhaustion and make sure that people are kept at a pretty tired level.

Officers are still with the blokes at this point – throughout the first stage of selection everyone's in it together – and there's none of this Royal Marines-style 'the officers are expected to do better' bollocks – they're just expected to perform and the only time it becomes a marginal thing is if there's some doubt as to your ability later on. They look back and see how well you performed in the hills and that's where your perform-ance becomes specifically integral to your success or not – as opposed to just passing.

You start off on the course carrying a bergan with about 35lbs in it, and every day it's increasing. It's in a bog standard rucksack which is taking its toll on your back as well, ripping the skin off, knocking you about a bit. And this is still the early days of the course, and people are beginning to tweak on little injuries, the little strains here and there. You've got through the first week and there's a bit of bullshit and then we're off on the second week and you've got to start to navigate yourself about.

You get the weekends off – it's all very sensible – but you're eating like an absolute bastard, putting away quantities of scoff that even I am embarrassed about. And for the first week or so, provided you're not

---

8 Interview, Officer, 22 SAS.

injured you feel all right. But as you start getting into the hills and you're really going for it there's a constant feeling of nausea. It's a combination of eating a lot of bulky food and not having long enough to digest it peacefully, together with a certain amount of tension, I guess. It means you're always a little uncomfortable even when you're not actually walking. I was up in the hills thinking to myself: 'Fuck, I'd never tell anyone this was fun; this is hard work; it fucking hurts; I feel sick!' You're close to total fucking exhaustion, basically. It's the feeling you get when you're walking like a bastard and you've got a fucking big hill in front of you and you've covered several big ones already. You don't feel a little tired. like at the end of a run, you feel FUCKED – and you want to just sit down, and have a cup of tea and let some other fucker carry the stuff over the hills 'cause you don't want to do it. This is when it becomes a mental battle.

After this you're getting a steady stream of people jacking – injuries, attitude, and then of course there are those who simply can't move fast enough over the hills, 'cos the speed is crucial to everything. People are being rifted out, people are jacking, others aren't sure why they're there, they might have done selection simply to get time off for training away from Germany. One or two who were there were just not all that fussed by it. I mean, this is why the hills are such a good test. You've really got to want to do it because it's fucking hard work. It's not a fitness test as such – I mean, you've got to be fit but you can't *just* be fit – because unless you're unbelievably fit and can just take it in your stride it's all about motivation.

You can be as fit as a fiddle but when the sleet's coming in horizontally, knocking your feet all over the shop when you're trying to put them down on the ground, and you tread on a tuft and twist your ankle, that's really fucking miserable. You yearn for getting to the end of the walk, getting on the truck, having a cup of tea – you literally dream of that. You come off the hills and you just think, 'Fuck, that was depressing', and it really is. At one stage I thought, 'Fuck this for a game of soldiers,' and I swung my rifle over my head and knocked the butt off it. I told the staff that I'd dropped it in a stream.

The DS are great: they're very professional and they don't beast you. They just sit there in the RVs and, if you're not producing the goods you can fuck off as far as they're concerned. They ain't going to make a comment either way at this stage . . . it's when you get to the jungle and so on that people actually start rifting you specifically on your attitude. For now, all you've got to do is march at speed with a heavy pack on your back.

So you're doing a lot of tabbing, a lot of work in the Elan Valley, which is fucking depressing, and then you move into test week, which starts off relatively easily before you move into the much harder, longer walks. And they really are getting pretty hard by now – and any injuries you've got are really giving you gyp.

The line is you've got to make a minimum of 4km an hour – which doesn't sound much but when you're walking over undulating ground like that, that is quite a decent pace – but that's cutting it pretty fine. You really want to be looking at more like 5 or 6km an hour to really shift over the hills and to start putting in good times rather than just adequate ones. On 6km an hour you'll do well, but on 4km it depends what the instructor's time is that day. The times for the walks vary because you can't just say, 'This walk always takes seven hours'. If the weather's good and everybody's in within six and a half, except for one guy who just beats seven, they might still bin him.[9]

Two weeks of build-up leads into test week:

In test week, the walks are beasty bastards. They're long and they're independent, so people are walking about all over the shop and you can't follow each other. Some guys still can't navigate, and you find blokes popping up like misguided missiles. I remember one guy coming up to me and saying: 'Fuckin' 'ell boss, where's the next RV? What fuckin' route are you on?' I said: 'I'm on blue route,' so he says: 'Oh, fuck, I'm on red route. Oh, well, not to worry, boss, see you later.' Then vrooomm! He went off at the most incredible speed into the ulu, but whether he was going in the right direction or not is another question.

Navigation is absolutely crucial because if you pick the wrong valley and you end up going up it, you've got to work bloody hard to correct

---

9 Interview, Officer 22 SAS.

your mistake. You might be going at quite a pace but it doesn't matter, if you've gone up the wrong valley then you've fucked up – big style. So your navigation's going to be critical, especially on walks like 'sketch map'.

I did 'sketch map' in pea soup fog, which was a real hoot. The problem was that I was very competitive, so that if I saw the bergan of the guy in front I'd try and catch him, and if I thought anyone was trying to catch me, I'd make sure they didn't. So when the fog came in, I had a bit of a problem 'cause I couldn't see the opposition, so to speak. I just switched off a bit, so I'd walk, and do the navigation and then the fog would lift and I'd see someone and I'd think, 'Right, let's go and get the bastard,' and off I'd go.

It's very difficult to keep your mind focused on storming the Iranian Embassy in a black balaclava when the shit's coming in and you're up to your knees in mud and the back of your heels are blistered to the point where you cut the back of your boot off to stop the rubbing or, in my case, the tendon running down the front of my shin was so knackered that I walked with the boot flapping like a flip-flop on Endurance, which is the 72-kilometre walk.

Endurance – that's the last big horror-story walk. You start on the Thursday morning, and the day before you'll have finished about 4 or 5 o'clock so there's time to sort your kit out. You've got a really heavy bergan: all in all you're carrying about 80lbs on Endurance if you include your webbing, rifle and bergan. First thing in the morning, you all set off in a big gangfuck from Talybont Reservoir, and pretty soon the field breaks up. It's still just dark when you start and everyone's doing the same route. Everybody just goes around it and there's a sort of attitude of 'if we crack this, we've cracked it in the air' but you've basically still got to do it, you've got to come in within the time. It's not quite as intense, the attitude, the general frame of mind, as the rest of test week.

I kind of enjoyed it in a funny way. I started off walking with some other officers and then got a bollocking at the half-way mark for walking in a bunch – from the training officer – so I said 'OK' and said goodbye to the guys I was walking with, got a good second wind and off I went. I went solo, head down and actually felt strong for the remaining 35-odd kilometres. I never felt for a second that I would fail – arrogance apart, I was probably one of the strongest walkers on that selection – but I did want to set a good time. I'd started at the same time as this guy from the start point but he was an hour and a half ahead of me at the half-way. But to show how much I'd accelerated after I left my friends, I actually caught him: he came in two minutes in front of me by the end of it. As I was coming down the forest in the last bit I was thinking, 'I've got to do this in less that fifteen hours! Under fifteen hours! Under fifteen hours!' – 'cos I was a bit dazed by then, a bit stunned. And just as I emerged from the bushes, literally with 200 metres to go just across the dam, the guy in front of me looked back and literally couldn't believe his eyes – 'cos he'd had all this time to himself – and he started to try and break into a run, and he was FUCKED! His feet were fucked, his back was fucked, everything was fucked. And he said to me afterwards that the last thing he wanted at that stage was me turning up and putting him under any pressure. I think I did it a bit under fifteen hours and that got me in, what, early evening. The training staff are there and somebody gives you an egg banjo and everybody smiles at you. And then you sit there and you're kind of chuffed but you know this is just stage one.

You wait around a bit, I mean I was the second guy in and you have to wait for other people to turn up. The top time on my course? Well, about two minutes quicker than me, but the record is about twelve and a half hours which was done in winter when the surface was pretty smooth by some Marine officer, a fucking nutter.

So that's that! The selection part is over and you sit on the truck on the way home, and you try to sleep and your feet are just throbbing like fucking lighthouses![10]

The initial selection phase provides the SAS training staff with a group of men that they know to be extremely fit, highly motivated and reasonably competent with a map and compass, but it is the training that follows which turns them into SAS soldiers. At their Hereford barracks, at the SAS training area,

---

10 Interview, Officer, 22 SAS.

and at other training areas in England and Wales, the potential SAS soldiers are introduced to the techniques, skills, weaponry and drills that separate them from conventional infantrymen:

> Yeah, that was a real eye-opener. Being a Sapper I'd fired the SLR, the SMG, the GPMG and the LMG, and that was it: bust. I'd never even touched a pistol, let alone fired one. And even when we did go on the ranges, which wasn't that often, you wouldn't get to fire that many rounds. It was always a case of twenty or so to check the zero and then fire your APWT, or some buckshee shoot. So then we started on the M16, and the M79, and the 203, and the Minimi, and the Kalashnikovs, and the foreign weapons, and we're using grenades, and mortars, and pistols: it was what I'd joined for; soldier heaven. I thought: 'This is me!'[11]

The continuation training period can only inculcate the recruits with a basic knowledge of the skills that they will subsequently be required to learn in much greater depth. Subjects like signals, using the high-frequency PRC 319 radio and encryption kits, are taught but all recruits who pass through selection to the sabre squadrons will subsequently take the much more detailed signals cadre which forms the first of the 'patrol skills' required of every operational member of the Regiment. The same is true of first-aid and demolitions. The full-blown medic cadre includes a hospital attachment, normally in a suitably accommodating inner-city casualty department, where SAS troopers acquire the skills required to manage major physical trauma including serious fractures, burns and, for some 'lucky' Regiment personnel, gun-shot wounds. In the short space of time available to training wing, it is clear that only the basics can be taught.

One of the principal aims of the continuation phase is to prepare recruits for their jungle training, carried out at the British Army's Jungle Warfare School in Brunei. The modern SAS was founded to fight communist guerrillas in Malaya, and jungle warfare skills are considered an essential element in SAS training. According to one long-serving SAS officer:

---

11 Interview, NCO, 22 SAS.

There is a fallacy that the spiritual home of the SAS is the desert. Certainly when I joined the regiment, in the 1960s, I'd been brought up on 'The Phantom Major' and 'Popski's Private Army', and I had an image of men in jeeps on sand-dunes, with beards and *keffiyahs*. I was quickly informed that I was wrong! 22 SAS, I was told, was about jungle warfare. And after my training, my first operational tour was in Borneo, which rather bore that out.

If you look at the history of the SAS, it was conceived as a special unit to operate in desert conditions, but it rather lost its way after the end of the desert campaign, and operations in Italy and north-west Europe weren't as successful. It wasn't until Malaya that the Regiment was able to really prove itself again, and Borneo only cemented that. The fact is that ever since then we've been selecting men to fight in the jungle, and the fact that they can adapt to desert conditions, or mountains or whatever, is by the by.[12]

For the jungle phase recruits are, for the first time, formed into stable patrols, with an SAS DS and, together with their military skills, their ability to function as an integral part of a tightly knit team is minutely examined. It is in the jungle that potential SAS recruits are subjected to the most intense scrutiny, and within training wing a recruit's performance in the jungle is regarded with much more interest than in the hills, where the more mundane skills of physical fitness and psychological motivation are on test:

I'd never been into jungle before I did selection and I hadn't actually soldiered outside the UK and Germany before either, so it was something that I was really looking forward to, but at the same time I was dead nervous about it as well. In the Guards, you got a lot of propaganda about how we were the elite of the British Army and all that, but actually we spent most of our time polishing our fucking boots and picking the fluff off our uniforms. Actual field soldiering seemed to come second for a lot of people in the battalion: they were more worried about whether the Queen Mother was upset because some-

---

12 Interview, Officer, 22 SAS.

body was slow saluting, or if Phil the Greek had spotted a loose thread on your tweeds. Although some of them were keen, a lot of the 'Ruperts' were just in it for the parties and the chance to shag a few debs, and they weren't interested in keeping their blokes fit, or turning them into good field soldiers.

All this meant that I was basically 'on my own' all through selection. I'd had to get myself fit, I'd had to dig out instructors to help me with my map-reading and first-aid, and I'd had to fit it all in around the ceremonial crap that we spent all our time doing. So the jungle had me worried, because it was here that my infantry skills were meant to come out, and I was meant to be helping the non-infantry boys along, and all the time I was thinking, 'Er . . . what infantry skills?'

It began to come to a head about two weeks in. We were doing patrols and trying to navigate around the place, and putting in ambushes and all this stuff, and I felt that I was just struggling with the basics. I'd had enough problems navigating around the Beacons on selection, and there you could see the horizon, but now I was getting lost trying to get from my basha to the admin area; it was fucking hopeless really.

I had a word with my patrol DS, and told him that I was struggling, and he was good about it. He told me to stick with it and that they took all these factors into account when they made the final assessment, but it was blatantly obvious to me that I wasn't going to pass, so the last couple of weeks were really miserable, what with being knackered, piss wet through and hot all the time, and getting bitten by all the world's insects.

So it was no surprise, when we got back, when I was called in to see the training major and binned. He said that I'd done well on the hills and I'd learnt quickly afterwards but that I didn't have the ability that they would expect from a lance sergeant in the infantry and that I'd been too slow on the uptake when we were in the jungle and hadn't adapted quick enough, and that he didn't think there was much point in trying again. Even so, he reckoned that I should congratulate myself for having got so far and told me to get in touch if I had any trouble for failing when I got back to the battalion. You know it's all bullshit, of course, but you do need to hear it when it's you that's failed.

So back I went after four months away and next morning it's 'report for interview with CO right away'. I turn up and there's the RSM waiting outside, giving it 'you were fucking disloyal to go off to the SAS like that, and now you've let the Regiment down by bloody well failing!' And the CO then tells me that if I buckle down for some 'proper soldiering', I might be able to build a career for myself – I'd been in seven years at this point – and I thought 'bollocks to you!' and put my papers in the next week.[13]

For others, the jungle phase is an epiphany:

When we got to Brunei, and got off the plane, and I smelt that smell for the first time, I fell in love with it. Remember, I was a fairly young Sapper and I just hadn't really been anywhere apart from Germany. It's the smell of warm, damp earth, and after a few hours you don't notice it, but every time you arrive in a tropical area, you smell it as you get off the plane.

That first night in the jungle, in my pit, I just lay there listening to the noise, the birds and the monkeys and the insects: let's face it, you don't get a lot of that in Preston.[14]

By the end of the jungle phase, the initial 150 or so recruits that started selection will normally have been reduced to less than twenty. But even now individuals are still under close scrutiny from the training wing staff, and their future in the SAS is by no means assured. Shortly after their return from Brunei, recruits must undergo the combat survival phase of their training, a course which includes the notorious 36-hour resistance to interrogation exercise.

The aim of the combat survival course is to teach students to survive for the relatively short periods that it might take for a crashed aircrew member, over-run special forces soldier, or escaped POW, to get back to his own lines. Students do learn to 'live off the land' but they soon find that this form of survival

13 Interview, NCO, Household Division.
14 Interview, NCO, 22 SAS.

is a near full-time occupation that is strictly for emergencies only. Together with soldiers, and former POWs, recruits are instructed by such diverse individuals as local poachers and market-gardeners. Nevertheless, although the skills being taught are new to most, it is the final week of the course that is fixed in the minds as the big test for the majority of those present:

We'd done all the business with the traps and snares and mushrooms and so on, but then it came to the big exercise at the end, which ends up with the interrogation, and I wasn't really looking forward to that. I'd heard all these stories about what went on: you got tied to railway lines; you got left out in the snow; there were nude women taking the piss out of the size of your dick, all that sort of crap; but really I had no idea what was going to happen.

The first phase is a big cross-country evasion in small patrols where you're meant to live off the land – which is a fucking bone idea! In fact you've got to make quite a reasonable pace between the RVs and there's just no way you can waste time going fishing, or putting out snares. Instead, the smart money was on pre-positioned caches in likely areas, and me and a couple of the selection lads cruised down to Tesco to buy in Mars bars and various bits and pieces, and then spent a free Saturday driving round south Wales planting them at various locations in the Beacons, the Black Mountains, the Elan Valley and Sennybridge where we reckoned we might be passing through. The other thing was to start eating really big to try to build up some reserves, in case we didn't manage to get to the caches.

Before the final exercise you had to sign a form, called a 'blood-chit', saying that you didn't mind being interrogated, and they told us that we were allowed to take one tobacco-tin worth of survival kit which had to include forty pence, I think, in ten-pence pieces, in case we had a no-duff fuck-up. We knew there was a big search before the start of the exercise, so some of the lads had got these small chargers and loaded them up, mostly with money, and stuck them up their arseholes. I thought about it, but in the end I didn't bother 'cos I reckoned that that would be one of the first places they'd look. But actually all the blokes who'd done it got through.

For the rest of us, it wasn't so much a search, they just took all our kit off us and gave us new stuff instead. I say new but in fact it was that World War II battledress, which is made out of material like blankets, didn't fit and fucking stank! They let us wear our own boots and socks, and our own underwear, but otherwise it was this nasty jacket and trousers, and a big greatcoat. For boots I wore the jungle-boots that I'd got for Brunei, which turned out to be a big mistake in Wales at the end of November because they got soaking wet after about ten minutes from the start, and stayed that way to the end.

The selection guys were all split up, and I got put in a patrol with an officer from the Paras, who was switched on, a bloke from the Danish SBS, who was also good – and fucking gigantic! – and a Navy pilot who was a nightmare. He was a nice enough bloke but his idea of physical fitness was a thirty-second jog from his dinner to the bar, and he didn't really have a clue about fieldcraft. All us selection lads had the same idea: that we'd ditch these 'sandbags' and go it alone at the first chance, but the DS were putting in a quiet word here and there, telling us that we had to show a bit of leadership, so we were stuck with them.

The first big shock was that the exercise wasn't in south Wales at all – it was way up north – so the caches had been a big waste. And the second was that the hunter force were fucking serious! They had dogs, vehicles and helicopters, and a bloody good idea about where we were going to be. I think it was a company, or two companies, of infantry, and there were rumours that they got extra leave if they caught us so they were really up for it. This meant that we couldn't afford to arse around, but the problem was that the sandbags didn't have anything riding on the outcome. I mean, as far as they were concerned, when they got caught, they got caught, but for us, if we were lifted in some bone fuck-up, we could be RTU.

Once we'd set off, the plan was to move down an escape line, going from agent RV to agent RV. Once we were going, we would only move by night and we'd use the days to lie-up. Navigation was a bit of a problem because the only maps we had were silk escape maps which covered the whole of Wales without a great deal of detail, so the 'agents' would have to give us the route when we met them.

Funnily enough, the only real problem I had on the walk was because I got a huge attack of the shits from drinking stream-water. I figured that after the jungle I must have cast-iron guts, 'cause I was one of the only blokes to have no problem out there, but a couple of mouthfuls from some dirty stream and I was crapping it out something rotten. This meant that I had to take it slowly, but it wasn't as bad as it could have been, and the pilot could keep up with us. We saw the hunter group a couple of times, when we were lying up in gorse or bracken during the day, but they never got that close, and I made sure that the Para always went forward to the RVs when we reached them, in case they got compromised.

We'd gone out, I think, on the Sunday, and it was the Friday evening when we reached the last RV. Everyone knew the deal which was that even if you made it right down the line, you still got interrogated, so I wasn't that surprised by what happened next.

We got loaded into a four-tonner for the drive back to Hereford which was a couple of hours away. There wasn't much talking, and nobody had anything to eat, so everyone just zonked out. When we arrived at the training area, they took us round to this building which is where the shit hit the fan. We were hauled out, blindfolded and stuck in the mud by the guards, just sitting there in the cold in this muddy puddle. After a bit, a couple of lads pulled me up and led me into the building and into a room there, which is where the fun started.

There were two guys in there, both middle-aged. One of them was a tiny little bloke with glasses who was wearing a green anorak, a blue shirt, shiny trousers and walking boots; the other one was this big monster. Apart from the fact that he was about six foot two and built like a brick shithouse, what I really noticed were his clothes. He was wearing a trilby hat, a green KF shirt with a stripy silk tie, a corduroy sports-jacket, breeches and this pair of brown Afrika Korps boots that laced all the way up to his knees. When the blindfold had come off and I saw him, the first thing I did was smile. Mistake. His opening line was the classic: 'What's so fucking funny then, sonny boy?' And I was about a millimetre away from answering: just saying 'nothing' or something equally dim.

Mr Big took his hat off and he had this white hair cut all round in a number two or three. Basically, he looked just like Robert Shaw in *From*

Russia with Love. Big and fucking hard. After that they started in with the name, rank, number and date-of-birth stuff, and got me to empty my pockets and frisked me. They took all the escape kit I had, except my map which I'd shoved into my shreddies when I was in the four-tonner, and put it in a brown envelope.

When they'd taken my gear, they'd made a list of it on this official-looking form, and they'd written my name, rank and number on it and on the envelope. Then they gave me the pen and told me to sign. Again, I fucking nearly did – I suppose I was tired and not concentrating – but in the army, you always sign for kit and you never hand anything over without a receipt or whatever, and so I nearly fell for it. There was a bit of verbal argy-bargey when I didn't sign but they seemed to get bored after a bit and stuck the blindfold back on me and I was taken back outside.

So, we sat there for a bit and every now and again you could hear someone else being taken in for the search, and I was thinking 'well, that's pretty fucking easy, you've got this cracked', and then – this is several hours later – there's a bit of an upheaval, and I'm pulled to my feet and led to the back of another truck.

This time, we didn't go that far. We weren't on the truck for more than ten minutes or so, and I knew that there was at least one of the other selection lads on it because I'd done a big cough as I was put in the back and one of the others had replied; this was something we'd worked out between us before it started.

This next place was obviously somewhere close by cbut I'd never been there before. There was no talking and you couldn't see anything, but it was warmer inside and from the sound of people's feet and that, you could tell it was quite big. I'd stood still for a bit and then someone grabbed my hands, someone else took my shoulders, and they kind of jogged me into this cold room. I remember that the floor was made up of stones, like gravel only bigger, and there was white noise being played. They put me in the classic stress position, feet apart, leaning against the wall, and then I started thinking 'Oh shit!' It wasn't that I didn't think I could stick it, but I did know that it was going to be one long hard slog and I really didn't fancy it at all. On the other hand, the stress position didn't seem that bad and the white noise wasn't a problem at all.

After about half an hour, someone grabbed me from behind and put me in a different position, sitting down with my back straight and my hands on my head. Standing against the wall had become a bit painful by then: your shoulders and upper-arms are on fire after a bit. but if you move. the guards come up and shove you back into position. Even so, I felt fairly good because I still had my map in my pants and a button compass which I'd hidden in the cuff of my jacket. so I figured that I might have got one over on them and there was an outside chance that I might be able to do a runner at some point.

One of the funny things was that although they were playing this white noise really loud, after a bit you just don't notice it. Instead you could hear these blokes' boots crunching on the floor, and coughing and farting and all sorts from the other 'prisoners'. Every few minutes there'd be this clattering on the rocks when they brought someone in or took someone out, and you'd hear the guards whispering to each other as well.

About this time, or it could have been before I went to the holding area actually, I'd been taken into this small carpeted room and someone had taken the blindfold off and there'd been a doctor, in uniform with a white armband, and a bloke in civvies with a white armband. The doctor had asked if I was OK, which I was, and the guy in civvies had written a number on my hand with a marker pen – something in the nineties, though I guessed that they must have started somewhere fairly high. Yeah, the first thing that happened from the holding area was being hauled off with one guy grabbing my hands and one holding my shoulders, away from the rocky bit and across what seemed like a big carpeted hall, and down a corridor into a small room. This was the first interrogation.

I still had the blindfold on but somebody very quietly told me to stand still, and then off it came. I was in this fairly small room which had a shit-brown coloured carpet, grey walls made out of that stuff with all the holes in it, a desk, a telephone and a couple of chairs. There was one bloke sitting behind the desk, and one standing next to me with the blindfold in his hands. Both of these guys were about my age: they were younger and fitter looking than the last two; they were in jeans and jumpers. that kind of gear, but when the blindfold came off it was all smiles.

These two kicked off by telling me that this was a search and that they were 'just going to check my gear in'. So off we went. I'd wondered if I might be going to keep hold of my clothes, with the map and the compass in them. but they did a very careful strip search right through everything, and at the same time they were running out a fairly slick crosstalk routine. Straight away I noticed that they were a bit shy about asking me direct questions, it was as if they were trying to involve me in all the patter, but it was obvious something was going on. They seemed to be trying to give the impression that they were just a pair of storemen, and most of the time their voices were pretty neutral, but then one of them would say something and I was thinking, 'Fucking got you, Rupert!' I haven't come across an army yet where you have officers working in the stores, so this was clearly some kind of set-up. They did the same 'kit signing' routine that the last two had done, but I didn't go for it.

One of the things that happened, as I was getting my kit off, was that they were commenting on the bad smell that was coming off me, and to be honest, I hadn't noticed it at all. But after a bit, I realized that I was pretty ripe, and I thought, 'The only time I've ever smelt this bad was when we came out of the jungle,' and for some reason this cheered me up: smelling like shit seemed to be an important part of what the Regiment was about.

Anyway, the search went on and I was down to my shreddies. These had once been a pair of white Y-fronts but they were minging! The front was deep yellow with old piss, and one of these two 'Ruperts' was putting a pair of rubber gloves on, and I was thinking. 'I wouldn't want your job, mate!' and that cheered me up as well. Then he told me to drop 'em so down they came, together with the scrunched-up silk escape map that I'd put in them. He told me to pass the pants over, so I did, and then he searched them as well. For fuck's sake! They were like one big skid-mark. I thought, 'That's real dedication!' But there was more. I was bollock-naked by now and all my gear had gone in a black bin-bag, but he got his torch out and I went through the bend over and spread your cheeks routine, then pull back my foreskin and show clear, then rub my hands through my hair to show I had nothing there, and then, last of all, he made me open my mouth and pull my lips around to show there was nothing there. This was after he'd had me do a rummage search of my own arsehole, so I guess it was his way of getting revenge for the shreddies.

They gave me a set of coveralls and a pair of odd-size right-foot plimsolls – the crap black army issue ones, without laces – and I got dressed. I was wondering what was going to happen next, and then one of these guys, the one who'd been behind the desk, offered me a fag: a Marlboro. I thought about it for a second and thought, 'Why the fuck not?' and lit up with his lighter. This was a serious fucking mistake because I hadn't had a fag for well over a week, and I was hungry, thirsty and tired. I almost keeled over there and then, and for the rest of the time I was there I was busting for a smoke!

When I'd finished the fag, and I was feeling a bit sick, one of these boys picks up the blindfold and walks behind me, but before he put it on he said something like, 'When the meals come round, do you want soup or stew?' It was such a normal question that I nearly replied, which was what he wanted. I nearly fucking kicked myself. I knew I was tired and it would just have been a slip, but that was the way it would work for real, I guessed, and once you've fucked up, you've fucked up. There's no going back. Anyway, he stuck the blindfold back on, the guards came in and got me, and back I went to the place with the white noise.

The next time round was about two hours later, I reckoned, because they'd changed my position four times. I heard the guards come up behind me, they grabbed my hands, and it was off again. Like before it was a relief to be moved, I wasn't too bothered by the thought of the interrogation, but I was hoping I would get a chance to sit down properly 'cause I was fucking shattered. When the blindfold came off, I was in the same sort of room, but it smelled different and this one had a couple of chains shackled to the floor: Christ knows why. Again there were two blokes, but one of them was middle-aged and the other was youngish. The young one was in the jeans, shirt and jumper order that the last two had been wearing, but the older guy had a black polo-neck and a blazer on, and a pair of 'Joe 90' specs.

This time, they went straight through the name, rank, number and date-of-birth stuff and then we got to 'unit?' I came out with the standard 'I can't answer that question', and they went fucking ballistic. It was funny really because it was like a weird double act. The older guy was a better actor, but his swearing was out of the 1950s, so he was giving it loads of, 'You're a bloody rotter!' whilst the younger one couldn't get too worked up but had a better vocabulary. The down side was they were shouting at me from about half an inch away, and the gob was shooting out of their mouths, and I could more-or-less taste the last meal they'd had. Even so, a lot of the time it was hard not to laugh, 'cause the older boy was taking his lead from the young one:

'Answer the damn question, you rotten scoundrel!'
'Yeah, answer it, you fucking arsewipe cunt, or we'll fill you in!'
'Yes, out with it, you rotten, scoundrelly, fucking arsewipe cunt, or we'll duff you up!'

This must have gone on for about half an hour, and the old boy was getting a bit red in the face, so they jacked their hand in and back I went. By this time, the stress positions were losing their appeal, and my arms, shoulders and back were roaring with agony all the time. Every time you tried to wriggle or stretch to ease them, one of these guards would come and give you a kick and push you back into the right position, which was no fun at all.

A couple of hours after the last one had finished, I was hauled off again to yet another room. This time there was only one bloke, and he made me sit in a chair and, for about two hours or so, he just asked me the same questions over and over, in this quiet, dull voice. At first it was OK, but as time went by, this one really got to me. The bloke was sitting behind me, so I couldn't look at him, and all I had to stare at was the wall of the room. The questions were my number, and my date of birth. Over and over. But every now and then he would slip in a tricky one, like age or unit, and I'd got so into the stream of answering that I'd have to catch myself, so as not to say anything. By the end I really wanted to punch his fucking teeth down his throat and I was nearly screaming with frustration, but then he just suddenly stopped and that was it.

The next one after that was the old Mr Nice, Mr Nasty routine, but that's like the oldest trick in the book and I can't say I was that bothered by it. In fact, just before that one, somebody had come up behind me in the holding place and made me lie down and told me to go to sleep, but I'd just got my head down when they woke me up again and I can't say I felt any better for it. I also got a piece of bread and a drink of water at one point, which was very nice of them.

I think there were two more after Nice and Nasty. One was a girl who kept saying that all my mates had talked so there was no point in me holding on, and another one was a bloke who was saying what a cunt I was for not talking. The only thing that was worrying me was that I was really fucking tired, which was partly the result of having had the shits, I think, because I had virtually no energy. The last time I got taken out of the holding area, I got to the room and the blindfold was taken off and it was Vince from Training Wing who was in his combats with a white armband, a plastic cup of minestrone soup and a slice of bread. With him was a bloke in civvies with a clip-board. Vince said something like, 'OK mate, that's ended, here's some soup; this gentleman is going to debrief you.' I said, 'Oh thanks,' or something like that, but I could have kissed him! I drank the soup: beautiful! Then we got started on the debrief. The bloke reckoned I'd done fine: I hadn't said anything I shouldn't have, then we went through it, stage by stage.

After that it was out to collect my black bag of kit, keeping quiet because the exercise was still going on, and back to the accommodation for several showers and a huge scoff-out. I don't think any of the selection lads fucked up on my course, though it wasn't unheard of, but some of the boys on the CSI course had been gobbing-off like nobody's business. Like I said though, they had nothing to lose.

What did I think of it? It wasn't a comfortable experience, and I didn't enjoy it at all, but having said that, there was no way I was going to break down and talk, there was too much at stake. The thing that I could easily have done, which probably would have got me binned, was answering one of the trick questions, like the 'soup or stew?' one. I was tired and fucked off, and you just lose your edge. You've really got to concentrate all the time, but that's the whole point of selection anyway: they only ever throw the fast-balls when you're knackered and don't want to know. Was it effective training? To be honest, when you know it's an exercise and it's going to come to an end in a set length of time, they can't put the pressure on you that the threat of, say, having half the Iraqi Gestapo hanging out of your arse would give you. The idea of sticking to the 'big 4' when you're being tortured is bollocks, there's no point in getting yourself killed to protect information that's going to be out of date soon anyway. What they ought to let you do is what they teach the 'Walts' for over the water – controlled release of a cover story – which is what the Bravo Two Zero team found themselves doing in Iraq. You give up enough to keep the interrogator happy and hope that he loses interest when he finds out what a low-level wanker you are.[15]

The student's perception is, however, regarded as being somewhat bleaker than the instructor's:

The SAS exercise comes up twice a year at [the SAS training area], in the bunker there. It's one of those things with a fearsome reputation which it probably doesn't deserve. Although it is an unpleasant ordeal for the people on it, it's extremely closely monitored with plenty of doctors, psychiatrists and so on lurking about, and the pressures which are applied to the prisoners are very restricted. Apart from being a tester for SAS selection and the CSI course, it's also the final exercise for the long interrogation course, so there's training value all round.

The interrogators who do it are mostly territorials or reservists from all three services. Generally speaking, they get selected to do the interrogation course because of their proficiency in languages and not because they are particularly fearsome characters, although some of them are. It's actually become a bit of a problem, because a lot of these old geezers who can do the language bit are so decrepit that they wouldn't survive the excitement of a real war; seriously, five years ago there were still World War II veterans doing it! What you have is a lot of elderly civvy academics trying to put the fear of God into potential SAS men in their late twenties: it doesn't work.

---

15 Interview, NCO, 22 SAS.

Despite what you hear, the idea isn't to 'break' the prisoners during these exercises, it's to expose them to different interrogation techniques. This means that the average prisoner will go through some sort of 'trick' approach, he'll get a screaming session, a sort of 'logical' persuasion session, a 'mutt and jeff' and one or two others. Theoretically, the interrogation exercise cannot be used as a means of selecting personnel, only for training them, and the individual reports on personnel aren't supposed to be shown to the SAS DS. But, of course, the training major and training wing sergeant major are in the control room for most of the exercise, so they usually know who has talked, and what they subsequently do is up to them. There's a whiteboard in the control room, and next to the name of any prisoner who talked they put a little red 'T', but this can mean various different things. I think it's fair to say that few SAS candidates talk during the interrogation; maybe one per course, rarely more, though you always get a handful of the CSI people to have a chat. Rather more rewarding are the courses for aircrew and such-like: aircrew seem to have a pathological aversion to keeping their mouths shut, and I would personally reckon to have about a fifty per cent hit rate with them.

The form is that you don't know who's doing selection and who isn't, though generally you can guess, particularly when they have sandal marks on their feet from sunbathing at the end of the jungle warfare course. For officers, you get to look at the Army List, and you can guess that if the guy's a second lieutenant in the Pay Corps, he's not doing selection. On Pilgrim's Progress all the runners are wearing old battledress uniforms and they don't carry military kit, and this masks one of the problems that faces SAS members for real. This is that, despite the fact that they don't wear badges and insignia on operations, they do wear special, high-quality uniforms and carry unusual weapons, and these are just as distinctive.[16]

After the combat survival and resistance to interrogation training, the SAS recruit has nearly made it, but there are still two elements of the course to go through: an introduction to the skills required for counter-terrorist and counter-revolutionary

16 Interview, Officer, JSIW.

warfare, and a parachute course for those who aren't already para-qualified.

> For everyone that joined the Regiment after the Iranian Embassy, the image you have is of guys in black overalls, respirators and HKs. Certainly that's how it was for me: I couldn't wait to get started.
>
> All through the CRW, when we got back at the end of the day, we'd be really stinking of cordite and oil, even after we'd showered and changed and gone down town, but I was still thinking: 'Yeah, this is great!' And I always kept that feeling. For me, the really special thing about the regiment is not all the macho shit, it's the fact that you are always, always doing something new. You get the odd slack period, when nothing much happens, but stick around and something completely unexpected will turn up.[17]

The parachute training for all operational members of the SAS is the basic military course for all British forces run by the RAF at Brize Norton, which lasts four weeks and consists of eight descents after a period of ground training. Despite the apparent advantages inherent in getting large numbers of troops onto the ground in a short period of time, airborne operations are at the mercy of increasingly sophisticated anti-aircraft defences and, on the face of it, opportunities for SAS units to use a conventional parachute insertion will be rare, nevertheless, it is a skill worth retaining for all operational squadrons.

On their return from Brize Norton, the course survivors are finally ready to join their squadrons as operational members of the Regiment. The last, pleasant, ritual of selection is 'badging' by the Commanding Officer or his second in command:

> Yes, on the last day we were told to report to the CO's office and we got there and the RSM was waiting outside. He gave us a sort of friendly pep-talk – you know the sort of thing: 'Never forget that you're soldiers, not supermen; keep your heads down, don't attract attention

---

17 Interview, NCO, 22 SAS.

from outsiders; you've still got a lot to learn . . .' et cetera, et cetera – then he took us into the CO's office, and [the CO] gave us our berets, and said the same sort of thing, and that was it. But I was so chuffed, the only time I've ever felt that way since was when the kids were born. I'd failed at school, and I hadn't been the greatest soldier in the battalion, but I'd set my heart on joining the Regiment: I'd trained on my own for six months; I'd gone balls-out through selection; and I'd finally been badged. I was walking on air, to tell you the truth.[18]

Out of the approximately 150 officers and other ranks that start selection, it is unusual for more than twenty to pass, and often considerably fewer get through. Those that make it are a very select group:

The Identikit guy is a very nice bloke, a genial team-worker who gets on with everybody – not necessarily extrovert – but friendly. Fit – not necessarily an athlete but strong and fit – and obviously a skilful soldier.

Basically the real key factors are A: he's hard, and B: he's a nice guy. You can be as hard as nails but if you're a cunt they won't want to know because you can't operate in a small team environment if you're a divisive influence. And that's what makes serving in the Regiment such a pleasure because the fact is that everybody is very pleasant because of this initial selection procedure which weeds out the tossers.[19]

---

18 Ibid.
19 Interview, Officer, 22 SAS.

17. **The Gulf War and the Balkans Conflict**

When Iraqi forces moved into Kuwait during the early hours of 2 August 1990 it did not come as a complete surprise to the Western intelligence community: American, British and other intelligence analysts had been noting suspicious Iraqi troop movements for some two weeks. But the signals from the Gulf had been confusing: only two days before, Saddam Hussein had promised King Fahd of Saudi Arabia and President Mubarak of Egypt that he wanted a negotiated settlement to his territorial and oil disputes with Kuwait; and, as a result, few military preparations had been made to meet the threat: there was no opportunity, as has been falsely claimed, to fly an SAS squadron into Kuwait City aboard a British Airways 747; there was no time for any form of pre-emptive airstrike against Iraqi targets; and there was no chance even to evacuate the small British Army training team attached to the Kuwaiti Armed Forces, which included a member of 22 SAS, but who were swiftly detained by the Iraqi military.

About a year or two after the Gulf War all these stories started to come out about how we managed to get a squadron into Kuwait just as the Iraqis were invading, and why a whole plane-load of civvies got stuck in Kuwait City and taken hostage by the baddies. Bollocks! People go off on secretive jobs in the Regiment and you aren't told about everything, but if anyone had been resisting the might of Saddam at the start of the invasion, you'd think we'd have heard about it by now: we've heard about every other fucking thing the Regiment did in the Gulf . . .'

In the weeks that followed the invasion, as diplomats painfully forged the anti-Iraqi coalition of European and Arab states that was so crucial to the eventual defeat of Iraq's army, the first SAS involvement began with the attachment of a handful of experienced NCOs to MI6, which had established a small camp to train members of the Kuwaiti resistance in eastern Saudi Arabia. More significantly, G Squadron of 22 SAS was dispatched to the United Arab Emirates for acclimatization and training for any operations that might come up. In mid-September, as G Squadron's turn as the Anti-Terrorist 'team' approached, they were replaced by D Squadron, which now became the focus of 22 SAS's desert preparations. D Squadron were subsequently joined in the Gulf by A Squadron and part of B squadron, who were originally intended for use as 'battle casualty replacements' but ultimately carried out one of the most famous operations of the war.

On 29 September Lieutenant-General Sir Peter de la Billière, who was then approaching retirement from active service and was serving as the Commander of the South Eastern Military District, was appointed Commander of all British Forces deployed in the Middle East area, and after his arrival in theatre in early October he gave orders that the SAS should examine the possibility of rescuing the large number of UK and foreign nationals being detained by Saddam Hussein as hostages. In fact this would have been a difficult mission to fulfil: the hostages were held in small groups scattered widely around installations deemed likely bombing targets by the Iraqis, ranging from military bases to oil refineries. In any event, the Iraqis spontaneously released the hostages on 6 December as a goodwill gesture and the rescue mission plans were abandoned.

This left the problem of how the SAS were to be employed. The traditional SAS tasks in conventional desert warfare,

---

1 Interview, NCO, 22 SAS.

harking back to World War II, encompass raiding, harassment and information reporting, but many senior officers in theatre felt that these could be achieved through air power (it was abundantly clear that the Allies would have overwhelming air supremacy), and, in any case, General Norman Schwarzkopf, the Commander-in-Chief of Allied Forces, was notoriously sceptical about the utility of special forces, having witnessed at first hand the disappointing performance of the US 'Green Berets' in Vietnam, as well as during the American invasion of Grenada in 1983 when a series of errors and failures by special forces units including Delta Force and the Navy SEALs had caused confusion and delay.

Ultimately the role that was given to the SAS was one that they developed for themselves. General de la Billière wrote that:

> Their task would be to cut roads and create diversions which would draw Iraqi forces away from the main front and sow fears in the mind of the enemy that some major operation was brewing on his right flank. At the back of my own mind was the idea that the SAS might also be able to take out mobile SCUD missile launchers . . .[2]

To a great extent, this role appeared to hark back to the glory days of L Detachment in the Western Desert:

> It seemed to me to be the obvious thing for us. As far as we could see, there was going to be a lot of empty space for us to move around in, and provided we didn't do anything too silly, we should be able to get away with it . . . Once we had air superiority, the Iraqis were going to have to be sharp to catch us, so it surprised me that the head-shed had to schmooze us into the role: we weren't going to do any harm to the Allies but we were planning to give the Iraqis the mother of all fuck-overs![3]

The first phase of the liberation of Kuwait began in the early hours of 17 January 1991 with a massive wave of aircraft and missile attacks aimed at destroying Iraqi air capability and suppressing

---

2 Sir Peter de la Billière, *Storm Command* 1995, p. 192.

3 Interview. NCO. 22 SAS.

air defences. Five days later, after a two-day delay, the first SAS patrols, drawn from B Squadron, crossed the border: Bravo 10, 20 and 30 were tasked to maintain watch on an Iraqi main supply route to the west of Baghdad, reporting significant sightings – and particularly SCUDs – back to the special forces headquarters at Al Jouf in Saudi Arabia. All three were eight-man patrols, but Bravo 30 was mounted in hastily converted Land Rovers whilst Bravo 20 and 10 had opted to operate on foot. Immediately after they landed, during the night of 22 January, it became apparent that a serious miscalculation had been made: instead of finding themselves in a relatively warm sand desert, in which they would have been able to construct secure and relatively comfortable observation posts (OPs), they were on a windswept rocky plateau with a night-time temperature around freezing point. The commander of Bravo 10, after consulting with their helicopter pilot, opted to turn around and fly straight back: he considered, almost certainly correctly, that there was little possibility of remaining in the area for long without compromise. Bravo 30 reached the same conclusion but opted to drive back into Saudi Arabia, a journey which took them two nights. Bravo 20's commander decided, after ascertaining that the patrol was close to an Iraqi military position and that cover was limited, that he would relocate.

In fact Bravo 20 were unable to make any immediate move because they discovered that their radio didn't appear to be working. Although the PRC 319 EMU appeared to be sending messages, they were not being acknowledged and there was no way to tell if they had got through. After lying up through the first day, and conducting recces of their immediate area during the next night, the patrol decided to rely on their 'lost comms' procedure – whereby a helicopter would fly to a pre-arranged location with a new radio – to solve the problem. This was not to be: during the second day a local civilian goatherd stumbled across the patrol's lie-up and raised the alarm.

Compromised, the patrol now attempted to evade across country towards Syria, which was 130 kilometres to the west. As is now very well known, three members of the patrol died, four were captured (and subjected to ferocious treatment by the

Iraqis) and one, almost incredibly, escaped and returned to Al Jouf via Damascus, Cyprus and Riyadh:

> A lot's been said about 'Bravo Two Zero': you'll find a lot of people in the Regiment saying this went wrong, or that went wrong, but ultimately it came down to comms. If they'd established good comms, they would have been in a position to extract or relocate or whatever, even after things started to go tits up. If the radio had shown any sign of working, they wouldn't have ditched it so quickly, and they wouldn't have been fucking around with TACBEs[4] trying to talk to passing aircraft. Without comms they were relying on their own resources and they had a long way to go: you can't blame them for what happened.

> Another criticism was the amount of medals handed out: the most decorated patrol in the history of the Regiment was actually a total fuck-up. Some of the old boys were comparing it to [the Battle of Mirbat] and saying it was a disgrace when you think that [Corporal Labalaba] only got an MID [Mention in Dispatches] for what he did. Well, maybe, but it's the head-shed that hands out medals so there's no point blaming 'Andy McNab' and his guys.

> But if you're looking for an example of good leadership, then getting the bulk of your patrol from a big balls-up right in the middle of Iraq, 200 miles to the Syrian border is it. 'McNab' made mistakes, no doubt about it, but he was basically on the right track. I think the real reason people got pissed off with him was he made a zillion pounds out of his books: that was his big mistake, as if he gives a shit.[5]

In the meantime, after a long period of build up training, A and D Squadrons deployed in force on 23 January in half-squadron sized fighting patrols into the 'Scud box', an area of several thousand square kilometres in the western Iraqi desert. On the same day, the SBS conducted Operation MAUDE, successfully cutting the fibre-optic communications cable connecting Baghdad with the port city of Basra.

The patrols of A and D Squadrons which deployed into the

---

4 A short-range VHF transceiver designed for downed aircrew to call in rescue aircraft.
5 Interview, NCO, 22 SAS.

western Iraqi desert were involved in hard fighting in challenging and difficult terrain. Details of many of their operations remain obscure, although published accounts by veterans describe successful attacks on a number of communications sites within Iraq. Nevertheless, despite claims made by some authors,[6] there is a degree of doubt over how many – if any – Scud missile launchers were actually put out of action. The United Nations Special Commission (UNSCOM), which was sent into Iraq after the war to supervise the elimination of Iraqi weapons of mass destruction, reached the conclusion that no mobile Scud launchers and no Scud missiles themselves were destroyed by any of the coalition forces,[7] and this conclusion was supported by an investigation by the United States House of Representatives Committee on Armed Services. Intelligence information collected after the war indicated that the Iraqis had possessed nineteen mobile Scud launchers and UNSCOM were able to account for all of them.

Between 17 and 26 January twenty-one Scuds were fired at Israel and twenty-two at Saudi Arabia. However, from 27 January, when the SAS (and later Delta Force) patrols became effective, to the end of the war, nearly a month later, only nineteen Scuds were launched at Israel and a further twenty-three at Saudi, largely because of the difficulty that the Iraqis had in getting the weapons to a safe launch site. This obviously represents a reduction in the numbers of missiles being launched, but not a huge one. It is reasonable to speculate that the SAS were responsible for a proportion of this reduction, nevertheless, it is also evident that the achievement of the SAS against the Scud threat, in particular, has been somewhat overemphasized.

When the final land assault was launched on 24 February it was evident that more than a month of bombardment by the most sophisticated air force ever assembled had almost completely disrupted Iraqi command and control, even if much of the weaponry and manpower that was believed to have been

---

6 Tony Geraghty in *Who Dares Wins* (Little, Brown, 1993) quotes an American officer who comments that the SAS were responsible for targeting US aircraft on to 'maybe one third' of their total Scud kills, and speculates that this would have meant twenty to thirty Scuds. Clearly this is nonsense.
7 An SAS intelligence NCO who served in the Gulf told the author in 1996 that he believed that 22 SAS had actually destroyed one Scud.

destroyed was actually intact. In less than a hundred hours the coalition achieved all of its aims: destroying the Iraqi forces within Kuwait; liberating Kuwait City itself; and massively reducing, if not eliminating, Iraq's ability to take offensive action against its neighbours for the near future. Within the compass of this enormous operation, the role of 22 SAS was clearly small and certainly not as influential on the outcome of the war as some have claimed. Despite this, the operations of A and D Squadrons represent a considerable technical achievement: it is no mean feat, in modern warfare, to maintain effective, aggressive and largely self-supporting patrols deep within enemy territory for weeks on end; and it is even more impressive that these patrols were able to repeatedly strike at Iraqi targets and live to fight another day. A former SAS officer who was not with the Regiment in the Gulf commented that:

The Gulf War, in my opinion, summed up what was best and worst about the Regiment. On the one hand we were desperate to be involved, trying to find something to do so that we could get stuck in, but it meant that some of our operations weren't as well prepared as they should have been.

For example, you had this situation with the B Squadron roadwatch going completely to pieces. The basic problem wasn't anything to do with the patrols themselves: they were doing what they were told; but they should not have been sent out there like that, dumped in the middle of Iraq on spec, with seriously inadequate intelligence. You then had two of the patrols quite rightly coming straight back out – I wouldn't criticize them for a moment for that, though a lot of people in the Regiment did – but the other one sticks around, gets compromised and suddenly you've got these poor buggers trying to E & E across a desert in mid-winter on foot: not good at all! . . .

But what you see in all of it – and this is the best side of the Regiment – is the quality of the blokes. It isn't any kind of macho heroism, though if you look at how Rob Consiglio died, or what 'Andy McNab' or 'Chris Ryan' went through, there's plenty of that. It's their determination, their intelligence and their flexibility – as well as the military skills – which means that if you give them a proper job to do, they will go balls out to get it right.

The thing with the SAS is that there's this fear that if we don't get involved in every scrap that's going we will be forgotten about, or we'll lose our budget, and that means that we're sometimes prepared to do things that don't fit in with our role; and that can get people killed and wounded for the wrong reasons. But we shouldn't have to do that. If the politicians don't realize by now what a huge national asset 22 SAS is. they're never going to. There is no other unit anywhere in the world that can do the range of tasks that we do as well as we do. That isn't big-timing, it's a fact.[8]

The major operational commitment for 22 SAS since the end of the Gulf War has been in the former Yugoslavia. Members of the Regiment first moved into the area in the wake of the first British deployments under the United Nations umbrella. In the words of one of the soldiers sent there:

. . . our objectives were first, to map out the front lines so that the UN would have a clear idea where each ethnic side was located; secondly, we had to report on the situation in the Muslim enclaves that were holding out against the Serbs. Horror stories had been coming back to UNHCR about malnutrition and atrocities in these designated areas, but nobody knew exactly what was happening because no observers had managed to get in or out. Our job was to report the truth.[9]

It is a role that 22 SAS have been conducting with some variations ever since. Observers in several Muslim enclaves became aware of the presence of SAS soldiers during the height of the sieges, and a member of 22 SAS died after being shot in the head by Serbian 'Cetniks' during heavy fighting. More recently, it has been claimed that SAS soldiers participated in the arrests of several war criminals: Bosnia is an operational theatre that remains both active and sensitive.

---

8 Interview, Officer. 22 SAS.
9 Mike Curtis, *CQB*, Bantam Press. 1997.

18. **Conclusion**

I first saw people from the Regiment when I was a baby Para in Northern Ireland in the late 1970s. I didn't really know what the SAS was or what it did, but they looked different: big hairy guys with weird and wonderful weapons. I didn't immediately think 'yeah, let's go', but I suppose I started to think about it in general terms, asked a few questions.

Then there was the Iranian Embassy. I was on leave, staying with my girlfriend in Croydon, watching some snooker match and there they were. I went down the pub that night and she told them all I was a Para and they were showing re-runs on the telly, so all the civvies were asking about the Regiment and I was getting bought a good few pints. And after that I started thinking: 'I could do that.' I was fit as a butcher's dog, did a lot of cross-country, never smoked in my life, loved the Army, loved the Para Reg, so I thought 'why the fuck not?' Then came the Falklands, where we lost a lot of good guys, and there was this funny atmosphere after: like 'we've done it now, why do we have to keep on training'. I thought the atmosphere had changed a lot.

So I kept on training, soldiered on, put in for selection, went through on my first attempt and there I was: in the Regiment. I haven't regretted it for one second since.

The funny thing is, when you tell people you've been in the Regiment, they're asking you about all the warry stuff, blood and guts, and you give 'em both barrels, get their toes curling. But that wasn't what it was like for me. Since I've been out, the thing I miss is the sense of adventure, not the operations or the . . . the glamorous bits. It's going into camp on a Monday and not knowing where you're going to be three days later: Africa, South America, wherever.

And you know you've got a set of mates who're going to be your mates for life: they'll die for you if they have to, and they know you'll do the same for them. Maybe that's the thing about the Regiment: it's fucking hard work getting in, and it can be fucking rough when you're in it, but you're all in it together . . . whatever happens.[1]

---

1 Interview, NCO, 22 SAS.

Glossary of Military Terms

9mm The ammunition calibre used by British forces in pistols and sub-machine guns. '9mm' is also the generic term in the Army for the Browning Hi-Power pistol, which was standard issue for SAS personnel for many years but which has now been superseded to a large extent by the Sig P-226.

44 pattern A type of canvas webbing equipment specially designed for jungle warfare and introduced into the British Army in 1944.

66 A light, portable, American-made, hand-held anti-tank rocket of 66mm nominal calibre and a maximum range of 200 metres. When fired accurately (no mean achievement), the 66 was found to have an impressive effect on static positions.

Adjutant An officer, normally of the rank of captain, who acts as the commanding officer's 'right-hand man' in peace and war, with special responsibility for personnel and discipline. In 22 SAS the post is normally held by an officer who has been commissioned through the ranks of the Regiment, in 21 and 23 SAS it generally goes to an officer attached to the Regiment from the regular army or Royal Marines.

Advance to Contact A form of operation in which a unit, or sub-unit, travels along a set route until it meets an enemy position, which it then engages. Normally used when the precise location of the enemy is unclear.

Bandolier A green plastic pouch issued to hold belts of 7.62mm machine-gun ammunition. An unpopular and fiddly item, the majority of soldiers prefer to carry belted ammunition slung around their bodies.

Basha An improvised shelter, normally constructed from the rainproof nylon poncho issued to all soldiers.

Battalion A military unit typically composed of between 500 and 1,000 soldiers commanded by a lieutenant-colonel.

Belt-kit Webbing equipment adapted to be worn without a shoulder harness or yoke and popular in the SAS because it does not interfere with the bergan.

Bergan The generic term in the British Army for any military-type rucksack, derived from the trade-name of a Norwegian rucksack manufacturer who supplied equipment to the Army in the 1950s.

Brigade A military formation comprising two, or more, battalions and commanded by a brigadier.

Brigadier A 1-star general of the British Army or Royal Marines.

C-130 A 4-engined turbo-prop driven aircraft used as a general transport and paratroop drop aircraft.

Captain Junior officer in the British Army and the lowest officer rank in 22 SAS where captains traditionally command troops or hold appointments on the Regimental staff.

Chinook Large twin-rotor transport helicopter which can transport up to half a company of infantry.

CO Commanding Officer. Normally a lieutenant-colonel, a CO in the British Army commands a unit of battalion size or its equivalent. 21, 22 and 23 SAS are the commands of lieutenant-colonels.

Combats Generic Army term for the heavy-duty camouflaged clothing worn in the field.

Company A sub-unit of an infantry battalion, normally comprising about a hundred men commanded by a major. Equivalent-sized units of other arms are squadrons, batteries, etc.

Compo Generic term for field rations issued by the British Army. In addition to the main meals, compo provides a selection of snacks, chocolate, biscuits, tea and coffee, and lavatory paper; this latter is known as 'John Wayne' because it is 'rough, tough and takes no shit from nobody'.

Corporal A junior non-commissioned officer, typically in command of a four-man SAS patrol.

DF A specific location onto which pre-arranged artillery fire can be brought.

Division A military formation comprising two, or more, brigades, and commanded by a major-general.

DMS 'Direct Moulded Sole', cheaply made, rubber-soled ankle boots issued by the British Army from the 1960s to the mid-1980s. They were supposedly waterproofed by the addition of cloth puttees, but in reality these made little difference. An example of the low-quality kit which used to be issued to British soldiers, the inadequacy of DMS boots was one of the reasons why the SAS has always allowed its members a good deal of latitude in selecting their own equipment for operations.

Dog-tags Metal discs worn by all soldiers in combat as a means of identifying their bodies afterwards. They bear the owner's name, number, religion and blood-group.

Doss-bag Military slang for sleeping-bag (also 'Gonk-bag', 'Green Maggot', etc).

DPM Disruptive Pattern Material. British-pattern camouflaged cloth.

DZ Dropping Zone (for paratroops).

Endex 'End of Exercise'. Used on completion of virtually every task.

FAP Final Assault Position. Sheltered location where attacking troops can 'shake out' into the formation that they will assault in.

Field Dressing Sterile pad with attached bandages issued to soldiers for emergency first-aid in the field.

FRV Final Rendezvous point.

Fleece Civilian-made thermal jackets worn by many soldiers underneath combat clothing.

FN/FAL Belgian-made 7.62mm automatic rifle used by Argentine forces.

FOO Forward Observation Officer. Artillery officer, normally a lieutenant or captain, who accompanies infantry troops and brings in aimed artillery fire onto targets at their request or on his own initiative.

FPF Final Protective Fire. A high-priority DF used as a last resort very close to a friendly position if it appears likely to be overrun.

G1 The military staff branch dealing with personnel.

G2 The military staff branch dealing with intelligence and security.

G3 The military staff branch dealing with operations and training.

G4 The military staff branch dealing with logistics.

Gazelle A light reconnaissance helicopter.

GPMG A belt-fed 7.62mm machine gun.

H Hour The specific time at which an operation starts.

HE High explosives.

Helly-Hansen   A popular brand of civilian-bought thermal clothing much used in the British Army.

HLS   Helicopter Landing Site.

Intelligence Corps   An arm of the British Army with responsibility for providing and analysing operational intelligence and advising on security. The Intelligence Corps provides 22 SAS with a specialist section of collators and analysts to support operations, collectively known as the 'Green Slime'.

Illum   Starshells and flares used to light up a battlefield.

IO   Intelligence Officer. In 22 SAS the intelligence officer is supplied by the Intelligence Corps, although he may well have operational SAS, or other special forces, experience.

IWS   Individual Weapon Sight. A bulky nightsight that can be mounted on a rifle or machine gun, or used like a telescope.

Kevlar   A fabric developed for the US space programme which has proved resistant to low-velocity bullets and shrapnel. Now used in body armour and helmets.

Lance-Corporal   The first rung on the promotion ladder. Often carries with it the appointment of second in command of a four-man patrol.

LUP   Lying Up Position.

M 16   An American-made 5.56mm assault rifle developed from the original 'Armalite AR15', which has become, in its M16A2 variant, the standard weapon of the SAS and other British special forces. Capable of firing in a fully automatic mode, its firepower can be augmented by the addition of the M 203 40mm grenade launcher.

Milan   A wire-guided anti-tank missile with a range of up to 1,950 metres. During the Gulf War these were fitted to SAS Land Rovers.

MO   Medical Officer.

Morphine   In combat, all soldiers are issued with a dose of morphine-based painkiller to use on themselves if they are wounded. It comes in the form of a 'syrette', a small tube with attached hypodermic needle, for intramuscular injection.

MT Mechanical transport.

ND Negligent discharge (of a weapon). An ND is a serious occurrence in the British Army; aside from being highly dangerous, it is indicative of sloppy drills and lack of professionalism.

NOD Night Observation Device.

O Group The O group is the means by which detailed operational orders are passed down the chain of command. It is, necessarily, a formal event which is usually carefully stage managed and controlled by the commander giving the orders. The sequence of events is as follows: the commander describes the ground over which the operation he is outlining will take place and follows this with a briefing on the situation (the intelligence picture, what 'friendly forces' are doing, who is attached and detached for the operation, etc.); once the situation has been described, the commander must then give a clear and simple mission; at this point, the commander gives an outline of his plan and then goes on to describe in detail what he wants of each individual sub-unit under his command, this is followed by co-ordinating instructions explaining such crucial matters as timings; these are followed by a round-up of essentially administrative points, and signals instructions. The formal structure and set format of an O group should mean that subordinate commanders will not miss any relevant orders or instructions.

OC Officer Commanding. The formal title of an officer in charge of a unit smaller than a battalion (i.e. squadrons and troops).

OP Observation post.

Ops Officer Operations Officer. The regimental ops officer is responsible for the co-ordination and administration of the regiment's operational tasks and for assisting the CO in his planning process.

PC Patrol Commander.

Pinkies Specially converted Land Rovers based on 1 SAS's desert jeeps. Pinkies are built on the Land Rover 110 chassis but carry some armour plating, special long-range fuel tanks and a variety of weapons fits. Their name is derived from the bizarre but effective 'desert pink' camouflage, which led to them being nicknamed 'Pink Panthers'.

Platoon Sub-unit of an infantry company, normally comprising about thirty men commanded by a lieutenant or second lieutenant.

Pucara Argentine-built turbo-prop bomber designed for counter-insurgency and close air support applications.

QM Quartermaster. The officer, normally commissioned through the ranks, who is responsible for the regiment's logistics

REMF Rear Echelon Mother Fucker. A non-combatant soldier.

RV Rendezvous Point.

RSM Regimental Sergeant Major.

RSO Regimental Signals Officer.

Sangar A defensive position constructed above ground using sandbags, earth, peat or rocks, as opposed to a trench, which is dug into the ground.

SBS Special Boat Squadron. A special forces unit recruited from the Royal Marine Commandos, with particular skills in amphibious and underwater infiltration of their targets. Now expanded, it is called the Special Boat Service.

Sea King Troop-carrying helicopter in service with the Royal Navy.

Second Lieutenant The most junior officers rank. In the SAS, second lieutenants are only to be found in the territorial regiments.

Section A sub-unit of an infantry platoon, normally comprising 8 to 10 men commanded by a corporal.

Sergeant Senior NCO, normally employed as second in command of a troop or commander of a patrol.

SLR Self Loading Rifle. Semi-automatic British variant of the fully-automatic 7.62mm FN/FAL and standard issue to all British units, including the SAS, from the late 1950s to the late 1980s.

SMG Sub-machine-gun. A small fully-automatic weapon which normally fires pistol ammunition. In the British Army this usually means the 9mm Sterling-Patchett carbine, but the SAS have a somewhat wider selection available, including the Heckler & Koch MP5 family of weapons.

Squadron Although the basic operational formation within 22 SAS remains the four-man patrol, the majority of training, operations and deployments are organized at squadron level. The four operational squadrons of 22 SAS, A, B, D and G, theoretically comprise about seventy members, including four troops of sixteen 'sabre' personnel, together with a small headquarters consisting of the officer commanding (a major), the SSM (see below), the SQMS and a small number of clerks and storemen. In reality, however, squadrons can be much bigger, particularly when they are deployed on their own, because they will acquire personnel from the Signals Squadron (264 SAS Signal Squadron: a Royal Signals unit permanently attached to the Regiment), the intelligence cell, and other administrative staff from HQ Squadron.

SSM Squadron Sergeant Major. A Warrant Officer Class 2 who acts as right-hand man to the squadron commander. In the SAS, the SSM is almost certainly the most experienced man in his squadron and might well take command of the squadron in the event of the OC being out of action.

Staff Sergeant Also known as a 'Colour Sergeant' in the infantry. Senior NCO, usually employed as SQMS or as a troop commander in the absence of an officer.

Tab Tactical Advance into Battle. Paras slang for a forced march ('like yomping only faster and harder').

TAOR Tactical Area of Responsibility.

Troop Each SAS squadron comprises four troops who, within 22 SAS at least, each maintain a particular specialization: parachuting, boats, vehicles and mountains. Troops are normally commanded by captains or staff sergeants and consist of sixteen members, broken down into four four-man teams.

Webbing The green canvas belt, harness and pouches used to carry ammunition, water and other essentials into battle. Also known as 'fighting order', 'belt-kit' and 'belt order'.

Welrod A silenced 9mm pistol originally developed for SOE (Special Operations Executive) during WWII. When used with subsonic ammunition the Welrod is virtually noiseless.

Windproof High-quality camouflaged combat jacket issued to the SAS and some other special forces.

Wombat 120mm recoilless anti-tank gun issued at battalion level. Superseded by the Milan system.

Zulu time Greenwich Mean Time. Used in all military operations in order to avoid confusion.

Index

Index

Index